One Pot **Comfort**

Meredith Laurence

Photography by Jessica Walker

Walah!, LLC | Publishers
Philadelphia

First Edition

Published in the United States by Walah!, LLC/Publishers

walah@me.com

Publisher's Cataloging-In-Publication Data
(Prepared by The Donohue Group, Inc.)

Names: Laurence, Meredith. | Walker, Jessica, 1975- photographer.

Title: One pot comfort / Meredith Laurence ; photography by Jessica Walker.

Other Titles: Blue Jean Chef | Make everyday meals in one pot, pan or appliance

Description: First edition. | Philadelphia : Walah!, LLC Publishers, [2018] | Includes index.

Identifiers: ISBN 9781948193146 | ISBN 1948193140 | ISBN 9781948193139 (ebook)

Subjects: LCSH: One-dish meals. | Comfort food. | Electric cooking, Slow. | Hot air frying. | Pressure cooking. | LCGFT: Cookbooks.

Classification: LCC TX840.O53 L38 2018 (print) | LCC TX840.O53 (ebook) | DDC 641.82--dc23

ISBN- 13: 978-1-948193-14-6
ISBN- 10: 1-948193-14-0

Printed in USA

Book design by Janis Boehm
www.bound-determined.com

Photography by Jessica Walker
www.jessicawalkerphotography.com

Food styling by Lisa Martin

Acknowledgments

Nobody writes a cookbook alone. I have many people to thank who helped me put this book together and it really says something that for most of the people on my team, this is our *sixth* project together. I am honored and proud.

Lisa Martin – you're not only my right hand, but my left leg as well and I wouldn't be able to stand up without you.

Janis Boehm – you can now add "jigsaw puzzle expert" to your resume and if I ever start playing chess, I want you on my team.

Jessica Walker – your grace and vision continue to calm and impress me.

Michele Pilone, Bill Hornaday and Lori Phelan – thank you for your dedication and long days of food styling.

Penny Markowitz – you did a lot of reading and re-reading for me. I appreciate your friendship.

Suzanne Smith, Virginia Puddicombe and Heidi Cooke – thank you for distributing so much recipe testing food to friends and neighbors, spreading a little sunshine around.

Tanya van Biesen – you've been right there for over thirty years and managed to test recipes on demand despite your busy schedule (even if you did bend the rules now and then). Thank you.

Linda Lisco – I truly feel your support every day. Thank you for listening and guiding me down the path gently.

Eric Theiss – we will always be there as each other's sounding boards.

To Annie. You put a lot of work into every aspect of this book – more than any partner should ever have to or want to. More importantly, you are always there to support me and keep life going when times get crazy. Thank you. I'm coming home from book-land now.

Table of Contents

Chicken

Beef

One Pot Penne Bolognese with Fennel Seed	68
Short Rib Ragu with Rigatoni	70
Tex Mex Skillet Dinner	73
Chili con Carne with Cornbread Dumplings	75
Sheet Pan Burgers with Pimento Cheese and Steak Fries	78
Skillet Lasagna	81
Soy-Ginger Beef and Broccoli Rice	84
Tea Braised Pot Roast	86
Sloppy Joe Casserole	88
Sesame Beef Noodles	91
New York Strip Steaks with Baked Potatoes and Asparagus	92
Cheese Stuffed Meatloaf with Roasted Russets and Carrots	95
Carne Asada with Onions and Peppers	98
Corned Beef with Cabbage, Potatoes and Split Pea Mash	101
Beef and Barley Stew with Horseradish	104
Classic Roast Beef with Smashed Potatoes, Green Beans and Onions	106

Pork and Lamb

Herb Crusted Pork Rib Roast with Root Vegetables	111
Pork Picatta with Capellini Pasta and Asparagus	112
Panko Crusted Pork Chops with Corn and Zucchini	115
Pork Tamale Pie	117
Chili Verde	118
Pork Chops, Apple and Cabbage	120
Moroccan Lamb Tagine with Orange, Olives and Couscous	123
Hearty Pork and Navy Bean Stew with Spinach	126
Easy Lamb Curry with Cauliflower and Chickpeas	128
Deep Dish Prosciutto, Spinach and Mushroom Pizza	130
Spicy Szechuan Pork and Jasmine Rice	133
Tuscan Pork Sausage with Kale, Butternut Squash and Toasted Bread	136
Fruit and Nut Stuffed Pork Loin with Pineapple Glaze, Roasted Cauliflower and Broccoli	139
Keilbasa, Pierogies and Sauerkraut Bake	141

Fish and Seafood

Vegetarian

Dessert

Introduction

I'm a lucky person. I'm lucky that I love to cook, because I love to eat. I'm also lucky that I have a great connection to others who love to cook and eat through my Blue Jean Chef social media community. Every day I hear from folks who want to show me what they've made in their kitchens, or who have questions for me about how to make something they are craving. As a result, I have a great sense of what many cooks across the country enjoy preparing and devouring.

People love comfort foods. This is not a revelation. People also seem to love one-pot cooking because it means one-pot cleaning. This is also not a revelation. What is a little more noteworthy is that there are so many "one pots" to use these days and that makes one-pot cooking more interesting. I can't tell you the number of times I get a question like "how would I make that in my pressure cooker or Instant Pot®?" or "could I do that recipe in my air fryer?" or "is there a way to use my slow cooker for that dish?" And all those questions led me to this cookbook.

In this cookbook, full of traditional and non-traditional comfort food recipes, I've given you a tried and true way to prepare dinner on the stovetop or in the oven. Every recipe in this book can be made with these two standard pieces of kitchen equipment. But then, for those of you who love your more modern kitchen appliances, those of you who are looking for a faster way to make something using a pressure cooker or a more convenient way to prepare dinner using your slow cooker, and those of you who are looking for a more health-conscious cooking method using your air fryer… I give you options (and it's always good to have options). Whenever it makes sense – when it's faster or more convenient AND gives you the same great results – the recipe has alternate cooking methods for how to make it using other kitchen appliances. If it doesn't make sense to prepare the recipe any other way, I tell you so.

All these recipes are intended to be the only thing you will need to cook for a complete dinner. You may want to supplement the meal with a piece of bread or a salad (and I do give you suggestions), but you won't need to cook anything else, unless of course you want to. The main rule for every recipe is that at the end of dinner, you'll only have one cooking vessel to clean up.

So, take inventory of your kitchen. You're about to make dinner YOUR way.

All About Kitchen Equipment

Stovetop Equipment

The majority of our cookware is intended for use on top of the stove. For the recipes in this book, you'll need three items for stovetop cooking. The first is a Dutch oven. My preference is for a cast iron Dutch oven because I love the way cast iron browns foods as well as how it distributes heat evenly for long slow braises. If you don't have a cast iron Dutch oven, however, a large stainless steel or aluminum stockpot will work for you as well. Just make sure that the pot is oven-safe (ideally broiler-safe). A 6-quart Dutch oven will work for all these recipes, but in many cases you will be able to get away with a smaller 4-quart size.

The other two items needed for the stovetop recipes are a large 12-inch skillet and a large sauté pan. These two items are often confused by people and for good reason. In the cookware industry, a "skillet" refers to a pan with sloped sides whereas a "sauté pan" has straight sides and usually comes with a lid. It's a little counterintuitive because when you sauté something, you toss it around and that is much easier to do in a skillet rather than a sauté pan. Makes no sense, but there you have it!

I do love a good cast iron skillet for the same reasons that I like a cast iron Dutch oven, but there are times when you'll want an aluminum or stainless steel skillet as well, which is easier to control on high heat. Whether or not you use cookware with a non-stick surface is entirely up to you. Obviously, a non-stick surface is easier to clean, but many people prefer a plain stainless steel interior.

Oven Equipment

The oven equipment that you will need for this book is also very straightforward. You will need a baking sheet. My favorite size of baking sheet is called a half sheet pan. It measures roughly 18-inches by 13-inches. A full sheet pan is twice the size and used only in professional kitchens. I don't specify "half sheet pan" in my recipes because I know that there are so many different sized baking sheets in home kitchens, but understand that for some of the quantities of food in the recipes, a large 18-inch by 13-inch pan is ideal and the most versatile.

You should also have the most common size of baking dish – a 9-inch by 13-inch baker. This could be a ceramic baker or a metal baking pan. The decision between the two really comes down to whether you intend to serve the food right out of the baking dish. Ceramic bakers are obviously more attractive at the table than a metal baking pan.

Finally, for some of the larger roasts, a roasting pan is very convenient, although in truth you could use one of the two vessels above as a substitute in a pinch.

Air Fryers

In the simplest of terms, an air-fryer is a compact cylindrical countertop convection oven. It's a kitchen appliance that uses superheated air that is blown around by a fan to cook foods, giving results very similar to deep-frying or high-temperature roasting. Air fryers use the same technology as convection ovens, but instead of blowing the air around a large rectangular box, it is blown around in a compact cylinder and the food sits in a perforated basket. This is much more efficient and creates an intense environment of heat from which the food cannot escape. The result is food with a crispy brown exterior and moist tender interior – results similar to deep-frying, but without all the oil and fat needed to deep-fry. In fact, when you air-fry, you usually use no more than one tablespoon of oil!

Better still, an air fryer doesn't just cook foods that you would usually deep-fry. It can cook any foods that you would normally roast, bake, grill, sauté or even microwave. It is a great tool for re-heating foods without making them rubbery, and is a perfect and quick way to prepare ingredients as well as make meals. It has become a valued helper in my kitchen.

You can get different sizes of air fryers these days. They range from two to six quarts in capacity. The most common size is a 3-quart, but if you do a lot of air-frying, the larger version is a wise investment. You'll do fewer batches of food and get dinner on the table faster.

Air fryers do come in different configurations. The recipes in this book were written for air fryers that have a pull out drawer and perforated basket, rather than the air fryer ovens that are either domed or have racks inside.

General Tips for Air-Frying

● **Don't overcrowd the basket.** I can't stress this enough. It's tempting to try to cook more at one time, but over-crowding the basket will prevent foods from crisping and browning evenly and take more time over all.

● **Flip foods over halfway through the cooking time.** Just as you would if you were cooking on a grill or in a skillet, you need to turn foods over so that they brown evenly.

● **Open the air fryer as often as you like to check for doneness.** This is one of the best parts of air fryers – you can open that drawer as often as you like (within reason) to check to see how the cooking process is coming along.

● **Shake the basket.** Shaking the basket a couple of times during the cooking process will re-distribute the ingredients and help them to brown and crisp more evenly.

● **Spray with oil part way through.** If you are trying to get the food to brown and crisp more, try spritzing it with oil part way through the cooking process. This will also help the food to brown more evenly.

● **Re-heating foods in the air fryer.** There's no hard and fast rule for time and temperature when re-heating leftovers because leftovers vary so significantly. I suggest re-heating in the air fryer at 350ºF and doing so for as long as it takes for the food to be re-heated to a food safety temperature of 165ºF. This is especially important for any potentially hazardous foods like chicken, pork and beef.

Pressure Cookers

A pressure cooker is a cooking vessel with a lid that locks on and prevents steam from escaping. As a result, the steam builds up pressure in the pressure cooker – about 12 to 15 pounds per square inch of pressure (psi) – and the temperature inside the cooker increases. At sea level, water boils at 212°F before it is converted into steam and it cannot get any hotter than that, regardless of the heat source below it. In a pressure cooker, with 15 psi of pressure added, water boils at 250°F before being converted into steam. That means that we are able to cook foods inside a pressure cooker at higher temperatures and they are therefore finished sooner – in about one third of the time it would take to cook on a regular stovetop. The time saved by using a pressure cooker is obviously a huge benefit, but that is secondary to how your foods taste out of the pressure cooker.

In a pressure cooker, the lid is sealed onto the pot letting nothing escape, and the flavors of the foods have nowhere to go but to mingle with each other. With flavor infused throughout, soups, stews, chilies, everything is intensely flavorful. Cuts of meat that usually need a long cooking time in order to become tender are transformed into spoon-tender, succulent meals. Because the lid prevents steam from escaping, foods remain moist too. The results of pressure-cooking are juicy, tender, moist and flavorful meals. All of that in one-third of the time it would normally take. You can't beat that!

Pressure cookers also come in different sizes, ranging from small 2-quart pressure cookers all the way up to 10-quart cookers and larger pressure canners. The recipes in this book were all tested in a 6-quart electric pressure cooker, but many can be made in a smaller model or a stovetop cooker. Just remember not to exceed the "max fill" line on the pressure cooker insert while ensuring that you still have 1 cup of liquid in the pot.

Converting from Electric Pressure Cookers to Stovetop Pressure Cookers

Stovetop pressure cookers get to pressure a little faster than electric pressure cookers and also drop their pressure a little faster than electric pressure cookers. Because of this, the actual cooking time of foods in a stovetop pressure cooker is shorter than when using an electric pressure cooker. However, stovetop pressure cookers often reach a higher pressure than electric pressure cookers, so it almost evens out. You won't find much difference in the timing for many recipes, but if you are cooking big pieces of meat, beans or grains, reduce the cooking time by a couple of minutes for stovetop cookers.

Converting to Smaller Pressure Cookers

Converting recipes for different sizes of pressure cookers can be tricky, but it doesn't need to be. The rule of thumb about pressure cookers is that you need to have at least one to one and a half cups of liquid in the recipe. (Check your pressure cooker manual for the minimum liquid requirement.) That liquid is needed to create the steam that will then create the pressure in the cooker. So, if you are decreasing the recipe, divide all the ingredients equally and then take a look at what you're left with. If there is less than one cup of liquid, increase just the liquid to the minimum amount required and leave the other quantities alone. Understand that you will probably have more sauce with your finished dish, or the final result of your cooking will be wetter than intended, but you can simply either reduce the liquid by simmering the sauce after the cooking time, or just use less of the sauce on the plate.

Converting for Pressure-Cooking at High Altitudes

Anyone cooking at a high altitude knows that water boils at a lower temperature because of the decreased atmospheric pressure. This affects the pressure inside a pressure cooker as well. So, when using a pressure cooker at higher altitudes, increase the cooking time by 5% for every 1000 feet over 2000 feet above sea level.

General Tips for Pressure-Cooking

● **Brown foods first.** For visual appeal as well as for flavor, it's important to brown your foods either before pressure-cooking, or after the food has been cooked. Many electric pressure cookers now have BROWN settings, which will allow you to sear foods before you add the liquid required for cooking. If your electric pressure cooker does not have a BROWN setting, simply brown the foods on the stovetop in a skillet first, add the liquid to the skillet to deglaze the pan, scrape up any brown bits that have formed on the bottom of the pan and pour everything into the pressure cooker along with the remaining ingredients. It's a small step that does take a little time, but it is important to the final result.

● **Natural-Release Method.** This method of releasing the pressure in the cooker involves simply turning your electric pressure cooker off. The temperature will slowly decrease in the cooker and the pressure will come back to normal. Understand that a natural pressure release can take as long as fifteen minutes, so account for that time in your meal planning. Use the natural-release method for meats in order to obtain tender results, for beans whose skins tend to burst otherwise, and for dishes with a lot of liquid where the liquid might spit out of the pressure release valve.

● **Quick-Release Method.** Electric pressure cookers have a release valve that you can turn to release the pressure manually. Steam will escape out of the valve until the pressure has returned to normal. Use the quick-release method for foods that are easily over-cooked, like grains, seafood or vegetables.

Multi Cookers

Multi cookers, as the name implies, have multiple functions. They almost always have pressure cooker as well as slow cooker functions, and often many other settings as well. The most popular multi cooker on the market these days is the Instant Pot®. It's become so popular, in fact, that it's almost become synonymous with multi cooker and people wonder about the difference between the Instant Pot® and a pressure cooker. All Instant Pot® multi cookers have multiple settings like browning, steaming, rice cooking and slow cooking but they are most often used as a pressure cooker. One quick word about the Instant Pot® slow cooker function: unlike most slow cookers, which have two temperature settings, the Instant Pot® has three settings – LOW, NORMAL and MORE. The MORE setting is equivalent to HIGH and the NORMAL setting is the same as LOW on other brands. Instant Pot®'s LOW setting is like a keep warm function.

Because browning foods before pressure- or slow-cooking is so important, having a multi cooker makes cooking much more convenient with fewer dishes to wash. If you don't have a multi cooker or a BROWN setting on your pressure or slow cooker, you can still make the recipes in this book by browning on the stovetop first, but it will mean you'll have to use another pan.

Slow Cookers

Slow cookers have been around so long that I probably don't even need to explain what they are, but I will anyway. A slow cooker is a round or oval electric pot, usually with a stoneware insert, that cooks foods at a very low temperature over a long period of time. Some have heating elements at the bottom of the unit only, while others have a base element as well as elements around the sides to heat more evenly and quickly. Slow cookers are always covered with a lid, which not only traps the heat and steam, but allows moisture to condense and fall back into your food. Some slow cookers have lids that clamp down on the pot, which are helpful for travel and to prevent any heat loss as the food cooks. Most slow cookers come with two cooking levels – LOW and HIGH – that keep foods around 190ºF to 200ºF or 250ºF to 300ºF, depending on the brand. You can usually set the cooker using LOW or HIGH based on how much time you have before you wish to eat. In general, LOW cooking times are about twice as long as HIGH cooking times. I have tried to give both options in the recipes that follow, but my recommended setting always comes first.

In my opinion, some starchy foods do not turn out very well in a slow cooker. Rice and pasta, in particular, do not have good results when slow-cooked. That's not to say that you can't make these foods in the slow cooker (many people do), but because I don't find the results as successful as in other cooking methods, I've chosen not to recommend them for the slow cooker.

General Tips for Slow-Cooking

● **Don't lift the lid.** This is by far the most important thing to remember when slow-cooking. When you lift the lid, you will lose a relatively enormous amount of heat from the pot. Lifting the lid out of curiosity will increase your cooking time. If you do need to open the slow cooker to check the food, do so as quickly as possible. Otherwise, resist the temptation.

● **Brown foods first.** Just as with pressure cookers, browning the foods first will enhance the appearance and the flavor of the final dish. If your slow cooker doesn't have a browning feature, do this on the stovetop and add the food to the cooker already browned.

● **No frozen foods.** Frozen foods bring the temperature of all your ingredients down and they don't heat fast enough in the slow cooker to avoid prolonged periods of time in the temperature danger zone. Make sure all your ingredients are thawed before adding to the cooker.

If you would like to learn more about
air-frying and pressure-cooking or would like
more recipes for your air fryer, pressure cooker
and other cooking tools, please visit me at
www.bluejeanchef.com.

Chicken
and
Poultry

Chicken with Orange, Peppers and Zucchini

Possible Cooking Methods: Stovetop and Oven   Pressure Cooker   Slow Cooker

I love a little orange flavor in foods. An orange has sweet as well as acidic qualities that make it such a great ingredient in savory dishes. This recipe is a beautiful summertime dish and would go nicely with a simple potato salad. The sauce that accompanies the chicken in this dish is brothy rather than thick and that gives it a lightness that makes it a delight even on the hottest summer nights. It would also be nice in the winter with some cooked rice, but for that you'll have to dirty another pot. 😊

1 tablespoon olive oil

1 (3½- to 4-pound) chicken, cut into 8 pieces

salt and freshly ground black pepper

1 onion, sliced

3 carrots, sliced ¼-inch thick

3 bell peppers (red, yellow or both), sliced

3 zucchini, sliced into half moons

1 sprig fresh rosemary, plus 1 teaspoon finely chopped fresh rosemary

2 sprigs fresh thyme

1 orange, zest and juice

½ cup chicken stock*

1 tablespoon butter

2 oranges, peeled and sliced

*Quantity changes for alternate methods

Stovetop and Oven Directions

Serves: 4   **Cooking Time:** 40 minutes

1. Pre-heat the oven to 375⁰F and pre-heat a large 12-inch sauté pan over medium-high heat.

2. Add the oil to the pan and brown the chicken pieces on both sides, seasoning with salt and freshly ground black pepper. Remove the browned chicken to a side plate and set aside.

3. Add the onion, carrots and peppers to the pan and sauté until they start to soften – about 5 minutes. Add the zucchini and continue to cook for another minute or two, tossing the vegetables occasionally. Add the rosemary and thyme, along with the juice of one orange (remember to zest the orange before you juice it – we'll use the zest later). Pour in the chicken stock and return the browned chicken to the pan. Transfer the pan to the oven.

4. Bake at 375⁰F for 30 minutes. Remove the pan from the oven and stir the butter into the sauce. Sprinkle the zest of one orange and the teaspoon of chopped fresh rosemary on top, scatter the slices of 2 peeled oranges all over the chicken and serve. Some bread on the side is nice to mop up the tasty jus.

Chicken with Orange, Peppers and Zucchini

Pressure Cooker Directions

Serves: 4   **Cooking Time:** 20 minutes

Change Ingredients: Remove skin from chicken pieces

1. Pre-heat a 6-quart multi-function presure cooker using the BROWN or SAUTE setting.

2. Add the oil to the cooker and brown the chicken pieces on both sides, seasoning with salt and freshly ground black pepper. Remove the browned chicken to a side plate and set aside.

3. Add the onion, carrots and peppers to the cooker and sauté until they start to soften – about 5 minutes. (If your cooker doesn't have a brown setting, use a skillet on the stovetop for the steps above and transfer the contents to the cooker now.) Add the zucchini, rosemary and thyme, along with the juice of one orange (remember to zest the orange before you juice it – we'll use the zest later). Pour in the chicken stock and return the browned chicken to the cooker. Cover and lock the lid in place.

4. Pressure cook on HIGH for 4 minutes.

5. Release the pressure using the QUICK-RELEASE method and carefully remove the lid. Remove the chicken to a serving dish and stir the butter into the sauce in the cooker before pouring it over the chicken. Sprinkle the zest of one orange and the teaspoon of chopped fresh rosemary on top, scatter the slices of 2 peeled oranges all over the chicken and serve. Some bread on the side is nice to mop up the tasty jus.

Slow Cooker Directions

Serves: 4   **Cooking Time:** 3 to 4 hours on LOW

Change Ingredients: Omit chicken stock; remove skin from chicken pieces

1. Pre-heat a 6-quart multi-function slow cooker using the BROWN or SAUTE setting.

2. Add the oil to the cooker and brown the chicken pieces on both sides, seasoning with salt and freshly ground black pepper. Remove the browned chicken to a side plate and set aside.

3. Add the onion, carrots and peppers to the cooker and sauté until they start to soften – about 5 minutes. (If your cooker doesn't have a brown setting, use a skillet on the stovetop for the steps above and transfer the contents to the cooker now.)

Add the zucchini, rosemary and thyme, along with the juice of one orange (remember to zest the orange before you juice it – we'll use the zest later). Return the browned chicken to the cooker, cover and slow cook on LOW for 3 to 4 hours (or 1½ to 2 hours on HIGH).

4. Remove the chicken to a serving dish and stir the butter into the sauce in the cooker before pouring it over the chicken. Sprinkle the zest of one orange and the teaspoon of chopped fresh rosemary on top, scatter the slices of 2 peeled oranges all over the chicken and serve. Some bread on the side is nice to mop up the tasty jus.

Chipotle Turkey Burgers
with Sweet Potato Wedges

Possible Cooking Methods: Oven   Air Fryer

Here's a recipe that although it is easy to make in your oven, I prefer the results when made in the air fryer. The intense convection heat of the air fryer helps to brown the burgers a little and gives you the best results on the sweet potato wedges. If you have a convection setting on your oven, I highly recommend you use it, reducing the temperature to 400ºF. This recipe will make four burgers, but the size of the burger depends on you. If you only want quarter-pound burgers, you'll start with 1 pound of turkey. If you'd prefer a 6-ounce burger, go for the 1½ pounds of ground turkey. The slight increase in the size of the burger won't make much of a difference to the cook time.

1 to 1½ pounds ground turkey

½ onion, finely chopped (about ½ cup)

1 to 2 cloves garlic, minced

2 tablespoons chipotle peppers in adobo, finely chopped

2 teaspoons fresh thyme, finely chopped (or ½ teaspoon dried thyme leaves)

1 teaspoon salt

vegetable or canola oil

2 sweet potatoes, scrubbed and cut into ½-inch wedges

freshly ground black pepper

4 hamburger buns

¼ cup mayonnaise

1 lime, juiced (about 2 teaspoons)

2 tablespoons chopped fresh cilantro

Oven Directions

Serves: 4   **Cooking Time:** 20 minutes

1. Place an 18-inch by 13-inch sheet pan in the oven and pre-heat the oven to 450ºF.

2. Combine the ground turkey, onion, garlic, chipotle peppers, thyme and salt in a large bowl and gently mix the ingredients together with your hands. Divide the mixture into 4 equal portions and then form the hamburgers, being careful not to over-handle the meat. The burger mixture will be sticky. Try wetting your hands before you shape them so that the meat doesn't stick to your hands while you shape it into patties. Make an indentation in the center of each patty to help keep the burger flat as it cooks.

3. Brush a little oil on both sides of the patties (use a spray bottle or your fingers) and set them aside. Toss the sweet potato wedges with a little oil and season with salt and freshly ground black pepper. Remove the hot sheet pan from the oven and place the burger patties close together on one side of the pan, and the sweet potatoes on the other side (wedges pointing upwards will give you the best results).

4. Return the sheet pan to the oven and bake for 10 minutes. Flip the burgers over and toss the sweet potato wedges. Return the pan to the oven and continue to bake for another 5 minutes. Turn on the broiler and finish the burgers and sweet potatoes under the broiler for another 5 minutes. You can brush the burger buns with a little oil and toast them under the broiler at the same time. When everything is cooked through, the sweet potato wedges should be soft in the center with lightly browned edges, the burgers should have an internal temperature of 165ºF on an instant read thermometer, and the buns should be lightly toasted.

5. Combine the mayonnaise, lime juice and cilantro in a small bowl. Serve the burgers with the cilantro lime mayo or any of your choice of toppings – tomato ketchup, mustard, relish, onions, tomatoes, lettuce or salsa – along with the sweet potato wedges.

Chipotle Turkey Burgers with Sweet Potato Wedges

Air Fryer Directions

Serves: 4   **Cooking Time:** 14 + 20 minutes

1. Combine the ground turkey, onion, garlic, chipotle peppers, thyme and salt in a large bowl and gently mix the ingredients together with your hands. Divide the mixture into 4 equal portions and then form the hamburgers, being careful not to over-handle the meat. The burger mixture will be sticky. Try wetting your hands before you shape them so that the meat doesn't stick to your hands while you shape it into patties. Make an indentation in the center of each patty to help keep the burger flat as it cooks.

2. Pre-heat the air fryer to 370⁰F.

3. Brush a little oil on both sides of the patties (use a spray bottle or your fingers) and place them in the air fryer. Air-fry at 370⁰F for 8 minutes. Flip the burgers over and air-fry for another 6 minutes or until the internal temperature of the burger reaches 165⁰F. Remove the burgers to a side plate and set aside while you make the sweet potato wedges.

4. Toss the sweet potato wedges with a little oil, season with salt and freshly ground black pepper and transfer them to the air fryer. Air-fry at 400⁰F for 15 to 20 minutes, shaking the basket occasionally during the cooking process. You may need to do this in batches depending on the size of your air fryer.

5. When the fries are tender with lightly browned edges, remove them from the air fryer and pop the burger patties back in for 2 minutes along with the burger buns (cut side up).

6. Combine the mayonnaise, lime juice and cilantro in a small bowl. Serve the burgers with the cilantro lime mayo or any of your choice of toppings – tomato ketchup, mustard, relish, onions, tomatoes, lettuce or salsa – along with the sweet potato wedges.

Balsamic Chicken
with Summer Vegetables

Possible Cooking Methods: Stovetop and Oven   Pressure Cooker

We often think of comfort food in the winter, but make this recipe in the summertime when the zucchini and cherry tomatoes are ripe in the garden and you will definitely get that cozy comfort food feeling. The pressure cooker version of this recipe really intensifies the balsamic flavor by infusing it into the food under pressure. If you want a more intense balsamic vinegar flavor for the stovetop version, finish this dish by drizzling some balsamic glaze over the top, which conveniently you can buy in most grocery stores these days.

4 (5-ounce) boneless, skinless chicken breasts

salt and freshly ground black pepper

2 tablespoons all-purpose flour

olive oil

½ cup diced onion

1 teaspoon Italian seasoning

¼ cup white wine

½ cup balsamic vinegar*

1 tablespoon brown sugar

1 teaspoon Dijon mustard

1½ cups dried orzo

1 zucchini, sliced into ½-inch thick, half moons

1 yellow squash, sliced into ½-inch thick, half moons

2 cups chicken stock

1½ cups cherry tomatoes, halved

4 ounces fresh mozzarella cheese, sliced

1 tablespoon fresh chopped basil

Quantity changes for alternate methods

Stovetop and Oven Directions

Serves: 4   **Cooking Time:** 35 minutes

1. Pre-heat the oven to 350ºF.

2. Season the chicken breasts with salt and freshly ground black pepper, and lightly dredge each breast in flour. Pre-heat a 12-inch skillet over medium-high heat. Add the olive oil and brown the chicken for 5 minutes on each side. Remove the browned chicken breasts from the pan and set aside.

3. Add the onion and Italian seasoning to the skillet and sauté until the onion starts to brown – about 5 minutes. Pour in the white wine and deglaze the pan by scraping up any bits of brown on the bottom of the skillet. Add the balsamic vinegar, brown sugar and Dijon mustard and mix well. Simmer for a few minutes until the liquid starts to reduce. Add the orzo and stir to coat the pasta. Cook for another minute or two and then add the zucchini, yellow squash and chicken stock. Season with salt and freshly ground black pepper and simmer the orzo and vegetables uncovered for 5 minutes.

4. Stir in the cherry tomatoes and return the chicken breasts to the skillet, turning them over to coat each breast with the sauce. Top the chicken breasts with the fresh mozzarella cheese and transfer the pan to the oven. Bake at 350ºF for 10 minutes, until the cheese has melted and is starting to brown on top.

5. Serve the chicken breasts on a bed of the orzo and vegetables, with a little fresh basil on top.

Balsamic Chicken with Summer Vegetables

Pressure Cooker Directions

Serves: 4   **Cooking Time:** 20 minutes

Change Ingredients: Reduce balsamic vinegar to ⅓ cup

1. Pre-heat a 6-quart multi-function pressure cooker using the BROWN or SAUTE setting.

2. Season the chicken breasts with salt and freshly ground black pepper, and lightly dredge each breast in flour. Add the olive oil to the cooker and brown the chicken for 5 minutes on each side. Remove the browned chicken breasts from the cooker and set aside.

3. Add the onions and Italian seasoning to the skillet and sauté until the onion starts to brown – about 5 minutes. Pour in the white wine and deglaze the pan by scraping up any bits of brown on the bottom of the skillet. Simmer for a few minutes until the liquid reduces. (If your cooker doesn't have a brown setting, use a skillet on the stovetop for the steps above and

transfer the contents to the cooker now.) Add ⅓ cup balsamic vinegar, brown sugar, and Dijon mustard and stir well. Add the orzo, zucchini, yellow squash, chicken stock, and cherry tomatoes. Season with salt and freshly ground black pepper and return the chicken to the pot, nestling it into the orzo and vegetables. Cover and lock the lid in place.

4. Pressure cook on HIGH for 5 minutes.

5. Release the pressure with the QUICK-RELEASE method and carefully remove the lid. Immediately top the chicken breasts with fresh mozzarella cheese and return the lid to the cooker. Let the chicken sit in the warm cooker for a few minutes to melt the cheese.

6. Serve the chicken breasts on a bed of the orzo and vegetables, with a little fresh basil on top.

Skillet Chicken Enchilada Rice

Possible Cooking Methods: Stovetop   Pressure Cooker

Here's a quick and easy dinner for those busy weeknights. While it's not exactly like eating enchiladas, this recipe has all of the same flavors. You could warm up tortillas, spoon some chicken enchilada rice inside, roll it up and eat it like a burrito too.

---

1 tablespoon chili powder

1 teaspoon salt

¼ teaspoon freshly ground black pepper

1½ pounds chicken tenders
(or sliced chicken breasts)

olive oil

½ onion, diced

½ red bell pepper, diced

½ green bell pepper, diced

1 Jalapeño pepper, seeded and minced

1½ cups basmati rice*

2 cups chicken stock

1 (19-ounce) can enchilada sauce

1 (2.25-ounce) can sliced black olives, drained

2 cups grated Cheddar cheese

Cilantro Cream:

½ cup sour cream

2 teaspoons milk

juice of ½ lime

2 tablespoons chopped fresh cilantro

salt

avocado, diced (for serving)

*Quantity changes for alternate methods

Stovetop Directions

Serves: 4   **Cooking Time:** 35 minutes

1.   Combine the chili powder, salt and freshly ground black pepper in a small bowl. Rub this spice mixture on the chicken tenders and set them aside while you prepare the rest of the ingredients.

2.   Pre-heat a 12-inch skillet over medium-high heat. Add the olive oil and brown the chicken on both sides, making sure the spice mixture does not get too dark in the pan. Remove the browned chicken and set aside.

3.   Add the onion and peppers to the skillet, along with a little more oil if necessary and sauté for a few minutes. Add the rice and continue to sauté for another 2 minutes. Pour in the chicken stock and enchilada sauce and stir well. Lower the heat, cover the pan and simmer for 10 minutes.

4.   While the rice is cooking, make the cilantro cream by whisking the sour cream, milk and lime juice together in a bowl until smooth. Stir in the chopped cilantro and season with salt. Set this cream aside.

5.   Add the olives to the skillet and return the chicken tenders to the pan, nestling them gently into the rice. Cover the skillet and continue to simmer for 10 to 15 minutes, until the rice is fully cooked. Top the chicken and rice with grated Cheddar cheese, cover and leave the pan on low heat until the cheese has melted.

6.   Serve the chicken and rice with a drizzle of the cilantro cream and sprinkle the diced avocado on top.

Skillet Chicken Enchilada Rice

Pressure Cooker Directions

Serves: 4   **Cooking Time:** 15 minutes

Change Ingredients: Reduce the basmati rice to 1 cup

1. Pre-heat a 6-quart multi-function pressure cooker using the BROWN or SAUTE setting.

2. Combine the chili powder, salt and freshly ground black pepper in a small bowl. Rub this spice mixture on the chicken tenders and set them aside while you prepare the rest of the ingredients.

3. Add the chicken to the cooker and brown the chicken on both sides, making sure the spice mixture does not get too dark in the cooker. Remove the browned chicken and set aside.

4. Add the onion and peppers to the cooker, along with a little more oil if necessary and sauté for a few minutes. Add 1 cup of rice and continue to sauté for another 2 minutes. (If your cooker doesn't have a brown setting, use a skillet on the stovetop for the steps above and transfer the contents to the cooker now.)

Add the chicken stock, enchilada sauce, olives and browned chicken tenders to the cooker, nestling the chicken gently into to the rice. Cover and lock the lid in place.

5. Pressure cook on HIGH for 5 minutes.

6. While the rice is cooking, make the cilantro cream by whisking the sour cream, milk and lime juice together in a bowl until smooth. Stir in the chopped cilantro and season with salt. Set this cream aside.

7. Release the pressure using the QUICK-RELEASE method and carefully remove the lid. Sprinkle the grated Cheddar cheese on top and return the lid to the cooker for a few minutes to allow the cheese to melt.

8. Serve the chicken and rice with a drizzle of the cilantro cream and sprinkle the diced avocado on top.

Zuni Style Roast Chicken and Bread Salad

Possible Cooking Methods: Oven   Air Fryer

Zuni Café is a famous San Francisco restaurant known for many dishes, but perhaps their roast chicken is the most celebrated of all of them. I worked at Zuni back in the 1990s and roasted many a chicken there! You can't completely replicate the famous Zuni chicken without having a wood-fired brick oven in your house (which I do not!), but roasting the best small chicken you can find and salting it a day ahead of time certainly gets you closer to the goal. This recipe also includes their delicious bread salad. Using a 9-inch by 13-inch baking pan is critical to the success of this recipe. If you only have bigger sheet pans to use, double the recipe so that the torn bread is covered by the chicken pieces. You won't be sorry. Those bread pieces that soak up all the chicken juice are the best ones and no-one is sorry to have leftover chicken the next day – especially when it tastes this good!

1 (3- to 3½-pound) chicken, cut into 6 pieces (2 breasts, 2 thighs, 2 drumsticks)*

salt

½ pound rustic sourdough (levain) bread (about half a large round loaf)

1 tablespoon red wine vinegar

¼ cup extra virgin olive oil, plus extra for coating bread

salt and freshly ground black pepper

2 tablespoons dried cherries, soaked in 2 tablespoons of red wine vinegar for 15 minutes and then drained

2 tablespoons pecans or hazelnuts

6 fresh sage leaves

2 cups arugula

Quantity changes for alternate methods

Oven Directions

Serves: 4   **Cooking Time:** 45 minutes

1. A day ahead of time, season the chicken pieces generously with salt, cover and refrigerate. Keep the chicken in your refrigerator for 24 hours. Before you are ready to roast the chicken, rinse it and dry the pieces very well with paper towel.

2. Pre-heat the oven to 450ºF.

3. Cut the crusts off the sourdough bread chunks and tear the bread into 2-inch pieces. You should have about 3 cups of random shaped bread chunks. Toss the bread chunks with a little olive oil and place them in a 9-inch by 13-inch baking pan. Use a pan that is only as big as you need to have the bread chunks in one layer. Place the bread in the oven for 10 minutes, tossing once halfway through.

4. While the bread is toasting, make the vinaigrette with red wine vinegar, olive oil, salt and pepper. Drizzle half of this mixture over the bread pieces and set the remaining half aside. Scatter the soaked dried cherries and pecans into the pan.

5. Season the chicken with freshly ground black pepper. Use your fingers to separate the skin from the chicken on the thighs and breasts and push the sage leaves under the skin. Place the chicken pieces on top of the bread so that they are quite close together and cover the bread well. Drizzle a little olive oil on top of the chicken pieces and transfer the pan back to the oven.

6. Roast the chicken and bread together in the oven for 35 minutes. When the chicken is nicely browned and cooked through (it should have an internal temperature of 165ºF on an instant read thermometer), remove the chicken pieces to a resting plate, loosely tented with foil. Transfer the bread, cherries and nuts to a large bowl, add the arugula and toss in the remaining vinaigrette. Serve the chicken and bread salad together with a Caesar salad à la Zuni Café.

Zuni Style Roast Chicken and Bread Salad

Make sure you use the right size pan for the job. A 9-inch by 13-inch pan for this recipe is perfect, or you can double the recipe and use a sheet pan.

Air Fryer Directions

Serves: 4   **Cooking Time:** 30 minutes

Change Ingredients: Be sure to buy a small 3-pound chicken to fit into your 5-quart air fryer. Alternatively, you can cook just two breasts (cut in half) and two thighs OR cook the chicken in batches.

1. A day ahead of time, season the chicken pieces generously with salt, cover and refrigerate. Keep the chicken in your refrigerator for 24 hours. Before you are ready to roast the chicken, rinse it and dry the pieces very well with paper towel.

2. Pre-heat the air-fryer to 400ºF.

3. Season the chicken with freshly ground black pepper. Use your fingers to separate the skin from the chicken on the thighs and breasts and push the sage leaves under the skin. Place the chicken pieces into the air fryer basket and spray or drizzle with olive oil.

4. Air-fry at 400ºF for 12 minutes, skin side up. Turn the chicken over and air-fry for another 8 minutes. Remove the chicken to a resting plate, loosely tented with foil. Pour the drippings from the bottom of the air fryer drawer into a glass measure or small bowl and set the drippings aside.

5. Cut the crusts off the sourdough bread and tear the bread into 2-inch pieces. You should have about 3 cups of random shaped bread chunks. Toss the bread chunks with some of the chicken drippings and place them in the air fryer basket. Air-fry at 400ºF for 3 minutes.

6. While the bread is toasting, make the vinaigrette with red wine vinegar, olive oil, salt and pepper. Drizzle half of this mixture and scatter the dried cherries and pecans over the bread. Air-fry for another 2 minutes, tossing partway through. Return the chicken to the air fryer, laying it on top of the bread and air-fry for a final 2 minutes.

7. Remove the chicken to a serving platter. Transfer the bread salad from the air fryer to a big bowl. Add the arugula and toss with the remaining vinaigrette. Serve the chicken and bread salad with a Caesar salad à la Zuni Café.

Honey Mustard Chicken Breasts
with Potato Galette and Green Beans

Possible Cooking Methods: Oven Air Fryer

This sheet pan dinner is a great go-to meal for 4. The potato galette (a savory tart) is so elegant and delicious that once you learn how easy it is to make, it could become a side dish staple for you, whether you use the oven or the air fryer to make it. The key to making the galette is using a mandolin slicer so you get thinly (and evenly) sliced potatoes. Substituting asparagus for the green beans would be a nice change in the spring. Although this recipe comes out beautifully in your air fryer, you will need to air-fry the chicken and the vegetables in separate batches.

2 tablespoons Dijon mustard

2 tablespoons honey

1 teaspoon olive oil

1 teaspoon Worcestershire sauce

1 teaspoon salt

freshly ground black pepper

4 (5-ounce) boneless, skinless chicken breasts

1 pound Yukon gold potatoes (about 2 large), thinly sliced ⅛-inch thick

¼ cup butter, melted

½ shallot, minced

2 tablespoons fresh thyme leaves

4 ounces grated Gruyère cheese

12 ounces fresh green beans, (about 3 to 4 cups)

sprigs of fresh thyme

Oven Directions

Serves: 4   **Cooking Time:** 60 minutes

1. Combine the Dijon mustard, honey, olive oil, Worcestershire sauce, salt and freshly ground black pepper in a large bowl. Add the chicken breasts to the bowl, toss to coat both sides and pierce the chicken breasts several times with a fork to tenderize and help the marinade penetrate. Refrigerate the marinating chicken for 1 to 3 hours.

2. While the chicken is marinating, make the potato galette. Use a mandolin slicer to thinly slice the potatoes into ⅛-inch slices. Place the potato slices in a large bowl and add the melted butter, shallot, fresh thyme, salt and freshly ground pepper. Toss to coat well.

3. Pre-heat the oven to 375°F.

4. Brush or spray one quarter of a large sheet pan with oil. Shingle the potato slices on the greased sheet pan in three overlapping rows to make a 12-inch by 7-inch rectangle. Sprinkle one third of the cheese on top of the potatoes. Add two more layers of potato slices and grated cheese. In the end you should have one 12-inch by 7-inch rectangle made up of three layers of potato and cheese. Transfer the sheet pan to the oven.

5. Bake the potato galette for 25 minutes. Remove the pan from the oven and tilt the pan slightly to distribute the melted butter evenly over the empty section of the sheet pan. Toss the green beans with olive oil, salt and freshly ground black pepper and place them next to the potato galette. Place the marinated chicken breast on the empty portion of the sheet pan next to the beans and spoon the extra marinade on top of the chicken. Return the pan to the oven and bake for 30 minutes, tossing the green beans once during the cooking process.

6. After 30 minutes of baking, turn on the broiler. Broil the dinner for an additional 5 minutes, until the galette is golden brown and the chicken is cooked through (the internal temperature of the chicken should be 165ºF).

7. To serve, cut the potato galette into four pieces and garnish with fresh thyme sprigs. Transfer the chicken breasts to a platter, spooning any sauce on the tray over the top. Serve the chicken breasts with a portion of the potato galette and green beans on the side.

Honey Mustard Chicken Breasts with Potato Galette and Green Beans

Slicing the breast makes for a prettier presentation of this quick and easy chicken dinner.

Air Fryer Directions

Serves: 4 **Cooking Time:** 50 minutes

1. Combine the Dijon mustard, honey, olive oil, Worcestershire sauce, salt and freshly ground black pepper in a large bowl. Add the chicken breasts to the bowl, toss to coat both sides and pierce the chicken breasts several times with a fork to tenderize and help the marinade penetrate. Refrigerate the marinating chicken for 1 to 3 hours.

2. While the chicken is marinating, make the potato galette. Use a mandolin slicer to thinly slice the potatoes into ¹/₈-inch slices. Place the potato slices in a large bowl and add the melted butter, shallot, fresh thyme, salt and freshly ground pepper. Toss to coat well.

3. Place a 12-inch long piece of aluminum foil on the counter top. Arrange one third of the potatoes on the foil in a 7-inch circle overlapping each other. Make sure the circle is the same size or smaller than the air fryer basket. Sprinkle one third of the cheese over the potatoes. Repeat with 2 more layers of potato slices and grated cheese.

4. Pre-heat the air fryer to 380°F.

5. Use the aluminum foil to lower the potatoes (and foil) into the air fryer basket. Fold the foil loosely over the potatoes. Air-fry at 380°F for 30 minutes. Reduce the temperature of the air fryer to 340°F. Open the aluminum foil and poke some holes in the bottom of the foil for the fat to drain away. Air-fry for an additional 5 minutes to brown the top layer of the potatoes. Remove the potato galette from the air fryer and close the foil on top to keep the potatoes warm. (If desired, hold the potatoes in a 200°F oven to keep warm.) Discard any grease from the bottom of the air fryer drawer.

6. Cut the green beans in half and transfer them to the air fryer basket. Drizzle the beans with olive oil and season with salt and freshly ground black pepper.

7. Air-fry the green beans at 400°F for 5 to 7 minutes. Transfer them to a bowl and cover with foil.

8. Place the chicken breasts in the air fryer basket and pour the extra marinade over the top. Air-fry at 380°F for 6 to 8 minutes, flipping the breasts over halfway through the cooking process.

9. To serve, cut the potato galette into four pieces and garnish with fresh thyme sprigs. Transfer the chicken breasts to a platter, spooning any sauce from the bottom drawer over the top. Serve the chicken breasts with a portion of the potato galette and green beans on the side. Note: If needed, return the green beans to the air fryer for 1 to 2 minutes to warm them up.

Turkey Tetrazzini with Broccoli

Possible Cooking Methods: Stovetop   Pressure Cooker

Turkey Tetrazzini is a classic leftover turkey dish, but it's so much better if made with fresh turkey, browned before adding it to the sauce. This is a one-pot pasta dish, where the pasta cooks right in the pot with the sauce ingredients. You can make it in a pressure cooker too, with a short 3-minute cooking time, but I don't recommend it in the slow cooker because the pasta can get too soft very quickly.

1 pound turkey breast, cut into 1-inch pieces	1 teaspoon dried thyme	4 cups dry egg noodles (about 8 ounces)
salt and freshly ground black pepper	1 teaspoon salt and freshly ground black pepper	$^2/_3$ cup heavy cream
¼ cup all-purpose flour	¼ cup dry white wine (or vermouth or sherry)	1 cup grated Parmesan cheese, plus more for garnish
2 tablespoons olive oil, divided	3 cups chicken stock*	¼ cup chopped fresh parsley
1 onion, chopped	2 cups broccoli florets	1 to 2 tablespoons finely chopped lemon zest
3 ribs of celery, chopped		
12 ounces button mushrooms, sliced		*Quantity changes for alternate methods*

Stovetop Directions

Serves: 4   **Cooking Time:** 25 minutes

1. Pre-heat a large 12-inch sauté pan over medium-high heat.

2. Season the turkey pieces with salt and freshly ground black pepper. Toss the turkey with the flour, coating every piece thoroughly (tossing everything together in a zipper sealable plastic bag makes quick work of this). Add 1 tablespoon of olive oil to the sauté pan. Shake off any excess flour from the turkey pieces and add them to the pan, browning them well on all sides. Remove the browned turkey and set aside.

3. Add another tablespoon of olive oil to the pan and sauté the onion, celery, mushrooms, thyme, salt and freshly ground black pepper for 6 to 8 minutes, or until the vegetables start to soften. Add the white wine and let it come to a boil. Add the chicken stock and bring it to a boil. Stir in the broccoli and egg noodles, submerging the noodles in the liquid as well as you can. Return the browned turkey to the pan on top of the noodles. Then, cover and lower the heat to medium-low.

4. Simmer for 5 minutes, stirring occasionally, until the noodles are almost cooked al dente. Remove the lid, add the cream and continue to simmer uncovered for a few more minutes. Turn off the heat and add the Parmesan cheese and parsley. Stir well, season to taste with salt (you shouldn't need much because the Parmesan cheese is salty), freshly ground black pepper and lemon zest. Serve with a crusty roll and more Parmesan cheese to sprinkle on top at the table.

Turkey Tetrazzini with Broccoli

Pressure Cooker Directions

Serves: 4   **Cooking Time:** 18 minutes

Change Ingredients: Reduce the chicken stock to 2 cups

1. Pre-heat a 6-quart multi-function pressure cooker using the BROWN or SAUTE setting.

2. Season the turkey pieces with salt and freshly ground black pepper. Toss the turkey with the flour, coating every piece thoroughly (tossing everything together in a zipper sealable plastic bag makes quick work of this). Add 1 tablespoon of olive oil to the cooker. Shake off any excess flour from the turkey pieces and add them to the cooker, browning them well on all sides. Remove the browned turkey and set aside.

3. Add another tablespoon of olive oil to the cooker and sauté the onion, celery, mushrooms, thyme, salt and pepper for 6 to 8 minutes, or until the vegetables start to soften. Add the white wine and let it come to a boil. (If your cooker doesn't have a brown function, use a skillet on the stovetop for the steps above and transfer the contents to the cooker now.)

4. Add the chicken stock and egg noodles and stir well, submerging the noodles in the liquid as well as you can. Return the browned turkey to the pan on top of the noodles to help submerge the noodles in the liquid. Cover and lock the lid in place.

5. Pressure cook on HIGH for 2 minutes.

6. Release the pressure using the QUICK-RELEASE method and carefully remove the lid. Add the cream and broccoli and return the cooker to the brown setting for 3 minutes to simmer. Turn off the heat and add the Parmesan cheese and parsley. Stir well, season to taste with salt (you shouldn't need much because the Parmesan cheese is salty), freshly ground black pepper and lemon zest. Let the pasta sit to cool to an edible temperature. The broccoli will continue to cook and the sauce will thicken. Serve with a crusty roll and more Parmesan cheese to sprinkle on top at the table.

Chicken and Cashew Coconut Curry
with Potatoes, Cauliflower and Green Beans

Possible Cooking Methods: Stovetop Pressure Cooker Slow Cooker

This is an easy-to-please curry – it is not too spicy and has a gentle, sweet flavor that makes it popular with everyone. The puréed cashews help to make this curry smooth and creamy without adding dairy and the chopped toasted cashews give a nice crunch at the end. If you like spicy curries, feel free to increase the cayenne pepper in the recipe.

2 tablespoons vegetable or coconut oil*

1½ pounds boneless skinless chicken (breasts or thighs), cut into 2-inch chunks

1 sweet onion, finely chopped

1 clove garlic, minced

2 tablespoons grated fresh gingerroot

2 tablespoons curry powder

pinch (or more) cayenne pepper

1 pound red potatoes, ½-inch dice (about 3 medium potatoes)

3 cups chicken stock*

1 cup toasted cashews, divided

1 (13-ounce) can unsweetened coconut milk (not light coconut milk)

3 cups cauliflower florets, cut into bite-sized pieces

2 cups green beans, cut into 2-inch lengths

1½ to 2 teaspoons salt

¼ cup fresh basil, mint and/or cilantro leaves

Quantity changes for alternate methods

Stovetop Directions

Serves: 6   **Cooking Time:** 35 minutes

1. Pre-heat a 6-quart Dutch oven over medium-high heat.

2. Add the oil and brown the chicken pieces until they are no longer pink (no need to get serious browning here). Do this in batches so that you don't overcrowd the Dutch oven and then remove the chicken to a side plate. Add and sauté the onion until it starts to soften – about 5 minutes. Add the garlic and ginger and cook for 2 more minutes. Stir in the curry powder, cayenne pepper and potatoes and continue to cook for 1 minute longer. Pour in the chicken stock and bring the mixture to a simmer.

3. While the liquid is coming to a simmer, purée ¾ cup of the cashews with the coconut milk in a blender until smooth. Pour the cashew purée into the Dutch oven. Rough chop and reserve the remaining ¼ cup of cashews for garnish.

4. Return the chicken to the pot, along with the cauliflower and green beans.

5. Season with salt and continue to simmer with the lid askew for 20 minutes, until the vegetables are tender and the chicken has cooked through.

6. Season with salt to taste again and serve the curry with the chopped cashews and fresh herbs sprinkled on top. Serve with naan bread.

Chicken and Cashew Coconut Curry
with Potatoes, Cauliflower and Green Beans

Pressure Cooker Directions

Serves: 4   **Cooking Time:** 15 minutes

Change Ingredients: Reduce chicken stock to 2 cups

1. Pre-heat a 6-quart multi-function pressure cooker using the BROWN or SAUTE setting.

2. Add the oil and brown the chicken pieces until no longer pink (no need to get serious browning here). Do this in batches so that you don't overcrowd the cooker and then remove the chicken to a side plate. Add and sauté the onion until it starts to soften – about 5 minutes. Add the garlic, ginger, curry powder and cayenne pepper and cook for 2 more minutes. (If your cooker doesn't have a brown setting, use a skillet on the stovetop for the steps above and transfer the contents to the cooker now.)

3. Purée ¾ cup of the cashews with 1 cup of chicken stock in a blender until smooth. Pour the cashew purée into the cooker, along with the remaining 1 cup of stock. Rough chop and reserve the remaining ¼ cup of cashews for garnish.

4. Add the potatoes, cauliflower and green beans to the cooker. Return the chicken and season with salt and freshly ground black pepper. Cover and lock the lid in place.

5. Pressure cook on HIGH for 4 minutes.

6. Release the pressure with the QUICK-RELEASE method and carefully remove the lid. Stir in the coconut milk. Season with salt to taste and serve the curry with the chopped cashews and fresh herbs sprinkled on top. Serve with naan bread.

Slow Cooker Directions

Serves: 4   **Cooking Time:** 4 hours on LOW +
                                            2 hours on HIGH

Change Ingredients: Omit oil; reduce stock to 1 cup

1. Start by puréeing ¾ cup of the cashews with the coconut milk in a blender until smooth. Pour the cashew purée into a 6-quart slow-cooker. Rough chop and reserve the remaining ¼ cup of cashews for garnish.

2. Add the onion, garlic, ginger, curry powder, cayenne pepper, potatoes, 1 cup of chicken stock and the chicken to the cooker. Stir well to distribute everything evenly. Season with salt, cover and slow cook on LOW for 4 hours.

3. Add the cauliflower and green beans and nestle them down into the liquid, adding a little more chicken stock if necessary. Continue to slow cook on HIGH for another 2 hours.

4. Season with salt to taste and serve the curry with the chopped cashews and fresh herbs sprinkled on top. Serve with naan bread.

Italian Turkey Pot Pie with Parmesan Crust

Possible Cooking Methods: Stovetop and Oven

This recipe includes a few twists on a traditional pot pie. Turkey takes the main stage instead of chicken, the Italian spices and cheeses give it a boost of flavor, but it's the Parmesan crust that makes it special and delicious. While you could make the filling for the pot pie in a pressure cooker, you really won't save much time because you'll still need to transfer the filling to a baking dish and bake the top crust in the oven. So, there are no recommended alternative methods of cooking for this classic meal.

Cheese crust:

1½ cups all-purpose flour

¾ cup unsalted butter, chilled and cut into pieces

¾ cup grated Asiago or Parmesan cheese

2 to 2½ tablespoons water

Filling:

1 tablespoon olive oil

1½ pounds turkey breast, cut into 1-inch chunks

½ onion, chopped

1 clove garlic, minced

1 red bell pepper, chopped

8 ounces button mushrooms, sliced

2 zucchini, sliced into half moons

1 large Yukon Gold potato, diced ¼-inch (about 1 cup)

1 teaspoon Italian seasoning

½ teaspoon dried oregano

salt and freshly ground black pepper

3 tablespoons unsalted butter

4 tablespoons all-purpose flour

1½ cups milk

pinch of nutmeg

1 cup grated Fontina cheese

1 cup grated Parmesan cheese

1 tablespoon chopped fresh basil

1 egg, beaten

Stovetop and Oven Directions

Serves: 6   **Cooking Time:** 55 minutes

1. Combine the flour, butter and cheese in a food processor. Pulse the mixture into coarse crumbles and then slowly add the water through the feed tube, processing just until the dough comes together. Remove the dough from the food processor and shape it into a disk. Wrap the disk in plastic wrap and chill in the refrigerator for at least 30 minutes, or even overnight.

2. Pre-heat the oven to 425°F. Removed the chilled dough from the refrigerator and let it rest on the counter for 10 to 15 minutes.

3. Pre-heat a 12-inch double-handled skillet over medium-high heat. Add the olive oil and brown the turkey chunks on all sides. Do this in batches so that you don't overcrowd the pan, setting the browned turkey aside in a bowl. Add the onion to the skillet and sauté until it starts to brown – about 5 minutes. Add the garlic, red pepper, mushrooms, zucchini, potato, Italian seasoning and oregano and toss together. Season with salt and freshly ground black pepper and sauté for a couple of minutes, until the vegetables just start to soften. Transfer the vegetables to the bowl with the browned turkey.

4. Melt the 3 tablespoons of butter in the skillet. Stir in the flour and cook for a few minutes. Pour in the milk and whisk until smooth. Bring the mixture to a boil so that the sauce thickens and then turn off the heat. Add the nutmeg, Fontina and Parmesan cheeses and stir until all the cheese has melted. Add the fresh basil and return the turkey and vegetables to the pan with a slotted spoon, leaving the juices behind.

5. Roll the dough out on a floured surface into a 14-inch circle – one big enough to cover your skillet with a little extra. Transfer the dough to the top of the skillet and turn the extra inch around the edge underneath the dough, to make a crust. If you would like a decorative crust, press the back of a fork around the edge to make a pretty pattern and use extra dough to make decorations on top. Cut a small hole in the center of the dough to vent the pie and brush the entire surface with the beaten egg.

6. Transfer the skillet to the oven and bake for 40 minutes, until the crust is golden brown. Let the pie rest for 15 to 20 minutes before serving with a mixed green salad.

Creamy Tarragon Chicken and Egg Noodles

Possible Cooking Methods: Stovetop Pressure Cooker

This is a rich, creamy pasta dish that can be made on the stovetop or in the pressure cooker. The noodles cook right in the sauce, which not only flavors the noodles, but also helps to thicken the sauce at the same time. Tarragon and sherry pair so nicely together in this dish. You can use either sweet or dry sherry, but you'll end up with very different results. If you like foods on the sweeter side, go with a sweet sherry. Otherwise, I recommend a dry version. Either way, if you're looking for a warm, comforting pasta, this just might be your dish.

1 teaspoon olive oil

1½ pounds chicken breast (about 3), cut into cubes

salt and freshly ground black pepper

2 tablespoons butter

½ onion, diced

3 carrots, halved and sliced

8 ounces button mushrooms, sliced

2 tablespoons all-purpose flour

1 cup sherry

3 cups chicken stock*

⅔ cup heavy cream

4 cups dried extra wide egg noodles (12 ounces)

½ cup frozen peas

1 cup grated Swiss cheese

2 tablespoons chopped fresh tarragon

*Quantity changes for alternate methods

Stovetop Directions

Serves: 4 to 6   **Cooking Time:** 25 minutes

1. Heat the olive oil in a large 12-inch skillet. Season the chicken with salt and freshly ground black pepper. Brown the chicken cubes on all sides. Remove the browned chicken from the pan and set aside.

2. Add the butter, onion and carrots and sauté for a few minutes, until the onions start to soften. Add the mushrooms, season with salt and freshly ground black pepper and sauté for a few more minutes until all the vegetables begin to soften. Stir in the flour and cook for a minute or two. Add the sherry and bring it to a simmer until the mixture has thickened. Pour in the chicken stock and heavy cream, continue to simmer and stir until the sauce is completely smooth. Stir in the dried egg noodles.

3. Simmer uncovered for 10 minutes. Return the browned chicken to the pan, add the peas and cook for 2 to 3 more minutes, until the noodles are cooked. Remove the pan from the heat and stir in the Swiss cheese and tarragon. Let it sit for a few minutes. The sauce will thicken a little and it will cool to an edible temperature. Serve with a butter lettuce salad.

Creamy Tarragon Chicken and Egg Noodles

Pressure Cooker Directions

Serves: 4 to 6   **Cooking Time:** 25 minutes

Change Ingredients: Reduce chicken stock to 2 cups

1. Pre-heat a 6-quart multi-function pressure cooker using the BROWN or SAUTE setting.

2. Season the chicken with salt and freshly ground black pepper. Brown the chicken cubes on all sides. Remove the browned chicken from the cooker and set aside.

3. Add the butter, onion and carrots and sauté for a few minutes, until the onions start to soften. Add the mushrooms, season with salt and freshly ground black pepper and sauté for a few more minutes until all the vegetables begin to soften. Stir in the flour and cook for a minute or two. Add the sherry and bring it to a simmer until the mixture has thickened. Pour in the chicken stock and heavy cream, continue to simmer and stir until the sauce is completely smooth. (If your cooker doesn't have a brown setting, use a skillet on the stovetop for the steps above and transfer the contents to the cooker now.) Stir in the dried egg noodles. Return the chicken to the cooker, cover and lock the lid in place.

4. Pressure cook on HIGH for 6 minutes.

5. Release the pressure using the QUICK-RELEASE method and carefully remove the lid.

6. Stir in the peas, Swiss cheese and tarragon. Return the lid to the pot and let it sit for a few minutes. The sauce will thicken a little, the peas will heat through, the cheese will melt and everything will cool to an edible temperature. Serve with a butter lettuce salad.

Chicken Gumbo and Rice

Possible Cooking Methods: Stovetop Pressure Cooker

This is a delicious one-pot meal with great flavors and some kick. Feel free to tailor the spices to your preference if you are not a fan of spicy foods. The spice will come from the cayenne pepper and the sausage you choose. If there are any leftovers (this is doubtful), you will need to add a little liquid when you reheat the dish as the rice will continue to absorb the liquid. This dish is easily transportable and so easy to serve at the table – all the flavors you could ask for in one great pot.

1 tablespoon olive oil

1 pound Andouille pork sausage, cut into chunks

2 boneless skinless chicken breasts, cut into ½-inch pieces

1 onion, finely chopped

2 stalks celery, finely chopped

1 green bell pepper, finely chopped

4 cloves garlic, minced

¼ teaspoon cayenne pepper

½ teaspoon dried sage

½ teaspoon dried thyme

1 bay leaf

1½ cups long-grain white rice

4 cups chicken stock

1 (14-ounce) can chopped tomatoes

2 teaspoons Worcestershire sauce

1 teaspoon salt

freshly ground black pepper

6 ounces smoked ham, diced

4 scallions, sliced

Stovetop Directions

Serves: 6   **Cooking Time:** 40 minutes

1. Pre-heat a large Dutch oven over medium-high heat.

2. Add the oil and brown the Andouille sausage and chicken pieces in batches. Set the browned meats aside.

3. Add the onion, celery and green pepper and continue to cook until the onion is tender – about 5 minutes. Stir in the garlic, spices and rice and cook for another minute or two, stirring to coat all the rice with oil. Add the stock, tomatoes, Worcestershire sauce, salt and freshly ground black pepper. Return the browned sausage and chicken to the pot and bring the mixture to a simmer. Cover and simmer for 20 minutes on medium-low heat.

4. Season to taste with salt and freshly ground black pepper and stir in the ham. Serve in bowls with the scallions sprinkled on top, some crusty bread and a simple salad.

Chicken Gumbo and Rice

Pressure Cooker Directions

Serves: 6   **Cooking Time:** 25 minutes

Change Ingredients: Add 1 tablespoon of tomato paste

1. Pre-heat a 6-quart multi-function pressure cooker using the BROWN or SAUTE setting.

2. Add the olive oil and brown the Andouille sausage and chicken pieces in batches. Set the browned meats aside. Add the onion, celery, green pepper and garlic and continue to cook until the onion is tender. Stir in the spices and rice and cook for a minute or so, stirring to coat the rice with the oil. (If your cooker doesn't have a brown setting, use a skillet on the stovetop for the steps above and transfer the contents to the cooker now.)

3. Add the stock, tomatoes, tomato paste, ham, Worcestershire sauce, salt and pepper. Return the browned sausage and chicken to the pot, cover and lock the lid in place.

4. Pressure cook on HIGH for 6 minutes.

5. Reduce the pressure with the QUICK-RELEASE method and carefully remove the lid. Stir everything together and scatter the scallions on top. Serve in bowls with some crusty bread and a simple salad.

Greek Lemon Chicken
with Rice, Peppers and Olives

Possible Cooking Methods: Stovetop and Oven   Pressure Cooker

I love Greek flavors in foods – not just the obvious ones, like oregano and olives, but the subtle nuances from spices like cinnamon and allspice that make their way into so many savory Greek meals. Here the allspice gives that "what is that flavor?" quality and helps the chicken take on a nice deep brown color when seared. This recipe calls for chicken thighs and I often get questions about whether or not it's possible to substitute chicken breasts. You can substitute chicken breasts, but please leave the skin on. I tested this recipe in the pressure cooker both with the skin on and without skin. Keeping the skin on really helped to keep the chicken tender and moist, but the skin will not be crispy so feel free to remove the skin before eating.

1 cup basmati or long-grain white rice	8 chicken thighs, skin on and bone-in	1½ cups chicken stock*
1½ teaspoons dried oregano	2 tablespoons olive oil	½ cup pitted Kalamata olives
½ teaspoon ground allspice	1 onion, finely chopped	1 tablespoon chopped fresh oregano
1 tablespoon finely chopped lemon zest, plus 2 teaspoons for garnish	1 red bell pepper, sliced	lemon wedges (optional)
	1 yellow bell pepper, sliced	crumbled feta cheese (optional)
½ teaspoon salt	2 cloves garlic, minced	*Quantity changes for alternate methods*
freshly ground black pepper	½ cup white wine	

Stovetop and Oven Directions

Serves: 4 to 6   **Cooking Time:** 38 minutes

1. Start by soaking the rice. Place the rice in a bowl and cover with water. Let this sit while the oven pre-heats and as you prepare the rest of the ingredients.

2. Pre-heat a large 12-inch sauté pan over medium-high heat and pre-heat the oven to 350ºF.

3. Combine the oregano, allspice, 1 tablespoon of lemon zest, salt and freshly ground black pepper in a small bowl and then sprinkle this mixture on both sides of all the chicken thighs. Add the oil to the pan and sear the chicken on both sides until nicely browned – about 4 minutes per side. Remove the browned thighs and set aside them aside.

4. Add the onion and peppers to the pan and sauté until they start to soften – about 5 minutes. Add the garlic and sauté for another minute. Strain the rice and add it to the sauté pan, stirring to coat it with the residual fat in the pan. Add the white wine and let it come to a quick boil. Stir in the chicken stock and season the rice mixture with salt. Return the browned chicken to the pan, resting it on top of the rice. Cover with a tight-fitting lid and transfer the pan to the oven for 20 minutes. Remove the lid, add the olives and continue to bake uncovered for another 10 minutes.

5. Sprinkle the fresh oregano and remaining lemon zest on top. For extra lemon flavor, give the dish a squeeze of lemon. If you like feta cheese, a few crumbles on top will add a nice salty note to the meal. Serve with a Greek salad or Tzaziki (cucumber-yogurt salad).

Greek Lemon Chicken with Rice, Peppers and Olives

Pressure Cooker Directions

Serves: 4 to 6   **Cooking Time:** 35 minutes

Change Ingredients: Reduce the stock to 1 cup

1. Pre-heat a 6-quart multi-function pressure cooker using the BROWN or SAUTE setting.

2. Combine the oregano, allspice, 1 tablespoon of lemon zest, salt and freshly ground black pepper in a small bowl and then sprinkle this mixture on both sides of all the chicken thighs. Add the oil to the cooker and sear the chicken on both sides until nicely browned – about 4 minutes per side. Remove the browned thighs and set them aside.

3. Add the onion and peppers to the cooker and sauté until they start to soften – about 5 minutes. Add the garlic and sauté for another minute. Add the rice, stirring to coat it with any residual fat in the cooker. Add the white wine and let it come to a quick boil. (If your cooker doesn't have a brown setting, use a skillet on the stovetop for the steps above and transfer the contents to the cooker now.) Stir in the chicken stock and season the rice with salt. Return the browned chicken to the cooker, resting it on top of the rice, and scatter the olives around. Cover and lock the lid in place.

4. Pressure cook on HIGH for 8 minutes.

5. Release the pressure with the QUICK-RELEASE method and carefully remove the lid. Sprinkle the fresh oregano and remaining lemon zest on top. For extra lemon flavor, give the dish a squeeze of lemon. If you like feta cheese, a few crumbles on top will add a nice salty note to the meal. Serve with a Greek salad or Tzaziki (cucumber-yogurt salad).

Brandy-Glazed Stuffed Game Hens
with Roasted Fennel

Possible Cooking Methods: Oven   Air Fryer

This is a really nice one-pan recipe to serve on those special occasions when you are looking for something different to make for your guests. A Cornish game hen can serve one to two people depending on the size of the hen as well as the size of your appetite, so the serving size really varies here. If you'd like to serve one hen per person be sure to look for the smallest hens you can find. Either way, I like to cut the hens in half when I serve them, giving each person one or two halves. It's easier for your guests to manage that way, and the stuffing is exposed so you can have some with every bite. Since the size of the hens will vary remember the cooking time might vary a little too. If you have larger hens, be prepared to leave them in the oven or air fryer for a few minutes longer.

Stuffing:

6 cups toasted small bread cubes, ¼-inch (12 ounces)

1 cup warm chicken stock

4 tablespoons melted butter

½ cup dried cherries

½ cup dried apricots, chopped

½ teaspoon dried thyme

½ teaspoon dried sage

½ teaspoon onion powder

2 tablespoons chopped fresh parsley

1 egg

4 Cornish game hens

salt and freshly ground black pepper

1 teaspoon dried thyme

4 to 6 bulbs fennel, quartered

1 cup brandy

4 tablespoons melted butter

All quantities are halved for Air Fryer

The key to great browning on these game hens is to remember to glaze them with the brandy-butter glaze every 10 minutes.

Brandy-Glazed Stuffed Game Hens with Roasted Fennel

Oven Directions

Serves: 4 to 8   **Cooking Time:** 50 to 55 minutes

1. Pre-heat the oven to 425⁰F.

2. Combine the bread cubes, chicken stock, 4 tablespoons of the melted butter, dried cherries, apricots, thyme, sage, onion powder, parsley and egg in a bowl. Let the stuffing sit to absorb the liquid.

3. Rinse the Cornish hens and pat them dry with a clean kitchen towel. Divide the stuffing into 4 portions and fill the cavity of each hen. Tie the hens' legs together with kitchen twine and tuck the wings behind the neck. Rub olive oil all over hens and season with salt, freshly ground black pepper and thyme. Place the hens in a large roasting pan or on a sheet pan. Transfer the pan to the oven.

4. Roast at 425⁰F for 15 minutes. While the hens are roasting, whisk the brandy and melted butter together in a small bowl.

5. After 15 minutes, remove the pan from the oven and arrange the fennel wedges around the game hens. Drizzle the fennel with a little olive oil and season with salt and freshly ground black pepper. Brush the brandy mixture on the hens. Return the pan to the oven.

6. Roast for another 35 to 40 minutes, basting the game hens every 10 minutes with the brandy glaze. Flip the fennel over halfway through the cooking process. Roast until the internal temperature of the game hens reads 165°F on an instant read thermometer inserted into the thickest part of the thigh.

7. Let the hens rest for at least 20 minutes before serving. Split the hens in half and serve with the roasted fennel on the side and a spring greens salad.

Note – Time may be slightly longer if using large Cornish game hens.

Air Fryer Directions

Serves: 2 to 4   **Cooking Time:** 50 minutes

Change Ingredients: Cut ALL ingredient quantities in half

1. Combine the bread cubes, chicken stock, 4 tablespoons of the melted butter, dried cherries, apricots, thyme, sage, onion powder, parsley and egg in a bowl. Let the stuffing sit to absorb the liquid.

2. Divide the stuffing into 2 portions and fill the cavities of both hens. Tie the hens' legs together with kitchen twine and tuck the wings behind the neck. Rub olive oil all over the hens and season with salt and freshly ground black pepper.

3. Pre-heat the air fryer to 380⁰F.

4. Place the hens breast side down in the air fryer basket. Air-fry for 15 minutes. While the hens are air-frying, whisk the brandy and melted butter together in a small bowl. Start basting the game hens with glaze after the first 10 minutes of cooking time.

5. Flip the game hens over and brush more brandy glaze on the hens. Air-fry for an additional 15 to 20 minutes, basting every 10 minutes.

6. The hens have finished cooking when the internal temperature reads 165°F on an instant read thermometer inserted into the thickest part of the thigh. Remove the hens from the air fryer and set them aside, loosely tented with foil. Add the fennel to the air fryer basket, drizzle with olive oil and season with salt and freshly ground black pepper. Air-fry at 390⁰F for 15 minutes while the hens rest, turning the fennel over halfway through the cooking process.

7. Split the hens in half and serve with roasted fennel on the side and a spring greens salad.

Chicken Fricassée
with Wild Mushrooms and Spring Vegetables

Possible Cooking Methods: Stovetop   Pressure Cooker   Slow Cooker

This is a pretty dish to help celebrate the coming of spring. Wild mushrooms come in small packages but they can pack a lot of flavor. In this recipe, you'll re-hydrate the dried mushrooms in boiling water, creating your own mushroom stock. Be sure to strain the stock well to remove any silt. Then brighten the whole dish up with spring asparagus, scallions and a burst of lemon. I've removed the skin on the bone-in chicken thighs in this recipe because covered cooking on the stovetop makes getting a crispy skin impossible. To make browning skinless chicken thighs easier on the stovetop, don't skimp on the olive oil. This dish is particularly good in the slow cooker where the dried mushrooms have even more time to lend their flavor to the sauce.

1½ cups boiling water*	1 rib celery, thinly sliced	½ cup heavy cream
½ ounce, dried wild mushrooms	3 carrots, thinly sliced	½ bunch asparagus, cut into 1-inch lengths (about 2 cups)
8 skinless, bone-in chicken thighs	8 ounces brown or shiitake mushrooms, sliced	half a lemon, zest and juice
salt and freshly ground black pepper	3 sprigs fresh thyme*	chopped fresh scallions
1 tablespoon olive oil	2 tablespoons all-purpose flour	*Quantity changes for alternate methods*
1 onion, finely chopped	½ cup white wine*	

Stovetop Directions

Serves: 6   **Cooking Time:** 45 minutes

1.   Start by pouring boiling water over the dried mushrooms to rehydrate them. Let them sit for 15 minutes and then lift the mushrooms out of the liquid with a slotted spoon, chop them finely and set them aside in a bowl. Use a fine strainer to strain the soaking liquid into another bowl or glass measure to remove any silt or dirt. Set the wild mushroom stock aside as well.

2.   Pre-heat a large 12-inch sauté pan over medium-high heat. Season the chicken thighs well with salt and freshly ground black pepper. Add the oil to the sauté pan and brown the chicken thighs on all sides until nicely colored – about 5 minutes per side. Remove the browned thighs from the pan and set aside.

3.   Add the onion, celery and carrots to the pan and sauté until they start to soften – about 5 minutes. Add the mushrooms and fresh thyme sprigs and sauté for another 4 to 5 minutes. Add the flour to the pan and let it cook with the vegetables for another 2 minutes. Add the white wine to the pan and bring to a simmer, scraping up any brown bits that have developed on the bottom of the pan. Add the mushroom stock, the chopped wild mushrooms and heavy cream and return the chicken to the pan. Cover the pan with a lid and turn down the heat. Let the chicken simmer for about 15 minutes.

4.   Remove the lid and add the asparagus to the pan. Simmer uncovered for another 10 minutes or until the asparagus is tender. Season with salt and freshly ground black pepper to taste. Give the dish a squeeze of lemon juice and sprinkle the scallions and lemon zest on top. Serve with a hearty romaine salad.

Chicken Fricassée with Wild Mushrooms and Spring Vegetables

Pressure Cooker Directions

Serves: 6   **Cooking Time:** 40 minutes

Change Ingredients: Reduce boiling water to ¾ cup; reduce white wine to ¼ cup; add 1 tablespoon of room temperature butter

1. Start by pouring boiling water over the dried mushrooms to rehydrate them. Let them sit for 15 minutes and then lift the mushrooms out of the liquid with a slotted spoon, chop them finely and set them aside in a bowl. Use a fine strainer to strain the soaking liquid into another bowl or glass measure. Set the wild mushroom stock aside as well.

2. Pre-heat a 6-quart multi-function pressure cooker using the BROWN or SAUTE setting. Season the chicken thighs well with salt and freshly ground black pepper. Add the oil to the cooker and brown the chicken thighs on all sides until nicely colored – about 5 minutes per side. Remove the browned thighs from the pan and set aside.

3. Add the onion, celery and carrots to the cooker and sauté until they start to soften – about 5 minutes. Add the mushrooms and thyme sprigs and sauté for another 4 to 5 minutes. Add the white wine to the cooker and bring to a simmer, scraping up any brown bits that have developed on the bottom of the cooker. (If your cooker does not have a brown setting, use a skillet on the stovetop for the steps above and transfer the contents to the cooker now.) Add the mushroom stock, the chopped wild mushrooms and heavy cream and return the chicken to the cooker. Cover and lock the lid in place.

4. Pressure cook on HIGH for 6 minutes.

5. While the chicken is cooking, combine the flour with 1 tablespoon of softened butter in a small bowl to form a paste. Set this aside.

6. Release the pressure with the QUICK-RELEASE method and carefully remove the lid. Remove the chicken to a side plate and loosely tent with foil. Whisk the butter and flour mixture into the sauce and add the asparagus to the cooker. Return the lid, but do not lock it. Let the stew sit like this for 10 minutes. That should cook the asparagus, thicken the sauce and let the stew cool to an edible temperature. Season with salt and freshly ground black pepper to taste. Serve the chicken with the vegetables and sauce over top. Give the dish a squeeze of lemon juice and sprinkle the scallions and lemon zest on top. Serve with a hearty romaine salad.

Slow Cooker Directions

Serves: 6   **Cooking Time:** 3 to 4 hours on LOW
                                    +30 minutes on HIGH

Change Ingredients: Reduce boiling water to ¾ cup; omit white wine; remove thyme leaves from sprigs and chop

1. Start by pouring boiling water over the dried mushrooms to rehydrate them. Let them sit for 15 minutes and then lift the mushrooms out of the liquid with a slotted spoon, chop them finely and set them aside in a bowl. Use a fine strainer to strain the soaking liquid into another bowl or glass measure. Set the wild mushroom stock aside as well.

2. Pre-heat a 6-quart multi-function slow cooker using the BROWN or SAUTE setting. Season the chicken thighs with salt and freshly ground black pepper. Add the oil to the cooker and brown the chicken thighs on all sides until nicely colored – about 5 minutes per side. Remove the browned thighs from the pan and set aside. (If your cooker does not have a brown setting, use a skillet on the stovetop for the steps above and transfer the contents to the cooker now.)

3. Add the onions, celery, carrots, mushrooms, chopped wild mushrooms, mushroom stock and heavy cream to the cooker and stir to combine well. Return the chicken to the cooker, nestling it into the vegetables, cover and slow cook on LOW for 3 to 4 hours (2 hours on HIGH).

4. While the chicken is cooking, combine the flour with 1 tablespoon of softened butter. Set this aside.

5. Remove the lid and add the asparagus. Slow cook on HIGH for 30 minutes or until tender.

6. When you are ready to serve, remove the chicken to a side plate and whisk the butter and flour mixture into the sauce. Return the multi-cooker to the BROWN or HIGH setting, add the thyme leaves and let the sauce simmer and thicken. Season with salt and freshly ground black pepper to taste. Serve the chicken with the vegetables and sauce over top. Give the dish a squeeze of lemon juice and sprinkle the scallions and lemon zest on top. Serve with a hearty romaine salad.

Apple Butter Glazed Chicken
with Brussels Sprouts, Apples, and Fingerling Potatoes

Possible Cooking Methods: Oven   Air Fryer

This is a beautiful sheet pan dinner for the fall when apples and Brussels sprouts are abundantly available. This is the time of year when many of our lives tend to pick up the pace a little after a lazy summer so it's nice to have the entire meal made on one baking sheet, leaving only one cooking vessel to clean. It's also the time of year when we welcome turning our ovens back on and having those great aromas waft through the house. There are so many great reasons to serve this for dinner. Although the results for this recipe in the air fryer are great, you will need to air fry the chicken and vegetables in two separate batches, but not to worry - it will just take a couple of minutes to re-heat the chicken at the end.

½ cup apple butter

2 tablespoons chicken stock or water

2 tablespoons olive oil

½ teaspoon dried thyme

4 bone-in, skin-on chicken thighs

salt and freshly ground black pepper

12 ounces Brussels sprouts, halved

1½ pounds fingerling potatoes, halved lengthwise

1 tablespoon chopped fresh rosemary

1 Gala or Pink Lady apple, peeled and cut into 1-inch cubes

Oven Directions

Serves: 4   **Cooking Time:** 55 minutes

1. Pre-heat the oven to 375°F.

2. Combine the apple butter, chicken stock (or water), olive oil and dried thyme in a small bowl. Season the chicken thighs on both sides with salt and freshly ground black pepper and place them on one half of a large sheet pan. Brush the apple butter mixture on the chicken thighs.

3. Toss the Brussels sprouts with a little olive oil and season with salt and freshly ground black pepper. Place them in a single layer on one quarter of the sheet pan with the chicken. Toss the fingerling potatoes with a little olive oil, fresh rosemary, salt and freshly ground black pepper and place the potatoes on the other quarter of the sheet pan. Transfer the pan to the oven.

4. Bake at 375°F for 25 minutes. Turn the fingerling potatoes over. Add the apple to the Brussels sprouts and toss them together. Continue baking for an additional 25 to 30 minutes, until the chicken has an internal temperature of 160°F on an instant read thermometer inserted into the thickest part of the thigh. Turn the oven to broil and broil for 3 to 5 minutes to crisp the chicken skin and vegetables.

5. Serve family style, or transfer the chicken and vegetables to 4 individual dinner plates.

Apple Butter Glazed Chicken with Brussels Sprouts, Apples, and Fingerling Potatoes

Air Fryer Directions

Serves: 4   **Cooking Time:** 45 minutes

1. Pre-heat the air fryer to 380⁰F.

2. Combine the apple butter, chicken stock, olive oil and dried thyme in a small bowl. Season the chicken thighs on both sides with salt and freshly ground black pepper and place them skin-side down in the air fryer basket. Spoon some of the apple butter glaze over the chicken and air-fry at 380⁰F for 10 minutes.

3. Turn the chicken skin-side up and air-fry for 5 minutes. Then spoon the remaining apple butter glaze on top. Air-fry for an additional 5 minutes and then transfer the chicken to a plate, covering with foil to keep it warm. Discard any grease from the bottom drawer of the air fryer.

4. Toss the fingerling potatoes with a little olive oil, fresh rosemary, salt and freshly ground black pepper. Transfer the potatoes to the air fryer basket and air-fry at 400⁰F for 12 minutes, shaking the basket several times during the cooking process. Remove the potatoes from the air fryer and set aside.

5. Add the Brussels sprouts and apples to the air fryer basket. Drizzle with a little olive oil, season with salt and freshly ground black pepper and air-fry for an additional 10 to 12 minutes, until the sprouts are cooked through, tossing them halfway through the cooking process.

6. Transfer the vegetables to serving bowls, place the chicken back in the air fryer and air-fry at 380°F for 2 minutes (just to heat through), and serve the chicken with the vegetables on the side.

There is no butter in apple butter, which is a little confusing. Apple butter is a concentrated form of apple sauce, made by stewing apples until all the water evaporates and the sauce turns a deep brown.

Coq au Vin Blanc

Possible Cooking Methods: Stovetop Pressure Cooker Slow Cooker

Coq au vin blanc takes the traditional coq au vin and uses white wine instead of red. The white wine gives it a little lighter feel, even if you choose to finish it with the heavy cream listed in the ingredients as optional. I suggest using a wine from Burgundy for this recipe. That is what is traditionally used when cooking with red wine. Burgundy whites are usually Chardonnays, but they are much less oaky than American Chardonnays. You could also use a Pinot Gris or a French Sauvignon Blanc for this recipe very successfully. Whatever you use, remember that it's also nice to cook with wine in a glass as well, so be sure to pick one that you like! Traditional cooking on the stovetop is my recommended version of this recipe, although the pressure cooker is a close second.

1 tablespoon olive oil

6 strips of bacon, chopped

3 pounds bone-in skin-on chicken thighs (about 8 large)

salt and freshly ground black pepper

10 ounces button mushrooms, quartered or cut into chunks*

24 pearl onions, fresh and peeled, or frozen and thawed

1 onion, sliced

3 carrots, sliced

2 cloves garlic, minced

1 teaspoon dried thyme

1 bay leaf

1 sprig fresh rosemary

¼ cup all-purpose flour*

3 cups white wine*

½ cup chicken stock

¼ cup heavy cream (optional)

2 tablespoons chopped fresh tarragon

Quantity changes for alternate methods

Stovetop Directions

Serves: 6   **Cooking Time:** 60 minutes

1. Pre-heat a wide 5-quart braiser pan over medium heat.

2. Add the olive oil and bacon and cook until crisp. Remove the bacon and reserve, leaving the bacon fat in the pan. Season the chicken with salt and freshly ground black pepper and sear in batches until well browned on all sides. Remove the chicken to a side plate once browned.

3. Add the mushrooms to the pan and brown well – about 5 to 8 minutes. Once they are nicely browned, add the pearl onions, sliced onion and carrots to the pan and cook until starting to soften – about 5 minutes. Add the garlic, thyme, bay leaf and rosemary and cook for another 2 minutes. Sprinkle in the flour and continue to cook for a minute or two. Pour in the white wine and let it come to a simmer for a few minutes. Add the chicken stock, scraping up any brown bits on the bottom of the pan. Return the chicken to the pan and cover with the lid askew. Lower the heat to keep a gentle simmer in the pan and cook for 30 minutes.

4. Pre-heat the broiler.

5. Remove the lid from the pan and pop it under the broiler for 5 minutes to color and crisp the skin. Pour in the heavy cream (if using) and remove the rosemary sprig. Season to taste with salt and freshly ground black pepper and sprinkle the fresh tarragon and the cooked bacon on top. Serve with a mixed green salad – a salad with radicchio and fennel would be especially nice.

Additional Cooking Directions for

Coq au Vin Blanc

Pressure Cooker Directions

Serves: 6   **Cooking Time:** 40 minutes

Change Ingredients: Remove skin from chicken thighs; slice mushrooms instead of quartering; reduce wine to 2 cups; reduce flour to 2 tablespoons; add 1 tablespoon butter

1. Pre-heat a 6-quart multi-function pressure cooker using the BROWN or SAUTE setting.

2. Add the olive oil and bacon to the cooker and cook until crisp. Remove the bacon and reserve, leaving the bacon fat in the cooker. Season the chicken with salt and freshly ground black pepper and sear in batches until well browned on all sides. Remove the chicken to a side plate once browned.

3. Add the mushrooms to the cooker and brown well – about 5 to 8 minutes. Once they are nicely browned, add the pearl onions, sliced onion and carrots to the cooker and cook until the onions starts to soften – about 5 minutes. Add the garlic, thyme, bay leaf and rosemary and cook for another 2 minutes. Pour in the white wine and let it come to a simmer for a few minutes.

Add the chicken stock, scraping up any brown bits on the bottom of the cooker. (If your cooker doesn't have a brown setting, use a skillet on the stovetop for the steps above and transfer the contents to the cooker now.) Return the chicken to the cooker, cover and lock the lid in place.

4. Pressure cook on HIGH for 10 minutes

5. Release the pressure with the QUICK-RELEASE method and carefully remove the lid. Transfer the chicken to a side plate.

6. Mix the flour with 1 tablespoon of soft butter, making a paste. Bring the sauce to a simmer in the cooker using the BROWN setting and whisk the butter and flour paste into the liquid to thicken. Add the heavy cream (if using) and return the chicken to the cooker to warm through and coat with the sauce. Season to taste with salt and freshly ground black pepper and sprinkle the fresh tarragon and cooked bacon on top. Serve with a mixed green salad – a salad with radicchio and fennel would be especially nice.

Slow Cooker Directions

Serves: 6   **Cooking Time:** 4 to 6 hours on LOW
+30 minutes on HIGH

Change Ingredients: Remove skin from chicken thighs; slice mushrooms instead of quartering; reduce flour to 2 tablespoons; reduce wine to 2 cups

1. Pre-heat a 6-quart multi-function slow cooker using the BROWN or SAUTE setting.

2. Add the olive oil and bacon to the cooker and cook until crisp. Remove the bacon and reserve, leaving the bacon fat in the cooker. Season the chicken with salt and freshly ground black pepper and sear in batches until well browned on all sides. Remove the chicken to a side plate once browned.

3. Add the mushrooms to the cooker and brown well – about 5 to 8 minutes. Once they are nicely browned, add the pearl onions, sliced onion and carrots to the cooker and cook until

starting to soften – about 5 minutes. Add the garlic, thyme, bay leaf and rosemary and cook for another 2 minutes. Sprinkle in the flour and continue to cook for a minute or two. Pour in the white wine and let it come to a simmer for a few minutes. Add the chicken stock, scraping up any brown bits on the bottom of the cooker. (If your cooker doesn't have a brown setting, use a skillet on the stovetop for the steps above and transfer the contents to the cooker now.) Return the chicken to the cooker, cover and slow cook on LOW for 4 to 6 hours (or 2½ hours on HIGH).

4. Add the heavy cream (if using) and slow cook on HIGH for 30 minutes. Season to taste with salt and freshly ground black pepper and sprinkle the fresh tarragon and cooked bacon on top. Serve with a mixed green salad – a salad with radicchio and fennel would be especially nice.

Pennsylvania Dutch Chicken Pot Pie
with Leeks and Lemon

Possible Cooking Methods: Stovetop   Pressure Cooker

Chicken pot pie is a classic comfort meal, but Pennsylvania Dutch pot pie might not be what you're expecting. Instead of a pastry crust, this version of the classic has square egg noodles inside the thick stew, similar to the rolled dumplings in another comfort classic – chicken and dumplings. (If you're looking for the traditional "pot pie", check out the Italian Turkey Pot Pie with Parmesan Crust on page 40.) This recipe calls for 1½ pounds of chicken breasts and thighs. You can use any combination of breasts and thighs, but 2 chicken breasts and 4 chicken thighs would be about right.

2 tablespoons butter

3 large leeks, cleaned, halved, dark green parts removed, white and light green parts sliced ½-inch thick

3 carrots, sliced ¼-inch thick

3 ribs celery, sliced ¼-inch thick

4 sprigs fresh thyme

2 cloves garlic, minced

6 cups chicken stock*

1½ pounds boneless, skinless chicken breasts and thighs

1½ teaspoons salt

freshly ground black pepper

1 (12-ounce) can evaporated milk*

1 pound Yukon gold potatoes, peeled, halved or quartered and then sliced ¼-inch thick

12 ounces dried "pot pie" square egg noodles

1 cup corn kernels, fresh or frozen and thawed

1 tablespoon lemon zest

juice of ½ lemon

¼ cup chopped fresh parsley

Quantity changes for alternate methods

Stovetop Directions

Serves: 6 to 8   **Cooking Time:** 75 minutes

1. Pre-heat a large 6-quart Dutch oven over medium heat. Add the butter and sauté the leeks, carrots, celery, thyme and garlic for 2 to 3 minutes, until the vegetables start to soften.

2. Pour in the chicken stock and bring it to a boil. Cut the chicken breasts in half on the bias and add all the chicken pieces to the pot. Season with salt and freshly ground black pepper, cover and simmer for 45 minutes.

3. Stir in the evaporated milk and add the potatoes to the pot. Cook for 10 minutes and then remove the chicken pieces from the pot and set aside.

4. Add the dried egg noodles along with the corn and cook for 10 minutes. While the noodles are cooking, shred the chicken with two forks. Return the shredded chicken to the pot and continue to cook for 5 to 8 more minutes, until the noodles are soft.

5. Stir in the lemon zest, lemon juice and fresh parsley, season to taste with salt and freshly ground black pepper and serve in bowls with salad greens as an accompaniment.

Pennsylvania Dutch Chicken Pot Pie with Leeks and Lemon

Pressure Cooker Directions

Serves: 6 to 8   **Cooking Time:** 5 minutes

Change Ingredients: Cut chicken into bite-sized pieces; reduce chicken stock to 5 ½ cups; replace the can of evaporated milk with 1 cup of heavy cream

1. Pre-heat a 6-quart multi-function pressure cooker using the BROWN or SAUTE setting.

2. Add the butter to the cooker and brown the chicken pieces on all sides. Remove the chicken from the cooker and set aside. Add the leeks, carrots, celery, thyme and garlic and continue to sauté until the leeks start to soften – about 2 to 3 minutes.

3. Add the chicken stock, heavy cream, browned chicken, potatoes, corn and dried egg noodles. Season with salt and freshly ground black pepper, cover and lock the lid in place.

4. Pressure cook on HIGH for 5 minutes.

5. Release the pressure using the QUICK-RELEASE method and carefully remove the lid. Stir in the lemon zest, lemon juice, and fresh parsley, season to taste with salt and freshly ground black pepper and serve in bowls with salad greens as an accompaniment.

Summer Ale Chicken
with Onions, Baby Red Potatoes and Summer Corn

Possible Cooking Methods: Oven   Air Fryer

Though I may say so myself, this spice rub blend is a keeper! I use it on chicken all the time, but it's great on pork as well. When you're making this recipe, mix together a big batch of the spice mix and store it away in your spice drawer for a rainy day. Summertime ale and fresh corn, cut right off the cob, make this a really delightful summer meal. It's a crowd pleaser so you might want to think about making TWO sheet pans full.

Spice Mix:

2 tablespoons brown sugar

2 tablespoons paprika

1 teaspoon dry mustard powder

2 tablespoons coarse sea salt or kosher salt

2 teaspoons coarsely ground black pepper

vegetable oil

1 (4-pound) whole chicken, sliced in half and backbone removed

2 to 3 sweet onions, sliced

2 tablespoons butter, melted

3 sprigs fresh thyme

salt and freshly ground black pepper

1½ pounds baby red potatoes, halved

12 ounces summer ale beer (or any hoppy amber ale)

4 ears fresh corn on the cob, kernels cut off

1 tablespoon chopped fresh chives

Summer Ale Chicken with Onions, Baby Red Potatoes and Summer Corn

Oven Directions

Serves: 4   **Cooking Time:** 80 minutes

1. Pre-heat the oven to 425⁰F

2. Combine the brown sugar, paprika, dry mustard, salt and black pepper in a small bowl. Rub a little vegetable oil all over the chicken and rub the spice mixture on both sides of the chicken halves. Set the chicken aside.

3. Toss the sliced onions with the melted butter and thyme sprigs and season with salt and freshly ground black pepper. Place them onto a 15-inch by 10-inch sheet pan and roast in the oven for 20 minutes.

4. When the onions have roasted for 20 minutes, remove the pan from the oven. Move the onions to the center of the sheet pan to make a bed for the chicken. Place the chicken halves on top of the onions, skin side up. Arrange the baby red potatoes around the chicken, drizzle with a little olive oil and season with salt and freshly ground black pepper. Pour the ale into the pan and roast for 30 minutes.

5. After 30 minutes of roasting time, baste the chicken with the juices in the pan. Sprinkle the corn kernels around the chicken and toss them in with the potatoes. Return the pan to the oven and roast for another 25 to 30 minutes, until the chicken reaches an internal temperature of 165⁰F on an instant read thermometer inserted into the thickest part of the thigh.

6. Remove the pan from the oven. Transfer the chicken to a cutting board and let it rest. Transfer the onions to a serving bowl and pour all the juices from the pan on top. If you prefer your potatoes crispy, set the oven to broil and send the potatoes back to the oven for 5 minutes.

7. Cut the chicken into pieces and serve it with the onions and jus on top and the roasted baby red potatoes and corn on the side. Sprinkle the chopped chives over everything.

Air Fryer Directions

Serves: 2 to 3   **Cooking Time:** 60 to 70 minutes

Change Ingredients: For 3-quart air fryers only - Cut ALL ingredient quantities in half

1. Pre-heat the air fryer to 400⁰F.

2. Combine the brown sugar, paprika, dry mustard, salt and black pepper in a small bowl. Brush or spray the oil all over the chicken. Set aside 1 tablespoon of the spice mix and rub the remaining mix on both sides of the chicken. Set the chicken aside.

3. Toss the baby red potatoes with olive oil, salt and freshly ground black pepper in the air fryer basket. Air-fry at 400⁰F for 10 minutes. Remove the potatoes from the air fryer and set aside.

4. Toss the onions with the melted butter and season with salt and freshly ground black pepper. Transfer them to the air fryer basket and air-fry at 400⁰F for 8 minutes.

5. When the onions have air-fried for 10 minutes, give them a toss and pour the summer ale over the onions in the air fryer

– most of the beer will end up in the drawer below. Place the chicken on top of the onions, skin side down and air-fry the chicken and onions together at 360°F for 20 minutes. Flip the chicken over and sprinkle the reserved spice mix on top. Air-fry for an additional 15 to 20 minutes, until the internal temperature on an instant read thermometer inserted into the thickest part of the thigh registers 165⁰F.

6. Remove the chicken from the air fryer and let it rest. Transfer the onions to a serving bowl and pour the juices from the bottom drawer over the onions.

7. Place the potatoes back into the air fryer basket and add the corn kernels. Air-fry for 10 to 13 minutes, shaking the basket a couple of times during the cooking process.

8. Cut the chicken into pieces and serve it with the onions and jus on top and the roasted baby red potatoes and corn on the side. Sprinkle the chopped chives over everything.

Beef

One Pot Penne Bolognese
with Fennel Seed

Possible Cooking Methods: Stovetop   Pressure Cooker   Slow Cooker

Pasta with a Bolognese sauce is a classic recipe, but in this version the fennel seed adds a subtle twist. There are many ways to make a Bolognese sauce and you can use your stovetop, pressure cooker OR slow cooker. The stovetop and pressure cooker methods qualify as one-pot cooking because the pasta can cook right in the sauce. If you are using a slow cooker, however, just make the sauce in the cooker and serve it over cooked pasta. To add a little green vegetable to this one pot dish, you could add spinach or arugula to the sauce just before serving, or toss in a few broccoli florets near the end of the cooking time – just long enough for the broccoli to cook though and become tender. To simplify your shopping experience, buy the typical meatloaf mix of beef, pork and veal.

1 tablespoon olive oil	½ pound ground beef	1 cup white wine (or red wine if you prefer)
1 onion, finely chopped	½ pound ground pork	1 (28-ounce) can tomatoes, diced
2 carrots, finely chopped	½ pound ground veal (or turkey)	3 cups beef stock*
2 ribs of celery, finely chopped	1½ teaspoons salt	12 ounces dried penne pasta (about 4 cups)
1 tablespoon fennel seeds	freshly ground black pepper	grated Parmigiano-Reggiano cheese
4 sprigs fresh thyme	1 cup milk*	*Quantity changes for alternate methods*

Stovetop Directions

Serves: 6   **Cooking Time:** 3 hours

1. Pre-heat a large Dutch oven over medium heat.

2. Add the olive oil and sauté the onion, carrots and celery until the vegetables start to soften – about 6 minutes. Stir in the fennel seeds and fresh thyme and cook for another minute or so. Add the meats to the Dutch oven and season with salt and freshly ground black pepper. Break the chunks up with a wooden spoon as you brown the meat until there is no pink left visible.

3. Pour in the milk and stir, scraping the bottom of the Dutch oven to incorporate any bits of flavor. Increase the heat a little and simmer until the milk has almost entirely disappeared – about 8 to 10 minutes. Add the wine and continue to simmer until it too has almost disappeared – another 10 minutes.

4. Add the tomatoes and bring to a simmer. Simmer (with a lid askew) for at least 2 hours.

5. Thirty minutes before you are ready to serve, add the beef stock and the penne and return the mixture to a full simmer. Continue to simmer for another 25 minutes.

6. Season to taste with salt and freshly ground black pepper and serve with Parmesan cheese at the table.

One Pot Penne Bolognese with Fennel Seed

Pressure Cooker Directions

Serves: 6   **Cooking Time:** 25 minutes

Change Ingredients: Omit the milk; add 2 tablespoons tomato paste; reduce stock to 2 cups

1. Pre-heat a 6-quart multi-function pressure cooker using the BROWN or SAUTE setting.

2. Add the olive oil and sauté the onion, carrots and celery until the vegetables start to soften – about 6 minutes. Stir in the fennel seeds and fresh thyme and cook for another minute or so. Add the meats to the cooker and season with salt and freshly ground black pepper. Break the chunks up with a wooden spoon as you brown the meat until there is no pink left visible.

3. Add the wine and stir, scraping the bottom of the cooker to incorporate any bits of flavor. Bring the mixture to a boil for 2 minutes. (If your multi-cooker doesn't have a brown setting, use a Dutch oven on the stovetop for the steps above and transfer the contents to the cooker now.)

4. Add the tomatoes, tomato paste and beef stock and stir in the pasta, doing your best to get the pasta covered with liquid. Cover and lock the lid in place.

5. Pressure cook on HIGH for 7 minutes.

6. Release the pressure with the QUICK-RELEASE method and carefully remove the lid.

7. Season to taste with salt and freshly ground black pepper and serve with Parmesan cheese at the table.

Slow Cooker Directions

Serves: 6   **Cooking Time:** 6 to 8 hours on LOW

Change Ingredients: Omit the milk; add 2 tablespoons tomato paste; reduce stock to 1 cup; serve over cooked pasta

1. Pre-heat a 6-quart multi-function slow cooker using the BROWN or SAUTE setting.

2. Add the olive oil and sauté the onion, carrots and celery until the vegetables start to soften – about 6 minutes. Stir in the fennel seeds and fresh thyme and cook for another minute or so. Add the meats to the cooker and season with salt and freshly ground black pepper. Break the chunks up with a wooden spoon as you brown the meat until there is no pink left visible.

3. Add the wine and stir, scraping the bottom of the cooker to incorporate any bits of flavor. Bring the mixture to a boil for 2 minutes. (If your multi-cooker doesn't have a brown setting, use a Dutch oven on the stovetop for the steps above and transfer the contents to the cooker now.)

4. Add the tomatoes, tomato paste and beef stock and stir. Cover and slow cook on LOW for 6 to 8 hours (or 3 to 4 hours on HIGH).

5. Season to taste with salt and feshly ground black pepper and serve over cooked pasta with Parmesan cheese at the table.

Short Rib Ragu with Rigatoni

Possible Cooking Methods: Stovetop   Pressure Cooker   Slow Cooker

This hearty ragu is worth the time it takes to make on the stovetop. The pressure cooker version is a good alternative if you're short on time. When making the ragu in the slow cooker, however, I suggest you cook the rigatoni on the stovetop the traditional way, as cooking pasta in the slow cooker does not yield the best results.

3 pounds boneless beef short ribs

salt and freshly ground black pepper

1 tablespoon olive oil

½ small onion, diced

1 carrot, diced

1 clove garlic, minced

1 teaspoon dried basil

1 teaspoon dried oregano

1 tablespoon tomato paste

½ cup red wine

1 (28-ounce) can crushed tomatoes

1 (14-ounce) can diced tomatoes

2½ cups beef stock*

1 tablespoon balsamic vinegar

1 bay leaf

1 pound dried rigatoni pasta

2 tablespoons chopped fresh parsley

Parmesan cheese, for serving

*Quantity changes for alternate methods

Stovetop Directions

Serves: 6   **Cooking Time:** 4 hours

1.   Season the short ribs with salt and freshly ground black pepper. Pre-heat a large 6-quart Dutch oven over medium heat. Add the oil and brown the short ribs on all sides. Transfer the browned meat to a plate and set aside.

2.   Pour off all but 1 tablespoon of the grease. Add the onion and carrot to the pot and sauté for a few minutes, until the onion starts to soften. Add the garlic, basil, oregano and tomato paste and continue to sauté for a couple of minutes. Then de-glaze the pot with the red wine, scraping any brown bits on the bottom of the pot. Add the crushed tomatoes, diced tomatoes, beef stock, balsamic vinegar and bay leaf. Season with salt and freshly ground black pepper and bring the liquid to a simmer. Return the browned short ribs to the pot, nestling them down into the liquid. Cover with the lid, slightly askew. Reduce the heat and simmer on the stovetop for 3 hours.

3.   Remove the grease from the top of the sauce with a ladle or shallow spoon and discard. Transfer the short ribs to a cutting board. Add the dried pasta to the pot along with 1 cup of water. Cook at a low boil for 30 minutes, stirring occasionally. Shred the short ribs with two forks and return the shredded meat to the sauce. Cook for another 5 to 10 minutes, until the pasta has cooked through. Season with salt and feshly ground black pepper to taste and stir in the chopped fresh parsley.

4.   Serve with Parmesan cheese and a frisée salad.

Short Rib Ragu with Rigatoni

Pressure Cooker Directions

Serves: 6   **Cooking Time:** 80 minutes

Change Ingredients: Reduce beef stock to 2 cups

1. Pre-heat a 6-quart multi-function pressure cooker using the BROWN or SAUTE setting.

2. Season the short ribs with salt and freshly ground black pepper. Add the oil and brown the short ribs on all sides. Transfer the browned meat to a plate and set aside.

3. Pour off all but 1 tablespoon of the grease. Add the onion and carrot to the cooker and sauté for a few minutes. Add the garlic, basil, oregano, and tomato paste and continue to sauté for a couple of minutes. Then deglaze the cooker with the red wine, bringing the liquid to a boil and scraping any brown bits on the bottom of the cooker. (If your cooker doesn't have a brown setting, use a skillet on the stovetop for the steps above and transfer the contents to the cooker now.) Pour in the crushed tomatoes, diced tomatoes, beef stock, balsamic vinegar and bay leaf. Season with salt and freshly ground black pepper and return the browned short ribs to the cooker, submerging them in the liquid.

4. Pressure-cook on HIGH for 55 minutes.

5. Let the pressure drop NATURALLY and carefully remove the lid.

6. Remove the grease from the top of the sauce with a ladle or shallow spoon and discard. Transfer the short ribs to a cutting board. Add the dried pasta to the pressure cooker and return the lid to the cooker, locking it in place.

7. Pressure-cook on HIGH for 5 minutes.

8. Release the pressure using the QUICK-RELEASE method and carefully remove the lid.

9. While the pasta is cooking, shred the short ribs with two forks and return the meat to the pot with the cooked pasta. Season with salt and freshly ground black pepper to taste and stir in the chopped fresh parsley.

10. Serve with Parmesan cheese and a frisée salad.

Slow Cooker Directions

Serves: 6   **Cooking Time:** 5 to 6 hours on HIGH

Change Ingredients: Reduce beef stock to 1 cup; serve over cooked pasta

1. Pre-heat a 6-quart multi-function slow cooker using the BROWN or SAUTE setting.

2. Season the short ribs with salt and freshly ground black pepper. Add the oil and brown the short ribs on all sides. Transfer the browned meat to a plate and set aside.

3. Pour off all but 1 tablespoon of the grease. Add the onion and carrot to the cooker and sauté for a few minutes. Add the garlic, basil, oregano and tomato paste and continue to sauté for a couple of minutes. Then deglaze the cooker with the red wine, bringing the liquid to a boil and scraping any brown bits on the bottom of the cooker. (If your cooker doesn't have a brown setting, use a skillet on the stovetop for the steps above and transfer the contents to the cooker now.) Pour in the crushed tomatoes, diced tomatoes, beef stock, balsamic vinegar and bay leaf. Season with salt and freshly ground black pepper and return the browned short ribs to the cooker, submerging them in the liquid.

4. Cover and slow cook on HIGH for 5 to 6 hours (or 10 hours on LOW).

5. Remove the grease from the top of the sauce with a ladle or shallow spoon and discard. Transfer the short ribs to a cutting board. Shred the short ribs with two forks and return the meat to the cooker. Season with salt and freshly ground black pepper to taste and stir in the chopped fresh parsley.

6. When ready to serve, add cooked pasta to the slow cooker and toss to coat the pasta. Serve with Parmesan cheese and a frisée salad.

Tex Mex Skillet Dinner

Possible Cooking Methods: Stovetop   Pressure Cooker

This is a true comfort food dinner – a combination of macaroni and cheese and chili all together in one bowl. Because you cook the pasta right in the sauce you are making, there's no need for an extra pot of boiling water, plus the pasta absorbs the delicious sauce flavor as it cooks. This works really well in the pressure cooker, but the slow cooker is not a great option because the pasta can get so overcooked. If you do make this dinner in your pressure cooker, but would prefer to serve it family style, transfer the pasta to a warmed serving dish right after you add the first half of the Cheddar cheese. Sprinkle the remaining cheese on top and then cover the dish with foil or plastic wrap to trap the steam and let the cheese melt. Sprinkle the scallions on at the end and serve.

1 pound ground beef	$1/8$ teaspoon cayenne pepper	1 cup frozen or fresh corn kernels
½ onion, diced	1 teaspoon salt	2½ cups beef stock
½ green bell pepper, diced	freshly ground black pepper	½ pound dried wagon wheel or bow-tie shaped pasta
½ red bell pepper, diced	1 (14-ounce) can fire-roasted diced tomatoes	
2 tablespoons chili powder		3 cups grated Cheddar cheese, divided
1 teaspoon ground cumin	1 (15-ounce) can black beans, drained and rinsed	chopped scallions, for garnish

Stovetop Directions

Serves: 4   **Cooking Time:** 25 minutes

1.   Pre-heat a large 12-inch sauté pan or skillet over medium-high heat. Add the ground beef and onion to the pan and brown. Discard most of the fat from the pan. Add peppers to the pan and sauté for 2 minutes. Stir in the chili powder, cumin, cayenne pepper, salt and freshly ground black pepper and sauté for another minute. Add the diced tomatoes, black beans and corn and bring the mixture to a simmer.

2.   Pour in the beef stock and dried pasta. Stir to combine and bring everything to a boil. Reduce the heat, cover and simmer for 15 minutes, stirring occasionally.

3.   Gently stir in half of the Cheddar cheese until it is melted throughout. Turn off the heat and sprinkle the remaining cheese on top, do not stir. Return the lid to the pan to melt the cheese for a couple of minutes. Sprinkle with the chopped scallions and serve.

Pressure Cooker Directions

Serves: 4   **Cooking Time:** 11 minutes

Change Ingredients: Use bow-tie pasta – wagon wheel pasta doesn't hold up well in the pressure cooker

1. Pre-heat a 6-quart multi-function pressure cooker using the BROWN or SAUTE setting.

2. Add the ground beef and onions to the cooker and brown until the meat is no longer pink. Pour off most of the fat from the cooker, stir in the red and green peppers, chili powder, cumin, cayenne pepper, salt and freshly ground black pepper and cook for another minute or so. (If your cooker doesn't have a brown setting, use a skillet on the stovetop for the steps above and transfer the contents to the cooker now.) Add the diced tomatoes, black beans, corn, beef stock and dried bow-tie pasta. Cover and lock the lid in place.

3. Pressure cook on HIGH for 6 minutes.

4. Release the pressure with the QUICK-RELEASE method and carefully remove the lid.

5. Add half of the Cheddar cheese and gently stir until the cheese is melted throughout. Sprinkle the remaining cheese on top, return the lid to the cooker and let the pasta sit for a couple of minutes. This will melt the cheese and cool the pasta to an edible temperature. Transfer the pasta to serving bowls and sprinkle with the chopped scallions.

Chili con Carne
with Cornbread Dumplings

Possible Cooking Methods: Stovetop and Oven   Pressure Cooker   Slow Cooker

I love the smoky flavor of this bean-less chili. Most of that smoky flavor comes from the chipotle peppers in adobo, but the smoked paprika helps too. I believe that keeping the chili simple with no beans and no peppers lets that flavor really shine. There's nothing like cornbread to go with your chili so this recipe gives you both in one pot. The cornbread dumplings soak up some of the liquid in the chili making it extra flavorful and thickening the chili below into a thick stew. It's a hearty meal all in one pot.

2 tablespoons vegetable oil

3 pounds boneless chuck or round roast, cut into bite-sized pieces

salt

1 onion, chopped

3 cloves garlic, minced

2 to 3 chipotle peppers in adobo sauce, chopped (about 3 to 4 tablespoons)

1 tablespoon chili powder

1 teaspoon dried oregano

½ teaspoon ground cumin

½ teaspoon smoked paprika

1 (28-ounce) can tomatoes, chopped

1 cup beef stock*

¼ cup chopped fresh cilantro (or parsley)

Cornbread Dumplings:

1 cup cornmeal, white or yellow

1 cup all-purpose flour

2 teaspoons baking powder

½ teaspoon baking soda

1 teaspoon salt

1 tablespoon sugar

1 cup buttermilk (or plain yogurt)

1 egg, lightly beaten

4 tablespoons butter, melted

1 red or green Jalapeño pepper, sliced

fresh cilantro, chopped

*Quantity changes for alternate methods

Stovetop and Oven Directions

Serves: 6 to 8   **Cooking Time:** 2½ hours

1. Pre-heat a large oval Dutch oven over medium-high heat.

2. Add the oil and brown the beef in batches, seasoning with salt. Set the browned beef aside. Add the onion and sauté until it just starts to soften – about 5 minutes. Add the garlic, chipotle peppers and spices and cook for another 2 minutes. Add the tomatoes and the beef stock, scraping the bottom of the pot to pick up any brown bits. Return the beef to the pot and cover. Bring the chili to a simmer and lower the heat. Simmer the chili gently for 1½ hours on the stovetop.

3. Just before the simmering time is up, pre-heat the oven to 350ºF. Combine the cornmeal, flour, baking powder, baking soda, salt and sugar in a bowl. Combine the buttermilk, egg and butter in another bowl or measuring cup. Add the buttermilk mixture to the dry ingredients and mix until just combined. Set the mixture aside.

4. Taste the chili, season with salt and stir in the cilantro. Drop 8 mounds of the cornbread batter on top of the chili and scatter the Jalapeño pepper slices on top. Transfer the pot to the oven.

5. Bake the cornbread dumplings and chili for another 30 minutes, or until a toothpick inserted into the center of one of the dumplings comes out clean and the top is nicely browned.

6. To serve, scoop the cornbread dumpling and chili together and garnish with chopped cilantro. This would be nice served with a hearty bean salad.

Chili con Carne with Cornbread Dumplings

Pressure Cooker Directions

Serves: 6 to 8   **Cooking Time:** 40 minutes

Change Ingredients: **Use only as much of the dumpling batter as is reasonable in your pressure cooker. Because most pressure cookers are round, there is not enough surface area for 8 dumplings. You can bake any remaining batter in a cupcake pan, making a couple of corn muffins. The dumplings won't get brown on top in the pressure cooker, but they'll be tender and moist.**

1. Pre-heat a 6-quart multi-function pressure cooker on the BROWN or SAUTE setting.

2. Add the oil and brown the beef pieces in batches, seasoning with salt. Add the onion, garlic, chipotle peppers and spices and cook for another 2 minutes. Add the tomatoes and the beef stock, scraping the bottom of the pot to pick up any brown bits. (If your cooker doesn't have a brown setting, use a Dutch oven on the stovetop for the steps above and transfer the contents to the cooker now.) Return the beef to the cooker, cover and lock the lid in place.

3. Pressure cook on HIGH for 15 minutes.

4. While the chili is cooking, make the cornbread dumpling mixture. Combine the cornmeal, flour, baking powder, baking soda, salt and sugar in a bowl. Combine the buttermilk, egg and butter in another bowl or measuring cup. Add the buttermilk mixture to the dry ingredients and mix until just combined. Set the mixture aside.

5. Let the pressure drop NATURALLY and carefully remove the lid. Season the chili to taste again with salt and stir in the cilantro. Drop dollops of the cornbread dumpling batter into the chili. Cover with the lid and bring the chili back to a simmer using the BROWN or SAUTE setting. Simmer for 5 to 6 minutes or until the dumplings are fully cooked through.

6. Serve the chili in a bowl with a cornbread dumpling on top and a hearty bean salad on the side.

Slow Cooker Directions

Serves: 6 to 8   **Cooking Time:** 6 hours on LOW
                                      plus 1 hour on HIGH

Change Ingredients: **Reduce the stock to ½ cup. Many slow cookers are round in shape. If your cooker is round there will not be enough surface area for 8 dumplings, so use only as much of the batter as is reasonable in your slow cooker. You can bake any remaining batter in a cupcake pan, making a couple of corn muffins. The dumplings won't get brown on top in the slow cooker, but they'll be tender and moist.**

1. Pre-heat 5- to 6-quart multi-function slow cooker on the BROWN or SAUTE setting. Add the oil and brown the beef pieces in batches, seasoning with salt. (If your cooker doesn't have a brown setting, use a Dutch oven on the stovetop for the step above and transfer the beef to the cooker now.) Return all the browned beef to the cooker.

2. Add the onion, garlic, chipotle peppers, spices, tomatoes and beef stock to the cooker with the beef and mix well. Cover.

3. Slow cook on LOW for 6 hours (or 3 hours on HIGH).

4. While the chili is cooking, make the cornbread dumpling mixture. Combine the cornmeal, flour, baking powder, baking soda, salt and sugar in a bowl. Combine the buttermilk, egg and butter in another bowl or measuring cup. Add the buttermilk mixture to the dry ingredients and mix until just combined. Set the mixture aside.

5. Season to taste again with salt and stir in the cilantro. Drop dollops of the cornbread dumpling batter on top of the chili and cover with the lid. Slow cook on HIGH for 1 hour or until the dumplings are cooked through.

6. Serve the chili in a bowl with a cornbread dumpling on top and a hearty bean salad on the side.

Sheet Pan Burgers
with Pimento Cheese and Steak Fries

Possible Cooking Methods: Oven   Air Fryer

Pimento cheese spread on a burger turns ordinary burgers into something special. You can find a ready-made pimento cheese in your grocery store, but it's really easy to make your own. You can roast the potato wedges directly on the sheet pan without any trouble, but for fluffier potatoes, parboil them first on the stovetop for 3 minutes or microwave the potatoes in a bowl of water for 3 minutes. Drain away the water and be sure to pat the potatoes dry with a clean kitchen towel before baking them.

2 to 3 Russet potatoes, scrubbed and cut into wedges, lengthwise

canola or olive oil

salt and freshly ground black pepper

1½ pounds ground beef

1 teaspoon salt

½ teaspoon onion powder

1 tablespoon Worcestershire sauce

½ cup pimento cheese spread (see below)

4 hamburger or Kaiser rolls

sliced tomatoes

lettuce leaves

Pimento Cheese Spread:

1½ cups grated Cheddar cheese

2½ tablespoons diced pimentos

¼ cup mayonnaise

⅛ teaspoon cayenne pepper

salt

Oven Directions

Serves: 4   **Cooking Time:** 40 minutes

1. Pre-heat the oven to 450ºF.

2. Toss the potatoes with canola oil, season with salt and freshly ground black pepper and spread them out on a large sheet pan. Transfer the sheet pan to the oven and bake at 450ºF for 25 minutes.

3. While the potatoes are cooking, make the burger patties. Combine the ground beef, 1 teaspoon of salt, onion powder and Worcestershire sauce in a bowl, using your hands to mix all the ingredients. Divide the mixture into 4 equal portions and then form the hamburgers, being careful not to over-handle the meat. Make an indentation in the center of each patty to help keep the burger flat as it cooks.

4. Turn the potatoes over with a spatula and push them to one side of the sheet pan to make room for the burgers. Add the burgers to the sheet pan and return the pan to the oven. Cook for 5 to 10 minutes (5 minutes for rare, 7 minutes for medium and 9 minutes for medium-well burgers).

5. Remove the sheet pan from the oven and set the oven to broil. Remove the fat from the sheet pan by carefully tilting the pan and pouring off the grease from the corner. Flip the burgers and top each burger with spoonfuls of pimento cheese spread. Return the pan to the oven and broil for 3 minutes, until the pimento cheese spread has melted on the burgers and the potatoes are crispy.

6. Remove the pan from oven. Place the rolls, cut side up on the oven rack for 1 minute to the toast buns.

7. Serve the burgers on the toasted buns topped with sliced tomatoes and lettuce leaves and with the steak fries on the side.

Additional Cooking Directions for

Sheet Pan Burgers with Pimento Cheese and Steak Fries

Don't discount the importance of good lettuce and tomatoes on a burger. If it's a special burger, then it deserves special attention to all the ingredients - and isn't every burger special?

Air Fryer Directions

Serves: 4   **Cooking Time:** 43 minutes

1. Pre-heat the air fryer to 400⁰F.

2. Toss the potatoes with canola oil, season with salt and freshly ground black pepper and place them in the air fryer basket. Air-fry at 400⁰F for 18 minutes, tossing the potatoes a few times during the cooking process.

3. While the potatoes are cooking, make the burger patties. Combine the ground beef, 1 teaspoon of salt, onion powder and Worcestershire sauce in a bowl, using your hands to mix all the ingredients. Divide the mixture into 4 equal portions and then form the hamburgers, being careful not to over-handle the meat. Make an indentation in the center of each patty to help keep the burger flat as it cooks.

4. Remove the steak fries from the air fryer and set them aside, loosely tented with foil to keep them warm.

5. Pour a little water in the bottom of the air fryer drawer to prevent any grease from smoking. Add the burgers to the air fryer basket and air-fry at 370⁰F for 16 to 20 minutes, depending on the desired doneness of your burgers. Flip the burgers over halfway through the cooking process. When 2 minutes are left on the timer, spread the pimento cheese spread on top of each patty.

6. Remove the burgers and let them rest for a few minutes. Return the steak fries to the air fryer and air-fry for 2 to 3 minutes, until crispy.

7. To toast the buns, place the rolls cut side up in the air fryer and air-fry at 370⁰ for 1 to 2 minutes.

8. Serve the burgers on the toasted buns topped with sliced tomatoes and lettuce leaves and with the steak fries on the side.

Skillet Lasagna

Possible Cooking Methods: Stovetop and Oven   Slow Cooker

Making lasagna can leave you with a kitchen full of pots and pans to wash, but not this version. This recipe uses no-boil noodles and builds the lasagna in the same pan used to make the meat sauce, so at the end of the day, you'll only have one skillet to clean. If you plan on taking this dish to the table to serve rather than dividing it onto plates in the kitchen, a double-handled 12-inch skillet makes for a prettier presentation. Just make sure whichever skillet you use is oven-safe. This dish can be made in a slow cooker, but I veer away from using a pressure cooker. Pressure cookers require liquid in order to create the steam needed to build pressure. In order to get lasagna to work in a pressure cooker, you have to make the sauce quite thin and even then you run the risk of burning the bottom. So, in the spirit of playing it safe, use your stovetop or slow cooker for this dinner.

¾ pound ground beef

½ onion, finely chopped

1 clove garlic, minced

½ red bell pepper, finely chopped

½ teaspoon dried oregano

1 teaspoon Italian seasoning

salt and freshly ground black pepper

1 (28-ounce) can crushed tomatoes

½ cup red wine

24 ounces ricotta cheese

2 eggs, beaten

4½ cups grated mozzarella cheese, divided*

¼ cup + 2 tablespoons grated Parmesan cheese, divided

1 teaspoon salt

2 tablespoons chopped fresh parsley, divided

16 sheets no-bake lasagna noodles*

chopped fresh basil

Quantity changes for alternate methods

Stovetop and Oven Directions

Serves: 6 to 8   **Cooking Time:** 70 minutes

1. Pre-heat a deep 12-inch oven-safe skillet over medium-high heat. Brown the ground beef and onion, breaking up the beef chunks with a wooden spoon. Drain the grease from the skillet and discard. Add the garlic, red pepper, oregano and Italian seasoning. Season with salt and freshly ground black pepper and sauté for a few more minutes. Stir in the crushed tomatoes and red wine. Simmer for 20 minutes.

2. While the meat sauce is cooking, combine the ricotta cheese, eggs, 2 cups of mozzarella cheese, ¼ cup of Parmesan cheese, 1 teaspoon of salt, freshly ground black pepper and half of the chopped parsley in a bowl. Mix well.

3. When the sauce has simmered, remove the skillet from the heat and stir in the remaining fresh parsley. Transfer two thirds of the meat sauce to a bowl, leaving one third of the sauce in the skillet, spreading it evenly over the bottom of the pan.

4. Pre-heat the oven to 350ºF.

5. Build the lasagna in the skillet. Top the sauce already in the skillet with a layer of the no-bake lasagna noodles, breaking them to fit the round skillet, as necessary. Then layer the ingredients as follows: half the ricotta mixture, a layer of noodles, half the remaining sauce, a layer of noodles, the remaining ricotta mixture, a layer of noodles and the remaining sauce. Sprinkle the remaining mozzarella and Parmesan cheeses over top. Cover with a lid or piece of aluminum foil and transfer the skillet to the oven.

6. Bake at 375ºF for 30 minutes. Remove the lid or foil and bake for another 15 to 20 minutes, until the cheese has browned and the lasagna is bubbly.

7. Let the lasagna sit at least 20 minutes before serving. Garnish with chopped fresh basil.

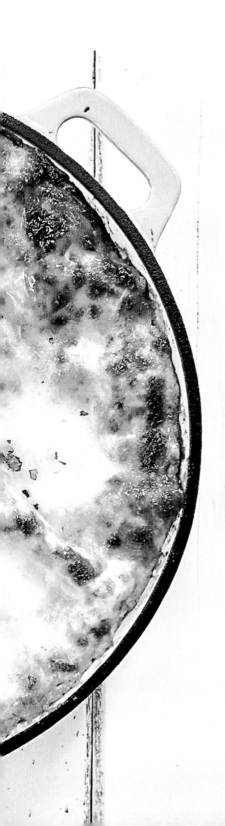

Slow Cooker Directions

Serves: 6 to 8   **Cooking Time:** 3 to 4 hours on HIGH

Change Ingredients: Use 12 regular lasagna noodles, cooked instead of the no-bake noodles; reduce the mozzarella cheese to 4 cups. If you want to make it ahead, you can build it in your pot the night before and slow cook it the next day. Add 1 hour to your cooking time if you are moving it right from the refrigerator to your slow cooker.

1. Pre-heat a 6-quart multi-function slow cooker using the BROWN or SAUTE setting.

2. Brown the ground beef in the cooker until no pink remains. Use a spoon or ladle to remove most of the grease from the cooker. Add the onions, garlic and red pepper, season with salt and freshly ground black pepper and sauté until the vegetables start to soften – about 5 minutes. Add the tomato sauce, diced tomatoes, red wine, Italian seasoning and oregano. Simmer for at least 15 minutes. (If your cooker doesn't have a brown setting, use a skillet on the stovetop for the steps above and transfer the contents to the cooker now.)

3. While the meat sauce is simmering, combine the ricotta cheese, eggs, 2 cups of mozzarella cheese, ¼ cup of Parmesan cheese, 1 teaspoon of salt, freshly ground black pepper and half of the chopped parsley in a bowl. Mix well.

4. When the sauce is ready, remove the insert from the cooker and stir in the remaining fresh parsley. Transfer two thirds of the meat sauce to a bowl, leaving one third of the sauce in the cooker, spreading it evenly over the bottom of the cooker.

5. Build the lasagna in the cooker. Top the sauce already in the cooker with a layer of the cooked lasagna noodles. You will need to cut a few noodles to fit the cooker. Then layer the ingredients as follows: half the ricotta mixture, a layer of noodles, half the remaining sauce, a layer of noodles, the remaining ricotta mixture, a layer of noodles and the remaining sauce. Sprinkle the remaining mozzarella and Parmesan cheeses over top. Cover with a lid and slow cook on HIGH for 3 to 4 hours (or 6 to 8 hours on LOW), until the cheese has melted and the noodles are soft.

6. Let the lasagna sit at least 20 minutes before serving. Garnish with chopped fresh basil.

Soy-Ginger Beef and Broccoli Rice

Possible Cooking Methods: Stovetop   Pressure Cooker

While you wouldn't find this dish on any Chinese restaurant menu, it does have all the Asian flavors that you'd expect from your favorite take-out. You can put the flank steak in the freezer for 15 minutes or so before you start your preparation – it will be much easier to slice. While I generally use beef stock for beef dishes, the chicken stock in this recipe is not a mistake. The soy flavor is so prominent here that using beef stock would make it a little too heavy. This dish is not winning any beauty pageant awards, but it's quick, easy and tasty, and uses one pan.

1 tablespoon canola oil	1 cup long-grain white rice	1 tablespoon sesame seeds, plus more for garnish
1½ pound flank steak, cut into thin strips	½ cup soy sauce	4 cups broccoli florets, cut into bite-sized pieces*
1 onion, finely diced	¼ cup honey	3 scallions, sliced
1 clove garlic, thinly sliced	1 tablespoon grated fresh ginger	*Quantity changes for alternate methods*
2 cups chicken stock*	½ teaspoon sesame oil	

Stovetop Directions

Serves: 2 to 4   **Cooking Time:** 25 minutes

1. Pre-heat a large 12-inch sauté pan over medium-high heat. Add the oil and sauté the beef strips in batches so you don't overcrowd the pan. Cook until browned on both sides – about 2 minutes per side. Remove the beef from the pan and set aside.

2. Add the onion to the pan and sauté until it just begins to soften – about 4 to 5 minutes. Add the garlic and continue to cook for 30 seconds. Pour in the chicken stock and deglaze, scraping up any brown bits that have formed on the bottom of the pan. Stir in the rice. Cover and decrease the temperature to medium-low so that the liquid is at a low simmer. Simmer for 15 minutes.

3. While the rice is cooking, combine the soy sauce, honey, ginger, sesame oil and sesame seeds in a small bowl.

4. Working quickly so that the lid is off the pan for as little time as possible, remove the lid from the pan and pop the broccoli florets on top of the rice. Cover and continue to cook for 5 minutes.

5. Remove the lid from the pan and increase the heat to medium. Return the beef to the pan and pour in the sauce. Stir everything together and cook for a few minutes to dry the rice a little and warm the beef back through. Serve with more sesame seeds and the scallions sprinkled on top. A cool cabbage salad would go nicely with this dish.

Soy-Ginger Beef and Broccoli Rice

Pressure Cooker Directions

Serves: 2 to 4   **Cooking Time:** 16 minutes

Change Ingredients: Reduce chicken stock to 1½ cups; use frozen broccoli florets

1.   Pre-heat a 5- to 6-quart multi-function pressure cooker using the BROWN or SAUTE setting.

2.   Add the oil to the cooker and, working in batches, brown the beef strips on both sides. Set the browned beef aside.

3.   Add the onion and garlic to the cooker and cook for a few minutes, until it just starts to soften. Add the stock, rice and broccoli florets and return the browned beef to the cooker. Stir well, cover and lock the lid in place.

4.   Pressure cook on HIGH for 6 minutes.

5.   While the rice is cooking, combine the soy sauce, honey, ginger, sesame oil and sesame seeds in a small bowl.

6.   Release the pressure using the QUICK-RELEASE method and carefully remove the lid. Return the cooker to the BROWN setting. Pour in the sauce, stir everything together and cook for a few minutes to dry the rice a little. Serve with more sesame seeds and the scallions sprinkled on top. A cool cabbage salad would go nicely with this dish.

Tea Braised Pot Roast

Possible Cooking Methods: Stovetop and Oven   Pressure Cooker   Slow Cooker

For many, a pot roast is the ultimate comfort food. It takes just a little time to prepare, but a long time cooking to make the meat tender and the sauce rich and delicious. That is unattended time, however, and you do have options. You could choose to extend the cooking time by using a slow cooker. That way, you can leave for the day and come back to a home-cooked meal. Or, you could speed up the time and use a pressure cooker, making this in just over an hour. Luckily, all three options are spelled out for you here. Instead of using the traditional red wine and beef stock braising liquid, this recipe uses strong black tea to braise the pot roast. This gives a rich but mellow result – one that is sure to please.

1 (3- to 3½-pound) chuck roast	2 bay leaves	2 parsnips, ½-inch sliced
salt and freshly ground black pepper	3 sprigs fresh thyme	1½ pounds Yukon gold potatoes, cut into 1-inch chunks
1 tablespoon olive oil	3 cups strong black tea	3 tablespoons all-purpose flour
1 onion, cut into large chunks	2 tablespoons Worcestershire sauce	2 tablespoons butter, room temperature
1 tablespoon tomato paste	1 tablespoon balsamic vinegar	chopped fresh parsley
1 cup beef stock	3 carrots, ½-inch sliced	

Stovetop Oven and Directions

Serves: 4 to 6   **Cooking Time:** 3½ hours

1. Pre-heat the oven to 325ºF.

2. Heat a 6-quart or larger cast iron Dutch oven over high heat. Season the chuck roast generously with salt and freshly ground black pepper. Add the olive oil to the Dutch oven and sear the roast on both sides until it is well-browned. Remove the roast from the pot and set it aside.

3. Add the onion and sauté until the chunks start to brown. Add the tomato paste and continue to sauté for a couple of minutes. Deglaze the Dutch oven with the beef stock, scraping up any brown bits from the bottom of the pan, and simmer for 2 minutes. Add the bay leaves, fresh thyme sprigs, black tea, Worcestershire sauce and balsamic vinegar. Return the browned beef to the pot, submerging it in the liquid.

4. Transfer the Dutch oven to the oven and cook at 325ºF for 3 hours. (Set a timer for 1½ hours, however.)

5. After 1½ hours of braising, add the carrots, parsnips and potatoes to the Dutch oven. Return the pot to the oven for the second half of the cooking time – another 1½ hours. After 3 hours, the meat should be fork tender and easy to pull apart. If you need additional cooking time, or prefer your pot roast falling apart, return the pot to the oven for another 30 minutes or so.

6. Mix the flour with the room temperature butter to form a paste. Set this mixture aside. This is called a beurre manié that will be used to thicken the gravy.

7. When the meat is tender to your liking, transfer the Dutch oven to the stovetop. Use a ladle to remove any grease that has risen to the surface. Transfer the meat to a serving platter. Add the beurre manié to the Dutch oven and bring the liquid to a simmer to thicken the gravy. Season with salt and freshly ground black pepper to taste.

8. Ladle the gravy and vegetables over the pot roast and garnish with chopped fresh parsley. This hearty meal needs nothing more than a side salad and perhaps a little bread to sop up any extra gravy.

Tea Braised Pot Roast

Pressure Cooker Directions

Serves: 4 to 6   **Cooking Time:** 1 hour 10 minutes

1. Pre-heat a 6-quart multi-function pressure cooker using the BROWN or SAUTE setting.

2. Season the chuck roast generously with salt and freshly ground black pepper. Add the olive oil to the cooker and sear the roast on both sides until it is well-browned. Remove the roast from the cooker and set it aside.

3. Add the onion and sauté until the chunks start to brown. Add the tomato paste and continue to sauté for a couple of minutes. Deglaze the Dutch oven with the beef stock, scraping up any brown bits from the bottom of the pan, and simmer for 2 minutes. (If your cooker doesn't have a brown setting, use a Dutch oven on the stovetop for the steps above and transfer the contents to the cooker now.) Add the bay leaves, fresh thyme sprigs, black tea, Worcestershire sauce and balsamic vinegar. Return the browned beef to the pot, submerging it in the liquid. Add the carrots, parsnips and potatoes. (If you add the vegetables now, they will be very tender at the end. If you prefer your vegetables a little firmer, start by cooking the roast on its own for 35 minutes, use

the quick-release method to open the cooker and then add the carrots, parsnips and potatoes. Pressure-cook on HIGH for an additional 15 minutes and proceed with the recipe.) Cover and lock the lid in place.

4. Pressure-cook on HIGH for 50 minutes.

5. While the roast is cooking, mix the flour with the room temperature butter to form a paste. Set this mixture aside. This is called a beurre manié that will be used to thicken the gravy.

6. Let the pressure drop NATURALLY and carefully remove the lid.

7. Use a ladle to remove any grease that has risen to the surface. Transfer the meat to a serving platter. Add the beurre manié to the cooker and bring the liquid to a simmer using the BROWN or SAUTE setting to thicken the gravy. Season with salt and freshly ground black pepper to taste.

8. Ladle the gravy and vegetables over the pot roast and garnish with chopped fresh parsley. This hearty meal needs nothing more than a side salad and perhaps a little bread to sop up any extra gravy.

Slow Cooker Directions

Serves: 4 to 6   **Cooking Time:** 6 hours on HIGH

1. Pre-heat a 6-quart multi-function slow cooker using the BROWN or SAUTE setting.

2. Season the chuck roast generously with salt and freshly ground black pepper. Add the olive oil to the cooker and sear the roast on both sides until it is well-browned. Remove the roast from the cooker and set it aside.

3. Add the onion and sauté until the chunks start to brown. Add the tomato paste and continue to sauté for a couple of minutes. Deglaze the Dutch oven with the beef stock, scraping up any brown bits from the bottom of the pan, and simmer for 2 minutes. (If your cooker doesn't have a brown setting, use a Dutch oven on the stovetop for the steps above and transfer the contents to the cooker now.) Add the bay leaves, fresh thyme sprigs, black tea, Worcestershire sauce and balsamic vinegar. Return the browned beef to the pot, submerging it in the liquid. Cover and slow cook on HIGH for 4 hours.

4. After 4 hours, add the carrots, parsnips and potatoes. Slow cook on HIGH for an additional 2 hours.

5. While the roast is cooking, mix the flour with the room temperature butter to form a paste. Set this mixture aside. This is called a beurre manié that will be used to thicken the gravy.

6. Use a ladle to remove any grease that has risen to the surface. Transfer the meat to a serving platter. Add the beurre manié to the cooker and bring the liquid to a simmer using the BROWN or SAUTE setting to thicken the gravy. Season with salt and freshly ground black pepper to taste.

7. Ladle the gravy and vegetables over the pot roast and garnish with chopped fresh parsley. This hearty meal needs nothing more than a side salad and perhaps a little bread to sop up any extra gravy.

Sloppy Joe Casserole

Possible Cooking Methods: Stovetop

Here's an old-time favorite and crowd pleaser with a twist. When I was young, I used to love Sloppy Joes, although my mother didn't make them very often. I remember trying to eat them very quickly before the bottom bun became too soggy. This recipe solves the problem by baking the buns on top of the casserole, keeping their texture intact.

2 pounds ground beef	3 to 4 tablespoons brown sugar	freshly ground black pepper
½ onion, chopped	¼ cup apple cider vinegar	3 cups grated Monterey Jack cheese, divided
1 green bell pepper, diced	2 tablespoons Worcestershire sauce	4 slider rolls
1 (14-ounce) can diced tomatoes	2 tablespoons yellow mustard	4 tablespoons melted butter
1 tablespoon tomato paste	1 teaspoon salt	

Stovetop Directions

Serves: 6 to 8   **Cooking Time:** 55 minutes

1. Pre-heat the oven to 350ºF and pre-heat a 4-quart sauté pan over medium-high heat. Add the ground beef and break it up with a wooden spoon as it browns. Add the onion and continue to cook until the meat is no longer pink. Drain the grease from the pan and then return it to the stovetop.

2. Add the green pepper, diced tomatoes, tomato paste, brown sugar, apple cider vinegar, Worcestershire sauce, mustard, salt and freshly ground black pepper. Bring the mixture to a boil and then reduce the heat and simmer for 20 minutes.

3. Remove the pan from the heat and sprinkle 2 cups of Monterey Jack cheese evenly over the beef mixture.

4. Split the slider rolls in half and arrange them in the pan on top of the meat and cheese with the cut side facing up. Brush the melted butter onto the cut surface of the rolls. Sprinkle the remaining Monterey Jack cheese on top and transfer the pan to the oven.

5. Bake at 350ºF for 25 minutes, or until the rolls are toasted brown and the cheese has melted.

Sesame Beef Noodles

Possible Cooking Methods: Stovetop

This recipe takes a little prep work, but once you have everything chopped and measured, it comes together very quickly. Partially freezing the steaks will make them very easy to slice into nice thin slices, which take just a minute or two on each side to cook. You can substitute other cooked noodles instead of the rice noodles, but rice noodles are so easy to cook by simply pouring boiling water over the top, that I think you'll appreciate them. If you can't find rice noodles, you can serve the beef over ramen noodles, lo mein noodles or even cooked linguine.

3 tablespoons soy sauce

3 tablespoons sesame oil

2 tablespoons rice wine vinegar

2 tablespoons brown sugar

1 clove garlic, minced

1 teaspoon fresh ginger, minced

1½ pounds sirloin steak, cut into thin 2-inch strips

1 tablespoon cornstarch

½ cup beef stock

10 ounces rice noodles

canola oil

½ onion, sliced into half moons

1 red bell pepper, julienned

2 carrots, julienned

1 cup snow peas, cut into 3 pieces

2 tablespoons toasted sesame seeds

Stovetop Directions

Serves: 4   **Cooking Time:** 25 minutes

1. Combine the soy sauce, sesame oil, rice wine vinegar, brown sugar, garlic and ginger in a bowl. Pour one third of the mixture over the sliced beef and marinate for 15 minutes. Whisk the cornstarch and beef stock into the remaining marinade and set it aside.

2. Bring 3 cups of water to a boil on the stovetop or in a kettle. Place the rice noodles in a large bowl and pour the boiling water over the top. Let the noodles sit for 5 minutes. Then, drain and rinse the noodles with cold water.

3. Heat a large 12-inch skillet or wok over high heat. Add some canola oil and sear the strips of beef in a single layer on both sides. You will need to do this in batches. Remove the browned beef and set it aside.

4. Add the onion, red pepper, and carrots to the skillet. Sauté for a few minutes and then add the cooked rice noodles and snow peas. Stir-fry for another 2 minutes.

5. Return the browned beef to the skillet and add the remaining marinade and stir-fry for a few minutes, until the sauce has thickened and the beef is heated through. Season to taste with soy sauce and sesame oil.

6. Serve in deep bowls with the toasted sesame seeds sprinkled on top.

New York Strip Steaks
with Baked Potatoes and Asparagus

Possible Cooking Methods: Oven Air Fryer

Steak and potatoes is a classic American dinner, but it usually takes three pans to prepare everything, including a vegetable. Here we use a large sheet pan to cook everything at once in the oven. The trick is to stagger the cooking by starting with the potatoes, adding the steak and asparagus closer to the end and then broiling everything together as the grand finale. Do remember that the timing of this recipe depends entirely on the thickness of the steaks and how you like your steak prepared. Be ready to flex in either direction with the timing to make dinner your way.

2 Russet potatoes, cut in half lengthwise	2 (1-inch thick) New York strip steaks	1 bunch of asparagus, trimmed
canola oil	olive oil	sour cream
salt and freshly ground black pepper	Worcestershire sauce	fresh chives, chopped

Oven Directions

Serves: 2 to 4   **Cooking Time:** 40 minutes

1. Pre-heat the oven to 450ºF.

2. Rub the potatoes with canola oil and season them with salt and freshly ground black pepper. Place the potatoes cut side down on the left-hand side of a large sheet pan. Pierce the potatoes several times with a fork and transfer the pan to the oven. Bake at 450ºF for 30 minutes.

3. Drizzle the steaks with olive oil and Worcestershire sauce and season with salt and freshly ground black pepper. Pierce the steaks several times with a fork on both sides and let them sit at room temperature while the potatoes are cooking.

4. Trim the asparagus stalks and toss them with olive oil and salt.

5. After 30 minutes of cooking, flip the potatoes over and add the steaks to the sheet pan, next to the potatoes. Place the asparagus on the right-hand side of the pan next to the steaks. Return the pan to the oven.

6. Roast at 450ºF for another 5 minutes. Flip the steaks over and toss the asparagus. Turn on the broiler and return the pan to the oven. Broil for 3 to 5 minutes, depending on how you like your steak cooked. (3 more minutes will cook a 1-inch thick steak to medium rare. Give or take a couple of minutes for less or more well-cooked steak.)

7. Let the steaks rest for five minutes before slicing and serving. While the steaks rest, continue to broil the asparagus for a few more minutes.

8. Top the baked potatoes with sour cream and chives and serve with the steaks and asparagus.

New York Strip Steaks with Baked Potatoes and Asparagus

Air Fryer Directions

Serves: 2 to 4   **Cooking Time:** 45 minutes

1. Pre-heat the air fryer to 400°F.

2. Rub the potatoes with canola oil and season them with salt and freshly ground black pepper. Place the potatoes cut side down in the air fryer basket. Air-fry at 400°F for 20 minutes. Flip the potatoes over and air-fry for an additional 10 minutes.

3. Drizzle the steaks with olive oil and Worcestershire sauce and season with salt and freshly ground black pepper. Pierce the steaks several times with a fork on both sides and let them sit at room temperature while the potatoes are cooking.

4. Trim the asparagus stalks and toss them with olive oil and salt.

5. When the potatoes have finished air-frying, remove them from the basket and tent them loosely with aluminum foil to keep warm.

6. Add the steaks to the air fryer basket and air-fry at 400°F for 9 minutes (medium-rare), 12 minutes (medium) or 14 minutes (well-done), flipping the steaks once halfway through the cooking time.

7. Let the steaks rest for 5 minutes before slicing and serving. While steaks are resting, place the asparagus in the air fryer basket and air-fry at 400°F for 5 minutes, shaking the basket a couple of times during the cooking process.

8. Top the baked potatoes with sour cream and chives and serve with the steaks and asparagus.

Cheese Stuffed Meatloaf
with Roasted Russets and Carrots

Possible Cooking Methods: Oven   Air Fryer

There are two ways to make a meatloaf – you can bake it in a loaf pan or you can do what this version does, which is bake it free form on a sheet pan. One of the advantages of using a sheet pan is that you don't trap all the fat that renders off the meat during the baking process. Instead, it can render away from the meat and it's perfect for roasting the vegetables along side, giving them a good flavor boost at the same time. Stuffing the cheese inside the meatloaf… well, that's just a bonus!

1 cup dry seasoned stuffing mix
(or coarse homemade toasted breadcrumbs)

¼ cup milk

⅓ cup ketchup

3 tablespoons dark brown sugar

1 pound ground beef

½ pound ground pork

½ pound ground veal

¼ cup chopped onion

½ teaspoon dried thyme

½ teaspoon dried sage

1 tablespoon Worcestershire sauce

2 eggs

¼ cup chopped fresh parsley

1 teaspoon salt

freshly ground black pepper

6 ounces Muenster cheese

2 Russet potatoes, cut into 1-inch chunks

½ teaspoon paprika

4 carrots, peeled and cut into 1-inch slices

Oven Directions

Serves: 4 to 6   **Cooking Time:** 60 minutes

1. Pre-heat the oven to 350ºF.

2. Combine the stuffing mix (or breadcrumbs) and milk in a large mixing bowl and let the stuffing soak while you prepare the rest of the ingredients. Whisk the ketchup and brown sugar together in a bowl until the sugar has dissolved and set aside.

3. Add the ground beef, pork and veal to the bowl with the stuffing mix. Grate the onion over the bowl right into the meat and add the thyme, sage, Worcestershire sauce, eggs, fresh parsley, salt and freshly ground black pepper. Combine everything well and then divide the meat into two equal portions.

4. Shape one portion of the meat into a long oval and place it in the middle of a large sheet pan. Cut the cheese into slices and layer it in the center of the meatloaf, leaving a rim around the edges. Shape the remaining portion of meat into a second long oval and place it on top of the cheese, patting the meat together to seal the edges.

5. Spread the ketchup mixture on top of the meatloaf and transfer the pan to the oven. Bake at 350ºF for 20 minutes.

6. After 20 minutes, toss the potatoes with a little olive oil, paprika, salt and freshly ground black pepper and add them to the pan, placing them around the meatloaf. Return the pan to the oven and bake for another 10 minutes. Then, add the carrots to the pan with the potatoes and cook for 30 more minutes, flipping the vegetables a few times during the cooking time. Cook until an instant read thermometer inserted into the center of the meatloaf registers 160ºF.

7. Let the meatloaf rest for at least 5 minutes before slicing, and serve with the roasted potatoes, carrots and some leafy greens.

Note: If you like your veggies a little crispier, transfer the meatloaf to a cutting board to rest. Increase the oven temperature to 400ºF. Spread the potatoes and carrots out on sheet pan and return it to the oven for about 5 minutes until you are ready to serve.

Cheese Stuffed Meatloaf with Roasted Russets and Carrots

Air Fryer Directions

Serves: 4 to 6   **Cooking Time:** 75 minutes

1. Pre-heat the air fryer to 400ºF.

2. Toss the potatoes and carrots with olive oil, paprika, salt and freshly ground black pepper. Transfer the vegetables to the air fryer basket and air-fry at 400ºF for 20 minutes, shaking the basket several times during the cooking process.

3. While the vegetables are cooking, prepare the meatloaf. Combine the stuffing mix (or breadcrumbs) and milk in a large mixing bowl and let the stuffing soak while you prepare the rest of the ingredients. Whisk the ketchup and brown sugar together in a bowl until the sugar has dissolved and set aside.

4. Add the ground beef, pork and veal to the bowl with the stuffing mix. Grate the onion over the bowl right into the meat and add the thyme, sage, Worcestershire sauce, eggs, fresh parsley, salt and freshly ground black pepper. Combine everything well and then divide the meat into two equal portions.

5. Shape one portion of the meat into a 7-inch circle. Cut the cheese into slices and layer it in the center of the meatloaf, leaving a rim around the outside. Shape the remaining portion of meat into a second 7-inch circle and place it on top of the cheese, patting the meat together to seal the edges.

6. When the vegetables have finished air-frying, transfer them to a bowl and cover with aluminum foil.

7. Pour a little water into the bottom of the air fryer drawer. (This will help prevent the grease that drips into the bottom drawer from burning and smoking.) Transfer the meatloaf to the air fryer basket and run a spatula around the side of the meatloaf to create a space about ½-inch wide between the meat and the side of the air fryer basket.

8. Air-fry the meatloaf at 350ºF for 20 minutes. Carefully invert the meatloaf onto a plate (remember to remove the basket from the air fryer drawer so you don't pour all the grease out) and slide it back into the air fryer basket to turn it over. Re-shape the meatloaf with a spatula if necessary. Air-fry for another 20 minutes at 350ºF.

9. Spread the ketchup mixture on top of the meatloaf and air-fry for another 5 to 10 minutes, until an instant read thermometer inserted into the center of the meatloaf registers 160ºF.

10. Remove the meatloaf from the air fryer and let rest for at least 5 minutes. Discard the grease and water from the air fryer drawer and return the potatoes and carrots to the basket. Air-fry for 5 minutes to re-heat the vegetables. Slice the meatloaf and serve with the roasted potatoes, carrots and some leafy greens.

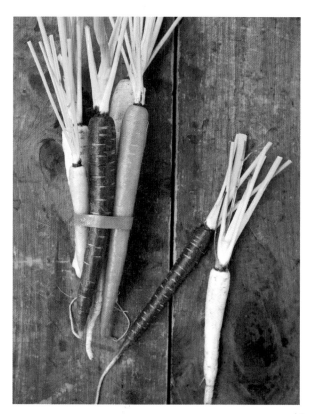

Carne Asada with Onions and Peppers

Possible Cooking Methods: Oven   Air Fryer

This version of carne asada (literally "roast beef") is a sheet pan dinner. It takes very little time in the oven, but there is some time needed to marinate the beef, so do take that into consideration. Chipotle peppers in adobo make up the bulk of the flavor in this marinade. You can usually find these in a can in the ethnic section of your grocery store, but if you can't, you can substitute 2 tablespoons of toma-to paste, 2 tablespoons of rice wine vinegar, 1 teaspoon ground cumin, ½ teaspoon smoked paprika, ½ teaspoon cayenne pepper, a big pinch of dried oregano and a pinch of garlic salt all combined with three dried chipotle peppers. Let it all sit together for several hours and then chop it finely. Use that mixture along with the lime juice and olive oil as your marinade. I've only given internal temperatures for steak cooked to medium rare and medium in this recipe. That's because flank steak cooked beyond this point tends to be dry and tough. If you prefer your beef medium-well or well done, this probably isn't the right recipe for you.

4 cloves garlic, minced

3 chipotle peppers in adobo, chopped

⅓ cup chopped fresh parsley

⅓ cup chopped fresh oregano

1 teaspoon ground cumin

juice of 2 limes

⅓ cup olive oil

1 to 1½ pounds flank steak
(depending on your appetites)

2 sweet onions, sliced

1 red bell pepper, sliced

1 yellow bell pepper, sliced

1 green bell pepper, sliced

1 tablespoon olive oil

salt and freshly ground black pepper

flour tortillas, wrapped in aluminum foil

1 avocado, diced

fresh tomato salsa

shredded lettuce

Oven Directions

Serves: 6 to 8   **Cooking Time:** 20 minutes

1. Make the marinade: Combine the garlic, chipotle peppers, parsley, oregano, cumin, lime juice and olive oil in a non-reactive shallow dish. Coat the flank steak with the marinade and then pierce the meat with a needle style meat tenderizer or the tip of a paring knife. Let the beef marinate for 2 to 8 hours in the refrigerator.

2. Place a sheet pan in the oven and pre-heat the oven to 450ºF.

3. Toss the onions and peppers in a bowl with olive oil, salt and freshly ground black pepper. Spread the onions and peppers out over half of the pre-heated sheet pan.

4. Remove the steak from the marinade, letting any excess drip off and place it on the hot sheet pan next to the vegetables. Season the steak with salt and transfer the sheet pan to the oven.

5. Roast for 10 minutes. Remove the pan from the oven and flip the steak over, seasoning again with salt. Stir the peppers and onions. Return the pan to the oven and turn on the broiler for 5 to 10 minutes, or until the steak has reached your desired level of doneness. Check the internal temperature of the steak with an instant read thermometer. Medium rare = 130ºF, Medium = 140ºF.

6. Remove the steak to a cutting board to rest. Mix the onions and peppers with the juices from the steak on the sheet pan and pop them back under the broiler for another 5 minutes while the steak rests. While you are doing that, place the packet of tortillas wrapped in aluminum foil in the oven to warm.

7. Thinly slice the steak, place a few slices in each tortilla, and top with the onions and peppers, avocado, salsa and shredded lettuce.

Air Fryer Directions

Serves: 6 to 8   **Cooking Time:** 30 minutes

1. Make the marinade: Combine the garlic, chipotle peppers, parsley, oregano, cumin, lime juice and olive oil in a non-reactive shallow dish. Coat the flank steak with the marinade and then pierce the meat with a needle style meat tenderizer or the tip of a paring knife. Let the beef marinate for 2 to 8 hours in the refrigerator.

2. Pre-heat the air fryer to 400ºF.

3. Remove the steak from the marinade, cut it in half if necessary to fit it into your air fryer and place it in the air fryer basket. It's ok if the pieces need to overlap slightly. Season the steak with salt and air-fry at 400ºF for 13 to 15 minutes, turning the pieces over halfway through the cooking time and seasoning again with salt. This should cook the steak to medium-rare or medium. Remove the steak from the air fryer and place on a cutting board loosely tented with foil to rest while you cook the onions and peppers.

4. Toss the onions and peppers with olive oil, salt and freshly ground black pepper and place them in the air fryer basket. Air-fry at 400ºF for 10 to 15 minutes, shaking the basket a few times during the cooking process. If desired, pop the tortillas into the air fryer for a couple of minutes to warm them.

5. Thinly slice the steak, place a few slices in each tortilla, and top with the onions and peppers, avocado, salsa and shredded lettuce.

Corned Beef
with Cabbage, Potatoes and Split Pea Mash

Possible Cooking Methods: Stovetop   Pressure Cooker   Slow Cooker

This is a version of a New England boiled dinner with the addition of split peas, cooked in a cheesecloth bag in the delicious corned beef broth. It's a traditional Sunday night dinner in Newfloundland, Canada, known as Jiggs Dinner, although salt beef is used in that part of the world rather than corned beef. The convenience of having everything – vegetables, meat and a mash – all in one pot makes this very easy to prepare. You do have to commit some time to making this meal, although the time is all unattended. If you use a pressure cooker, however, you'll cut your time in half. This could be your go to dinner around St. Patrick's Day, of course, but I think it's delicious any day of the year.

1 (3- to 3½-pound) corned beef brisket	10 coriander seeds	1 small to medium head cabbage, cut into 6 wedges
4 cups beef stock	2 teaspoons brown or yellow mustard seeds	6 large carrots, cut into large pieces
1 onion, quartered	8 allspice berries	6 medium white potatoes, halved
3 cloves garlic, smashed	6 cloves	2 tablespoons butter
2 bay leaves	1 cup dried yellow split peas	salt and freshly ground black pepper
10 peppercorns	cheesecloth or a "pudding bag"	
1 cinnamon stick		

Stovetop Directions

Serves: 4   **Cooking Time:** 2 hours

1. Rinse the corned beef brisket and place it in a large stockpot. Cover with beef stock and add the onion, garlic and spices to the pot. (If your corned beef comes with a seasoning packet, you do have the option of using that instead of the spices listed here.) Place the dried split peas into a pudding bag, or wrap them in the cheesecloth, tying the cheesecloth loosely so that the peas have room to expand. Push the bag down into the liquid, adding a cup or two of water to make sure everything is submerged. Cover the pot with a lid and bring everything to a simmer. Lower the heat and simmer for 1½ hours.

2. Add the cabbage wedges, carrots and potatoes, return the lid and continue to simmer for 30 minutes.

3. When all the vegetables are tender, transfer the cooked split peas to a bowl. Remove the cheesecloth and discard. Mash the peas with a wooden spoon, stirring in the butter and season with salt and lots of freshly ground black pepper.

4. Slice the beef, transfer the slices to a large platter with the vegetables and serve the mashed split peas on the side.

Corned Beef with Cabbage, Potatoes and Split Pea Mash

Pressure Cooker Directions

Serves: 4   **Cooking Time:** 68 minutes

1. Rinse the corned beef brisket and cut it into large chunks – just so they fit into your cooker. Cover with beef stock and add the onion, garlic and spices to the cooker. (If your corned beef comes with a seasoning packet, you do have the option of using that instead of the spices listed here.) Lock the lid in place.

2. Pressure cook on HIGH for 55 minutes.

3. Let the pressure drop NATURALLY and carefully remove the lid. Transfer the beef to a serving platter and tent with aluminum foil.

4. Place the dried split peas into a pudding bag, or wrap them in the cheesecloth, tying the cheesecloth loosely so that the peas have room to expand. Push the bag down into the broth. Add the carrots, potatoes and cabbage to the cooker, adding a cup or two of water to make sure everything is submerged. Lock the lid in place.

5. Pressure cook on HIGH pressure for 8 minutes.

6. Release the pressure using the QUICK-RELEASE method and carefully remove the lid. Remove the vegetables and transfer to a serving platter. Leave the pudding bag in the cooker, lock the lid in place and pressure cook on HIGH for an additional 5 minutes.

7. Release the pressure using the QUICK-RELEASE method and carefully remove the lid. Transfer the cooked split peas to a bowl. Remove the cheesecloth and discard. Mash the peas with a wooden spoon, stirring in the butter and season with salt and lots of freshly ground black pepper.

8. Slice the beef, transfer the slices to a large platter with the vegetables and serve the mashed split peas on the side.

Slow Cooker Directions

Serves: 4   **Cooking Time:** 10 hours on LOW

1. Place the onion, garlic, carrots, potatoes and spices in the cooker. (If your corned beef comes with a seasoning packet, you do have the option of using that instead of the spices listed here.) Rinse the corned beef brisket and add it to the cooker along with the beef stock. Place the dried split peas into a pudding bag, or wrap them in the cheesecloth, tying the cheesecloth loosely so that the peas have room to expand. Push the bag down into the liquid, adding a cup or two of water to make sure everything is submerged. Cover and slow cook on LOW for 8 hours (or 4 hours on HIGH).

2. Add the cabbage wedges and continue to slow cook on LOW for 2 hours (or 1 hour on HIGH).

3. Transfer the cooked split peas to a bowl. Remove the cheesecloth and discard. Mash the peas with a wooden spoon, stirring in the butter and season with salt and lots of freshly ground black pepper.

4. Slice the beef, transfer the slices to a large platter with the vegetables and serve the mashed split peas on the side.

Beef and Barley Stew
with Horseradish

Possible Cooking Methods: Stovetop Pressure Cooker Slow Cooker

This stew is hearty to begin with. As it sits, however, it gets thicker and thicker because of the barley that continues to swell and absorb liquid. You can use pearled, pot or hulled barley in this recipe but hulled barley will have a more nutritious impact. If you have leftovers, be sure to thin the stew with some water or stock.

1 tablespoon olive oil

2½ pounds beef chuck, cut into 2-inch cubes

salt and freshly ground black pepper

1 onion, sliced

3 carrots, peeled and sliced on the bias, about ½-inch thick

2 parsnips, peeled and diced ½-inch (or sliced if they are small)

3 cloves garlic, minced

2 teaspoons dried rosemary

1 teaspoon dried thyme

2 tablespoons tomato paste

2 cups red wine*

4 cups chicken stock

2 tablespoons Worcestershire sauce

1 cup hulled, pot or pearled barley

8 ounces button mushrooms, sliced

1 cup frozen peas

2 tablespoons prepared horseradish (not horseradish sauce)

Quantity changes for alternate methods

Stovetop Directions

Serves: 6   **Cooking Time:** 2½ hours

1. Heat a large Dutch oven or stockpot over medium heat. Add the olive oil and working in batches so you don't overcrowd the pan, brown the beef cubes, seasoning with salt and freshly ground black pepper – about 8 minutes per batch. Set the browned meat aside.

2. Add the onion, carrots and parsnips to the pot and cook until lightly browned - about 5 minutes. Add the garlic and dried spices and cook for another 30 seconds. Add the tomato paste and cook, stirring, for another minute or two. Then add the red wine and deglaze the pan by scraping up any browned bits on the bottom of the Dutch oven with a wooden spoon. Bring the liquid to a boil and let it simmer for a couple of minutes. Return the browned beef to the pot, add the stock and Worcestershire sauce and return the liquid to a simmer again.

3. Simmer for 1 hour.

4. Add the barley and mushrooms and continue to simmer for 1 hour.

5. Check the vegetables, meat and barley for tenderness. If needed, simmer for another 30 minutes. Otherwise, stir in the horseradish and frozen peas, and season to taste with salt and freshly ground black pepper. Sprinkle the parsley on top and serve with a piece of crusty bread.

Beef and Barley Stew with Horseradish

Pressure Cooker Directions

Serves: 6   **Cooking Time:** 40 minutes

Change Ingredients: Reduce wine to 1 cup

1. Pre-heat a 6-quart multi-function pressure cooker using the BROWN or SAUTE setting.

2. Add the olive oil to the cooker and working in batches so you don't overcrowd the pan, brown the beef cubes, seasoning with salt and freshly ground black pepper – about 8 minutes per batch. Set the browned meat aside.

3. Add the onion, carrots and parsnips to the cooker and cook until lightly browned - about 5 minutes. Add the garlic, mushrooms and dried spices and cook for another 30 seconds. Add the tomato paste and cook, stirring, for another minute or two. Then add the red wine and deglaze the cooker by scraping up any browned bits on the bottom of the cooker with a wooden spoon. Bring the liquid to a boil and let it simmer for a couple of minutes. (If your cooker doesn't have a brown setting, use a pot on the stovetop for the steps above and transfer the contents to the cooker now.) Return the browned beef to the cooker, add the stock and Worcestershire sauce and stir in the barley. Cover and lock the lid in place.

4. Pressure cook on HIGH for 20 minutes.

5. Let the pressure drop NATURALLY and carefully remove the lid. Stir in the horseradish and frozen peas, and season to taste with salt and freshly ground black pepper. Sprinkle the parsley on top and serve with a piece of crusty bread.

Slow Cooker Directions

Serves: 6   **Cooking Time:** 7½ to 8½ hours on LOW

Change Ingredients: Reduce wine to 1 cup

1. Pre-heat a 6-quart multi-function slow cooker using the BROWN or SAUTE setting.

2. Add the olive oil to the cooker and working in batches so you don't overcrowd the pan, brown the beef cubes, seasoning with salt and freshly ground black pepper – about 8 minutes per batch. Set the browned meat aside.

3. Add the onion, carrots and parsnips to the cooker and cook until lightly browned – about 5 minutes. Add the garlic, mushrooms and dried spices and cook for another 30 seconds. Add the tomato paste and cook, stirring, for another minute or two. Then add the red wine and deglaze the cooker by scraping up any browned bits on the bottom of the cooker with a wooden spoon. Bring the liquid to a boil and let it simmer for a couple of minutes. (If your cooker doesn't have a brown setting, use a pot on the stovetop for the steps above and transfer the contents to the cooker now.) Return the browned beef to the cooker, add the stock and Worcestershire sauce and stir in the barley.

4. Cover and slow cook on LOW for 7 to 8 hours (or 4 hours on HIGH).

5. Stir in the horseradish and frozen peas, and season to taste with salt and freshly ground black pepper. Sprinkle the parsley on top and serve with a piece of crusty bread.

Classic Roast Beef
with Smashed Potatoes, Green Beans and Onions

Possible Cooking Methods: Oven Air Fryer

A proper Sunday roast beef dinner with all the sides usually results in a sink full of dishes. This version uses just one pan by managing the timing of cooking the different parts of the meal. The potatoes and vegetables easily serve four people with some leftover roast beef for sandwiches during the week.

---

1 (3½- to 4-pound) eye of round roast beef

olive oil

1 tablespoon chopped fresh rosemary

1 tablespoon Montreal steak seasoning

1 large onion, thick sliced

salt and freshly ground black pepper

2 pounds red potatoes, cut into 1-inch chunks

14 ounces fresh green beans, halved

3 tablespoons butter

½ cup milk, warmed

3 tablespoons sour cream

2 scallions, finely chopped

Horseradish Sauce:

¾ cup crème fraîche (or sour cream)

3 tablespoons prepared horseradish

1 teaspoon chopped fresh thyme

1 tablespoon chopped fresh parsley

Oven Directions

Serves: 4   **Cooking Time:** 1 hour 15 minutes

1. Pre-heat the oven to 375ºF.

2. Rub the roast all over with olive oil. Combine the fresh rosemary and Montreal steak seasoning in a small bowl. Rub the spice mixture all over beef and transfer the beef to the center of a large roasting pan or sheet pan.

3. Toss the onion with olive oil and season with salt and freshly ground black pepper. Place the onion slices on one side of the pan, next to the roast. Toss the red potatoes with olive oil, season and add to the roasting pan on the other side of the roast. Transfer the roasting pan to the oven.

4. Roast at 375ºF for 40 minutes.

5. Add the green beans to the roasting pan, tossing them in with the onions. Give the potatoes a stir to turn them over and return the pan to the oven. Roast for another 20 minutes. When the potatoes are fork tender, remove them from the pan and set them aside in a bowl. Spread the beans and onions out around

the beef and continue to roast for an additional 10 minutes. Start checking the beef for your desired degree of doneness and remove the pan from the oven when an instant read thermometer registers 5ºF lower than your goal temperature. (Rare- 130ºF, Medium – 150ºF, Well done – 170ºF)

6. While the beef finishes roasting in the oven, finish the potatoes. Smash the potatoes with a fork and stir in the butter, milk and crème fraîche or sour cream, mixing well. Add the scallions and season with salt and freshly ground black pepper. Cover the mashed potatoes with aluminum foil to keep warm.

7. Make the horseradish sauce by combining all the ingredients in a bowl and whisking well.

8. Remove the roast from the oven and let it rest on a cutting board for 5 to 10 minutes. Transfer the onions and green beans to a serving bowl. Serve the sliced roast beef with horseradish, smashed potatoes, green beans and onions either family style or on individual dinner plates.

Classic Roast Beef with Smashed Potatoes, Green Beans and Onions

Air Fryer Directions

Serves: 4   **Cooking Time:** 77 minutes

1. Pre-heat the air fryer to 390ºF.

2. Rub the roast all over with olive oil. Combine the fresh rosemary and Montreal steak seasoning in a small bowl. Rub the spice mixture all over beef. Let the beef sit at room temperature while you cook the potatoes.

3. Toss the red potatoes with olive oil, salt and freshly ground black pepper and transfer them to the air fryer basket. Air-fry the potatoes for 20 minutes, shaking the basket a couple of times during the cooking process. Transfer the cooked potatoes to a bowl.

4. Toss the onions with olive oil, salt and freshly ground black pepper and transfer them to the air fryer basket. Place the roast beef on top of the onions and air-fry at 360ºF for 50 minutes, rotating the roast a few times during the cooking process.

5. Start checking the beef for your desired degree of doneness and remove the pan from the oven when an instant read thermometer registers 5ºF lower than your goal temperature. (Rare- 130ºF, Medium – 150ºF, Well done – 170ºF)

6. While the beef finishes air-frying, finish the potatoes. Smash the potatoes with a fork and stir in the butter, milk and sour cream, mixing well. Add the scallions and season with salt and freshly ground black pepper. Cover the mashed potatoes with aluminum foil to keep warm.

7. Make the horseradish sauce by combining all the ingredients in a bowl and whisking well.

8. Transfer the roast beef to a cutting board and let it rest. Place the onions in a bowl. Toss the green beans with olive oil, salt and freshly ground black pepper and transfer them to the air fryer basket. Air-fry at 400ºF for 5 to 7 minutes, shaking the basket a couple of times during the cooking process. Add the beans to the onions and toss together.

9. Serve the sliced roast beef with horseradish, smashed potatoes, green beans and onions either family style or on individual dinner plates.

Note: To keep the potatoes warm, they can be heated up in the microwave or can be held in a 200ºF oven while the beef cooks.

Pork
and
Lamb

Herb Crusted Pork Rib Roast with Root Vegetables

Possible Cooking Methods: Oven

If you're looking for a celebratory meal for a holiday or special occasion, and you don't want to default to turkey or ham, try a pork rib roast. The rib roast is made up of the pork loin, or 8 center-cut pork chops still attached together. A French-cut pork rib roast is one where the meat is removed from the bones, leaving the exposed ribs to make an impressive presentation. You can cut the meat away from the bones yourself, or just ask your butcher to do it for you. When it's holiday season, chances are you will find this cut of pork already prepared in the meat counter of your grocery store. If you can't find a rib roast, this recipe also works well with a boneless pork loin roast. Whichever you use, it is an easy way to feed eight people generously. If you would like a sauce with the roast, you will need to use a second pan. Simply whisk 2 tablespoons of melted butter with 2 tablespoons of flour in a small sauce-pan over medium heat. Add 1 cup of chicken stock, along with the juices from the roasting pan and some fresh thyme leaves. Bring it all to a simmer to thicken the sauce and season with salt and freshly ground black pepper.

2 tablespoons chopped fresh rosemary	1 (8-rib) French-cut pork rib roast	1 rutabaga, cut into large chunks
2 tablespoons fresh thyme leaves	salt and freshly ground black pepper	2 pounds fingerling potatoes, halved
2 tablespoons chopped fresh sage	¼ cup Dijon mustard	olive oil
2 tablespoons chopped fresh parsley	5 carrots, halved and cut into 3-inch pieces	½ teaspoon dried thyme
²/₃ cup coarse fresh breadcrumbs (preferably homemade)	5 parsnips, halved, cut into 3-inch pieces	

Oven Directions

Serves: 8 **Cooking Time:** 2 hours 15 minutes

1. Pre-heat the oven to 375ºF.

2. Combine the rosemary, thyme, sage, parsley and bread-crumbs in a small bowl. Generously season the rib roast with salt and freshly ground black pepper. Spread the Dijon mustard all over and press the herb and breadcrumb mixture on top to cover the top and sides of the roast. Place the roast in a large 12-inch by 15-inch roasting pan and transfer the pan to the oven. Roast at 375ºF for 30 minutes.

3. Toss the carrots, parsnips, rutabaga and fingerling potatoes with olive oil, dried thyme, salt and freshly ground black pepper. Once the pork has roasted for 30 minutes, add the vegetables to the roasting pan around the pork. Continue to roast for another 60 to 90 minutes (depending on the size of your roast), until the internal temperature of the pork reaches 145°F on an instant-read thermometer inserted into the thickest part of the roast. Toss the vegetables a few times during the cooking process to help them cook evenly.

4. Remove the roasting pan from the oven. Transfer the pork to a cutting board and let it rest for at least 20 minutes, loosely tented with foil. Return the vegetables to the oven for another 10 to 15 minutes, until they are cooked to your liking.

5. Slice the roast in between the bones into portions. Shingle the slices on a large platter and arrange the vegetable around them. Pour the jus from the pan over the meat and serve.

Pork Picatta
with Capellini Pasta and Asparagus

Possible Cooking Methods: Stovetop

This is such an easy dish to make and cooks in no time flat on the stovetop. As a result, it really only makes sense to cook this on the stovetop, rather than in an appliance. You won't save any time in a pressure cooker and the slow cooker would overcook the pasta. So, do your mise en place (all your measuring and chopping) first and then get ready to put this meal together in a jiffy.

1 pork tenderloin (about 1 pound)

salt and freshly ground black pepper

¼ cup all-purpose flour

2 tablespoons olive oil

½ lemon, sliced

½ shallot, thinly sliced

1 clove garlic, thinly sliced

3 cups chicken stock

8 ounces capellini or thin spaghetti pasta, broken in half if necessary

8 ounces asparagus, sliced on the bias into 1-inch slices (about ½ bunch)

1 to 2 tablespoons fresh lemon juice (about 2 lemons)

3 tablespoons capers, drained and rinsed

3 tablespoons butter

2 tablespoons chopped fresh parsley

1 tablespoon finely chopped lemon zest

Stovetop Directions

Serves: 4   **Cooking Time:** 20 minutes

1. Prepare the pork medallions. Slice the tenderloin into 1-inch slices and pound the slices gently with a meat pounder until they are approximately ¾-inch thick. Season the pork medallions with salt and freshly ground black pepper and lightly dredge them in the flour, shaking off any excess.

2. Heat a large 12-inch sauté pan over medium-high heat. Once the pan is hot, add the olive oil and sear the pork in batches for about 2 to 3 minutes per side. Remove the browned pork and set aside.

3. Reduce the heat to medium, add the lemon slices to the pan and brown lightly. Then, add the shallots and garlic to the pan and cook for another minute, taking care not to burn the drippings in the skillet. Add the chicken stock and scrape up any brown bits on the bottom of the skillet. Stir in the pasta and the asparagus, turn the heat down and simmer the liquid gently until the pasta is al dente and the asparagus is tender – about 4 to 5 minutes. (If you start to run out of liquid here, add more chicken stock or water and increase the heat.)

4. Add the lemon juice and capers to the skillet and return the pork cutlets (and any juices) to the pan. Continue to simmer gently for another 2 minutes to finish cooking the pork through and to blend the flavors. If you need more liquid, add a little more stock or lemon juice to taste.

5. Remove the pan from the heat and stir in the butter. Add the parsley and season to taste with salt and freshly ground black pepper. Serve the pork on a bed of the pasta and asparagus, spoon any extra sauce over the top and sprinkle with lemon zest.

Panko Crusted Pork Chops
with Corn and Zucchini

Possible Cooking Methods: Oven   Air Fryer

Here's another sheet pan meal for those summer weeknights when dishes are the last thing you feel like doing. These pork chops are the classic breaded chop that we all grew up with, but all our favorite summer side dishes get cooked right along side on the same pan.

---

2 tablespoons butter, softened	¼ cup all-purpose flour	olive oil
4 ears corn, husked	1 egg, beaten	2 zucchini, cut into ¼-inch thick half moons
salt and freshly ground black pepper	1½ cups panko breadcrumbs	½ teaspoon Italian seasoning
4 center cut, boneless pork chops, 1-inch thick	1 teaspoon paprika	1 cup cherry tomatoes, halved
	½ teaspoon garlic powder	*All quantities halved for alternate method*

Oven Directions

Serves: 4   **Cooking Time:** 45 minutes

1. Pre-heat the oven to 400⁰F.

2. Spread the butter all over the ears of corn and generously season with salt and freshly ground black pepper. Place the corn on one side of a 18-inch by 13-inch sheet pan and transfer the pan to the oven. Roast for 20 to 25 minutes, rotating the corn once halfway through the cooking time.

3. While the corn is roasting, prepare the pork chops. Place the pork chops on a cutting board, cover with plastic wrap and pound with the flat side of a meat pounder so that they are all ¾-inch thick. Set up a dredging station with three shallow dishes. Place the flour in the first dish, the beaten egg in the second dish and combine the breadcrumbs, paprika and garlic powder in the third dish. Season the pork chops with salt and freshly ground black pepper and then dredge them with the flour, then coat with the egg and finally press them into the breadcrumb mixture. Brush or spritz the breaded chops with a little olive oil.

4. Toss the zucchini with olive oil, Italian seasoning, salt and freshly ground black pepper. Once the corn has roasted for 20 to 25 minutes, add the pork chops and the zucchini to the sheet pan and return the pan to the oven for 10 minutes.

5. Flip the pork chops over and add the cherry tomatoes to the pan with the zucchini. Roast for an additional 5 to 7 minutes in the oven until the pork reaches an internal temperature of 165⁰F on an instant read thermometer inserted into the thickest part of the chop.

6. Serve the chops with the vegetables on the side.

Panko Crusted Pork Chops with Corn and Zucchini

Air Fryer Directions

Serves: 2   **Cooking Time:** 18 minutes

Change Ingredients: **Cut ALL ingredients in half**

1. Pre-heat the air fryer to 390ºF.

2. Spread the butter all over the ears of corn and generously season with salt and freshly ground black pepper. Toss the zucchini with olive oil, Italian seasoning, salt and freshly ground black pepper. Place the corn and zucchini in the air fryer basket and air-fry for 6 minutes, rotating the ears of corn and stirring the zucchini halfway through the cooking process. (Air-fry in two separate batches if the ears of corn and zucchini do not fit in your air fryer together.)

3. While the vegetables are air-frying, prepare the pork chops. Place the pork chops on a cutting board, cover with plastic wrap and pound with the flat side of a meat pounder so that they are all ³/₄-inch thick. Set up a dredging station with three shallow dishes. Place the flour in the first dish, the beaten egg in the second dish and combine the breadcrumbs, paprika and garlic powder in the third dish. Season the pork chops with salt and freshly ground black pepper and then dredge them with the flour, then coat with the egg and finally press them into the breadcrumb mixture. Brush or spritz the breaded chops with a little olive oil.

4. Remove the corn from the air fryer and wrap in aluminum foil to keep warm. Transfer the zucchini to a bowl.

5. Place the breaded pork chops in the air fryer basket and air-fry at 400ºF for 8 to 10 minutes, until the pork reaches an internal temperature of 165ºF on an instant read thermometer inserted into the thickest part of the chop. Flip the chops over halfway through the cooking process. Transfer the pork chops to a serving plate. Return the zucchini to the air fryer, add the cherry tomatoes and air-fry at 400ºF for 2 to 3 minutes, until the zucchini is fork tender.

6. Serve the chops with the vegetables on the side.

Pork Tamale Pie

Possible Cooking Methods: Stovetop and Oven

Here's a quick and easy dinner for those busy weeknights. While it's not exactly like eating tamales, this dish has the flavor of traditional pork tamales without all the work. For classic tamales, a flavorful filling (often pork) is encased in masa (a dough made from masa harina) and then wrapped in corn husks or plantain leaves and steamed to cook. When I was teaching cooking classes in San Francisco, the tamale class was the messiest one of all – we would end up with masa everywhere! In this pork tamale pie, we simply top a quick pork filling with the tamale dough and bake it in the oven. It's delicious and easy and, of course, there's only one pan to wash. For a more authentic taste, don't be tempted to try to substitute cornmeal or corn flour for the masa harina. Masa harina is a very fine corn flour that has been soaked in limewater and consequently gives a very distinct flavor to the masa dough.

1 tablespoon olive oil

2½ pounds ground pork

1 onion, chopped

1 poblano pepper, chopped

2 cloves garlic, minced

2 tablespoons chili powder

1 teaspoon ground coriander

1 teaspoon dried oregano

1½ teaspoons salt

1 (28-ounce) can stewed tomatoes, crushed by hand

3 tablespoons tomato paste

1½ cups corn kernels

1 cup grated pepper Jack cheese

Masa Crust:

1 cup instant masa flour or masa harina

1 cup hot water

4 tablespoons butter, softened

½ teaspoon baking powder

½ teaspoon chili powder

½ teaspoon salt

¼ cup chicken stock

Stovetop and Oven Directions

Serves: 6   **Cooking Time:** 60 minutes

1. Prepare the masa for the masa crust by combining the masa flour and hot water together in a bowl. Set it aside to soak for 20 minutes.

2. Pre-heat the oven to 350ºF.

3. Heat a large 12-inch oven-proof skillet over medium heat. Add the olive oil and brown the pork and onion together in the pan until the pork is no longer pink. Add the poblano pepper, garlic, chili powder, coriander, oregano, salt, stewed tomatoes, tomato paste and corn kernels. Bring the mixture to a boil, simmer for 5 minutes and then remove the pan from the heat.

4. Continue making the masa crust while the pork is simmering. Use an electric hand or stand mixer to beat the butter, baking powder, chili powder and salt together until fluffy. Gradually add the soaked masa mixture and pour in the chicken stock, beating until a soft, sticky dough is formed.

5. Spoon the dough over the pork mixture around the edges of the pan, spreading it out but leaving a 5-inch hole in the middle. Fill the hole with the pepper Jack cheese and transfer the pan to the oven.

6. Bake at 350ºF for 45 to 50 minutes, until the crust is golden brown.

Chili Verde

Possible Cooking Methods: Stovetop   Pressure Cooker   Slow Cooker

Chili Verde is usually made with roasted tomatillos. In this recipe, instead of roasting the tomatillos, they are simply sautéed and puréed. If the bottom of your pot gets a little brown, not to worry – that will give you more roasted flavor in your sauce – but don't let it burn. For a super shortcut, you could use a 24-ounce jar of tomatillo salsa instead of the tomatillos. Omit the Jalapeño peppers, garlic, and spices too, since the flavor will come from the salsa you choose. Make sure you choose a good one!

2 tablespoons vegetable oil, divided

3 pounds pork butt or shoulder, trimmed of fat and cut into 1½-inch cubes

salt, to taste

1 onion, rough chopped

2 Jalapeño peppers, rough chopped

1 hot red chili pepper, rough chopped

1 pound tomatillos, husked, rinsed and cut into quarters

2 to 3 cloves garlic, minced

1 teaspoon dried oregano

½ teaspoon ground dried cumin

½ teaspoon chili powder

10 sprigs fresh cilantro, stems and leaves

2 cups chicken stock*

1 red bell pepper, chopped

1 yellow or orange bell pepper, chopped

6 thick flour tortillas, wrapped in foil and warmed (optional)

¼ cup chopped fresh cilantro (or parsley)

1 cup sour cream

Quantity changes for alternate methods

Stovetop Directions

Serves: 6   **Cooking Time:** 1 hour 45 minutes

1. Pre-heat a Dutch oven over medium-high heat. Add 1 tablespoon of the oil and brown the pork in batches, seasoning with salt. Set the browned pork aside.

2. Add the remaining oil and sauté the onion until it starts to soften and color – about 5 minutes. Add the Jalapeño and hot peppers, tomatillos and garlic and continue to sauté, stirring frequently until the tomatillos are soft – 10 to 15 minutes. Add the oregano, cumin and chili powder and continue to sauté for another few minutes. Transfer the vegetables to a blender, add the cilantro sprigs and process until smooth.

3. Return the tomatillo purée and browned pork to the pot, add the chicken stock, red and yellow peppers and bring the mixture to a simmer. Cover with the lid askew and simmer for 1½ hours.

4. When the pork is tender, season again to taste. Serve the chili with warmed tortillas, fresh cilantro or parsley and a dollop of sour cream. This would go well with a cabbage and red pepper salad with orange segments and avocado.

Pressure Cooker Directions

Serves: 6   **Cooking Time:** 45 minutes

Change Ingredients: Reduce stock to 1 cup

1. Pre-heat a 6-quart multi-function pressure cooker using the BROWN or SAUTE setting.

2. Add 1 tablespoon of the oil and brown the pork in batches, seasoning with salt. Set the browned pork aside.

3. Add the remaining oil and sauté the onion until it starts to soften and color – about 5 minutes. Add the Jalapeño and hot peppers, tomatillos and garlic and continue to sauté, stirring frequently until the tomatillos are soft – 10 to 15 minutes. Add the oregano, cumin and chili powder and continue to sauté for another few minutes. (If your cooker doesn't have a brown setting, use a Dutch oven or sauté pan on the stovetop for the steps above.) Transfer the vegetables to a blender, add the cilantro sprigs and process until smooth.

4. Return the tomatillo purée and browned pork to the cooker, add the chicken stock, red and yellow peppers and bring the mixture to a simmer. Cover and lock the lid in place.

5. Pressure cook on HIGH for 15 minutes.

6. Let the pressure drop NATURALLY and carefully remove the lid. Season to taste with salt. Serve the chili with warmed tortillas, fresh cilantro or parsley and a dollop of sour cream. This would go well with a cabbage and red pepper salad with orange segments and avocado.

Slow Cooker Directions

Serves: 6   **Cooking Time:** 6 to 7 hours on LOW

Change Ingredients: Reduce stock to 1 cup

1. Pre-heat a 6-quart multi-function slow cooker using the BROWN or SAUTE setting.

2. Add 1 tablespoon of the oil and brown the pork in batches, seasoning with salt. Set the browned pork aside.

3. Add the remaining oil and sauté the onion until it starts to soften and color – about 5 minutes. Add the Jalapeño and hot peppers, tomatillos and garlic and continue to sauté, stirring frequently until the tomatillos are soft – 10 to 15 minutes. Add the oregano, cumin and chili powder and continue to sauté for another few minutes. (If your cooker doesn't have a brown setting, use a skillet on the stovetop for the steps above.) Transfer the vegetables to a blender, add the cilantro sprigs and process until smooth.

4. Return the tomatillo purée and browned pork to the cooker, add the chicken stock, red and yellow peppers and bring the mixture to a simmer. Cover and slow cook on LOW for 6 to 7 hours (or 3 to 4 hours on HIGH).

5. Season to taste with salt. Serve the chili with warmed tortillas, fresh cilantro or parsley and a dollop of sour cream. This would go well with a cabbage and red pepper salad with orange segments and avocado.

Pork Chops, Apple and Cabbage

Possible Cooking Methods: Stovetop   Pressure Cooker   Slow Cooker

This recipe is easy and quick especially if you pick up a package of pre-shredded coleslaw mix. If you don't have access to a package, you can substitute half a head of cabbage, thinly sliced and 2 carrots, shredded or julienned. Many braised cabbage recipes have sugar added. This recipe uses apple instead to sweeten the cabbage without adding sugar.

---

1 tablespoon olive oil

4 bone-in pork rib chops, 1-inch thick

1 onion, thinly sliced

1 (16-ounce) package coleslaw mix

2 apples, 1-inch dice (Gala, Fuji or Winesap would be good choices)

¾ cup apple cider vinegar

1 teaspoon caraway seeds

1½ teaspoons salt

1 cup chicken stock*

Quantity changes for alternate methods

Stovetop Directions

Serves: 4   **Cooking Time:** 40 minutes

1. Pre-heat a large 12-inch sauté pan over medium-high heat.

2. Add the oil and brown the pork chops well on both sides. Set the browned chops aside.

3. Add the onion to the pan and sauté until it starts to soften – about 5 minutes. Add the package of coleslaw mix and the apples and stir well. Add the apple cider vinegar, caraway seeds and salt to the pan and stir well. Pour in the chicken stock, scraping the bottom of the pan to incorporate any tasty bits.

4. Return the browned pork chops to the pan, resting them on top of the cabbage, and bring the liquid to a boil. Cover the pan with a lid and lower the heat to a simmer. Simmer gently on the stovetop for 30 minutes.

5. Transfer the pork chops to a serving platter and use tongs or a slotted spoon to remove the braised cabbage and apples. Serve with a spicy mustard and crusty rolls or rye bread.

Pork Chops, Apple and Cabbage

Pressure Cooker Directions

Serves: 4   **Cooking Time:** 11 minutes

Change Ingredients: Reduce the chicken stock to ½ cup

1. Pre-heat a 6-quart multi-function pressure cooker using the BROWN or SAUTE setting.

2. Add the oil and brown the pork chops well on both sides. Set the browned chops aside.

3. Add the onion to the cooker and continue to cook for a few minutes, until the onion begins to soften. (If your cooker doesn't have a brown setting, use a skillet on the stovetop for the steps above and transfer the contents to the cooker now.)

4. Add the coleslaw mix, apples, apple cider vinegar, caraway seeds, salt and chicken stock to the cooker. Stir well. Return the browned pork chops to the cooker, on top of the cabbage. Cover and lock the lid in place.

5. Pressure cook on HIGH for 6 minutes.

6. Let the pressure drop NATURALLY and carefully remove the lid. Transfer the pork chops to a serving platter and use tongs or a slotted spoon to remove the braised cabbage and apples. Serve with a spicy mustard and crusty rolls or rye bread.

Slow Cooker Directions

Serves: 6   **Cooking Time:** 5 to 6 hours on LOW

Change Ingredients: Reduce the chicken stock to ½ cup

1. Pre-heat a 6-quart multi-function slow cooker pressure cooker using the BROWN or SAUTE setting.

2. Add the oil and brown the pork chops well on both sides. Set the browned chops aside.

3. Add the onion to the cooker and continue to cook for a few minutes, until the onion begins to soften. (If your cooker doesn't have a brown setting, use a skillet on the stovetop for the steps above and transfer the contents to the cooker now.)

4. Add the coleslaw mix, apples, apple cider vinegar, caraway seeds, salt and chicken stock to the cooker. Stir well. Return the browned pork chops to the cooker, on top of the cabbage.

5. Cover and slow cook on LOW for 5 to 6 hours (or 3 hours on HIGH).

6. Transfer the pork chops to a serving platter and use tongs or a slotted spoon to remove the braised cabbage and apples. Serve with a spicy mustard and crusty rolls or rye bread.

Moroccan Lamb Tagine
with Orange, Olives and Couscous

Possible Cooking Methods: Stovetop   Pressure Cooker   Slow Cooker

This combination of subtle spices with the sweet raisins and salty olives is a Moroccan delight, and a nice change from the lamb stew that many of us are used to. The pearl-sized Israeli couscous is larger than traditional couscous and holds its shape well in the cooking process. My best friend, Tanya, tested this recipe and in a moment of rogue rebellion used orzo instead of the Israeli couscous. That's actually a great substitute if you can't find the couscous. Tanya, by the way, hates raisins and has ever since we were childhood friends, but she loved this recipe.

2½ pounds lamb shoulder, trimmed of fat and cut into 1½- to 2-inch cubes

salt and freshly ground black pepper

2 tablespoons olive oil, divided

1 onion, chopped

3 large carrots, sliced on the bias (½-inch slices)

2 cloves garlic, minced

4 teaspoons grated fresh ginger

½ teaspoon ground cumin

½ teaspoon ground cinnamon

¼ teaspoon ground allspice

⅛ teaspoon ground cayenne pepper

6 ounces orange juice

1 (28-ounce) can diced tomatoes

½ cup beef stock

1 cup raisins

½ cup pitted and halved green olives

½ cup Israeli couscous

2 tablespoons chopped fresh parsley

zest of 1 orange

Stovetop Directions

Serves: 6   **Cooking Time:** **90** minutes

1. Pre-heat a Dutch oven over medium-high heat.

2. Season the lamb with salt and freshly ground black pepper. Add 1 tablespoon of the olive oil to the Dutch oven and brown the lamb in batches, using more oil as necessary. Set the browned lamb aside.

3. Add the onion and carrots to the pot and continue to sauté for a few minutes. Add the garlic, ginger and dried spices and continue to cook for a minute. Pour in the orange juice and bring the liquid to a simmer for a minute. Return the lamb to the Dutch oven and add the tomatoes and stock. Bring the liquid back to a simmer and cover with a lid.

4. Simmer on medium-low to low heat for an hour. Stir in the raisins and olives and continue to simmer for another 30 minutes.

5. Season to taste with salt and freshly ground black pepper and stir in the couscous. Cover with the lid and let the stew sit for a 10 to 15 minutes, or until the couscous is tender and the stew has cooled to an edible temperature. Sprinkle with fresh parsley and orange zest. Serve with some warmed pita bread and a carrot salad.

Moroccan Lamb Tagine with Orange, Olives and Couscous

Pressure Cooker Directions

Serves: 6   **Cooking Time:** 30 minutes

1. Pre-heat heat a 6-quart multi-function pressure cooker on the BROWN or SAUTE setting.

2. Season the lamb with salt and freshly ground black pepper. Add 1 tablespoon of the olive oil to the cooker and brown the lamb in batches, using more oil as necessary. Set the browned lamb aside.

3. Add the onion, carrots and garlic to the cooker and continue to sauté for a few minutes. Add the ginger and dried spices and continue to cook for a minute. (If your cooker doesn't have a brown setting, use a skillet on the stovetop for the steps above and transfer the contents to the cooker now.) Return the lamb to the cooker and add the orange juice, tomatoes, stock, raisins, and olives. Cover and lock the lid in place.

4. Pressure cook on HIGH for 15 minutes.

5. Let the pressure drop NATURALLY and carefully remove the lid. Season to taste with salt and freshly ground black pepper and stir in the Israeli couscous. Cover with the lid and let the stew sit for 15 minutes. That will be enough time for the couscous to cook and for the stew to cool to an edible temperature.

6. Sprinkle with fresh parsley and orange zest. Serve with some warmed pita bread and a carrot salad.

Slow Cooker Directions

Serves: 6   **Cooking Time:** 6 to 7 hours on LOW
                                 + 30 minutes on HIGH

1. Pre-heat heat a 6-quart multi-function slow cooker on the BROWN or SAUTE setting.

2. Season the lamb with salt and freshly ground black pepper. Add 1 tablespoon of the olive oil to the cooker and brown the lamb in batches, using more oil as necessary. Set the browned lamb aside. (If your multi-cooker doesn't have a brown setting, use a skillet on the stovetop for the steps above and transfer the contents to the cooker now.)

3. Add the onion, carrots, garlic, ginger, dried spices, orange juice, tomatoes, stock, raisins, and olives to the cooker. Return the lamb to the cooker and stir well to combine. Cover and slow cook on LOW for 6 to 7 hours (3½ hours on HIGH).

4. Season to taste with salt and freshly ground black pepper and stir in the couscous. Increase the temperature to HIGH and slow cook for 30 minutes.

5. Sprinkle with fresh parsley and orange zest. Serve with some warmed pita bread and a carrot salad.

Hearty Pork and Navy Bean Stew
with Spinach

Possible Cooking Methods: Stovetop and Oven   Pressure Cooker   Slow Cooker

The famous French Cassoulet – a slow cooked pork and white bean stew with a thick crust on top – is the inspiration for this recipe. I used dried beans instead of canned beans here because I feel that they produce the best results. If you're short on time or forget to soak the beans overnight, you can use 2 (17-ounce) cans of navy beans instead. I won't hold it against you. Just remember to add them at the very end of cooking (when you stir in the spinach) so that they don't overcook. If you want to bake a crust onto this dish, follow the last optional step to bake very coarse fresh breadcrumbs on top.

1½ cups (about 1 pound) dried navy beans, soaked in water overnight

4 strips of bacon, chopped

1½ pounds (about 3 links) sweet Italian sausage, casings removed and broken into chunks

1½ pounds boneless pork shoulder, cut into 1½-inch cubes

salt and freshly ground black pepper

1 onion, diced

3 cloves garlic, smashed

2 carrots, sliced 1-inch thick

2 ribs celery, thinly sliced

¼ teaspoon ground nutmeg

4 sprigs fresh thyme

1 bay leaf

½ cup white wine

4 to 5 cups chicken stock*

1 (28-ounce) can tomatoes, chopped

4 ounces fresh baby spinach

4 cups very coarse fresh breadcrumbs (optional)

chopped fresh parsley

*Quantity changes for alternate methods

Stovetop and Oven Directions

Serves: 4 to 6   **Cooking Time:** 2½ to 3 hours

1. Pre-heat a large 6-quart Dutch oven over medium-high heat.

2. Add the bacon and cook until almost crispy. Remove the bacon with a slotted spoon and set it aside. Working in batches, brown the sausage chunks and pork shoulder in the pot, seasoning with salt and freshly ground black pepper. Set the browned meat aside.

3. Add the onion and cook until it starts to soften – about 5 minutes.

4. Add the garlic, carrots, celery, nutmeg, thyme and bay leaf and continue to sauté for another 4 minutes or so. Pour in the white wine and bring to a simmer. Let it simmer for a minute and then add the chicken stock and tomatoes. Return the browned meat to the pot, along with the soaked navy beans. Cover, leaving the lid askew, and simmer on low heat for 1½ hours.

5. Remove the pot from the heat. Remove the lid, skim some of the fat off the surface of the stew and set it aside. Stir in the spinach and reserved cooked bacon. Season to taste with salt and freshly ground black pepper. Serve with fresh parsley sprinkled on top, or proceed with the next optional step.

6. Toss the breadcrumbs with about 2 tablespoons of the reserved fat from the top of the stew. Spread the breadcrumb mixture over the top of the stew and finish by browning the top in a 425ºF oven for about 20 to 25 minutes.

Hearty Pork and Navy Bean Stew with Spinach

Pressure Cooker Directions

Serves: 4 to 6   **Cooking Time:** 30 minutes

Change Ingredients: Reduce stock to 2 cups

1. Pre-heat a 6-quart multi-function pressure cooker using the BROWN or SAUTE setting. Add the bacon and cook until almost crispy. Remove the bacon with a slotted spoon and set aside. Working in batches, brown the sausage and pork shoulder in the cooker, seasoning with salt and freshly ground black pepper. Set the browned pork aside.

2. Add the onion, garlic, carrots, celery, nutmeg, thyme and bay leaf to the cooker. Pour in the white wine and bring to a simmer. Let it simmer for a minute and then add the chicken stock and tomatoes. (If your cooker doesn't have a brown setting, use a Dutch oven on the stovetop for the steps above and transfer the contents to the cooker now.)

3. Return the browned meat to the pot, along with the soaked navy beans. Cover and lock the lid in place.

4. Pressure cook on HIGH for 20 minutes.

5. Let the pressure drop NATURALLY and carefully remove the lid. Skim some of the fat off the surface of the stew and set it aside. Stir in the spinach and reserved cooked bacon. Season to taste with salt and freshly ground black pepper. Serve with fresh parsley sprinkled on top, or proceed with the next optional step.

6. Combine the breadcrumbs and reserved fat. Toast the breadcrumbs in a skillet until crispy and sprinkle this crispy breadcrumb mixture on top of each bowl of stew.

Slow Cooker Directions

Serves: 4 to 6   **Cooking Time:** 8 to 10 hours on LOW

Change Ingredients: Reduce stock to 2 cups

1. Pre-heat a 6-quart multi-function slow cooker using the BROWN or SAUTE setting. Add the bacon and cook until almost crispy. Remove the bacon with a slotted spoon and set aside. Set any extra bacon fat aside. Working in batches, brown the sausage and pork shoulder in the cooker, seasoning with salt and freshly ground black pepper. Set the browned pork aside.

2. Add the onion, garlic, carrots and celery and sauté for a few minutes. Pour in the white wine and bring to a simmer. (If your cooker does not have a brown setting, use a Dutch oven on the stovetop for the steps above and transfer the contents to the cooker now.)

3. Return the browned meat to the cooker and add the nutmeg, thyme and bay leaf, chicken stock, tomatoes and the soaked navy beans. Cover and slow cook on LOW for 8 to 10 hours (or 4 hours on HIGH).

4. Remove the lid, skim some of the fat off the surface of the stew and set it aside. Stir in the spinach and reserved cooked bacon. Season to taste with salt and freshly ground black pepper. Serve with fresh parsley sprinkled on top, or proceed with the next optional step.

5. Combine the breadcrumbs and reserved fat. Toast the breadcrumbs in a skillet until crispy and sprinkle this crispy breadcrumb mixture on top of each bowl of stew.

Easy Lamb Curry
with Cauliflower and Chickpeas

Possible Cooking Methods: Stovetop   Pressure Cooker   Slow Cooker

This lamb is considered "easy" in my book because it doesn't require preliminary browning, which saves a huge step. This is also a great basic curry recipe that can be made with any meat – beef, chicken or pork. The only thing that would change is the cooking time for chicken (only 30 minutes).

---

3 to 4 tablespoons canola or coconut oil

1 onion, diced (about 1 cup)

1 cinnamon stick

2 carrots, sliced

2 ribs celery, sliced or finely diced

1 large clove garlic, minced

1 tablespoon minced fresh ginger

½ teaspoon turmeric

1½ teaspoons ground cumin

½ teaspoon brown mustard seed

½ teaspoon ground coriander

¼ teaspoon ground cayenne pepper

½ teaspoon garam masala

1 (28-ounce) can tomatoes, chopped

2 pounds lamb stew meat, trimmed of fat and in 2-inch cubes

1 teaspoon salt

freshly ground black pepper

1 cup beef stock or water*

½ head cauliflower, cut into florets*

1 (15-ounce) can chickpeas, drained

½ cup toasted almonds, rough chopped

fresh cilantro

naan bread, warmed
(optional, but not if you are gluten free)

*Changes for alternate methods

Stovetop Directions

Serves: 4   **Cooking Time:** 2 hours 35 minutes

1. Pre-heat a 5-quart Dutch oven over medium-high heat. Add the oil and sauté the onion and cinnamon stick gently for 5 minutes. Add the carrots, celery, garlic and ginger for another 5 minutes. Add the spices and cook for 2 minutes. Add the tomatoes and let the mixture simmer for at least 5 minutes.

2. Add the lamb to the pot and season with salt and freshly ground black pepper. Pour in the beef stock or water and bring the liquid to a boil. Reduce the heat and simmer for 2 hours.

3. Add the cauliflower to the pot and continue to simmer for 20 minutes. Stir in the chickpeas and turn off the heat.

4. Sprinkle the toasted almonds on top and garnish with fresh cilantro leaves. Serve with warmed naan bread.

Easy Lamb Curry with Cauliflower and Chickpeas

Pressure Cooker Directions

Serves: 4   **Cooking Time:** 45 minutes

Change Ingredients: Substitute frozen cauliflower for the fresh cauliflower

1. Pre-heat a 5-quart multi-function pressure cooker using the BROWN or SAUTE setting. Add the oil and sauté the onion and cinnamon stick gently for 5 minutes. Add the carrots, celery, garlic and ginger for another 5 minutes. Add the spices and cook for 2 minutes. Add the tomatoes and let the mixture simmer for at least 5 minutes. (If your cooker doesn't have a brown setting, use a Dutch oven or sauté pan on the stovetop for the steps above and transfer the contents to the cooker now.)

2. Add the lamb to the cooker and season with salt and freshly ground black pepper. Pour in the beef stock or water, cover and lock the lid in place.

3. Pressure cook on HIGH for 15 minutes.

4. Let the pressure drop NATURALLY for 15 minutes, then quick-release any residual pressure and carefully remove the lid.

5. Add the cauliflower and chickpeas and return the lid to the cooker. Let the curry sit for 10 minutes. This will be enough time to heat the cauliflower and chickpeas through and cool the curry to an edible temperature.

6. Sprinkle the toasted almonds on top and garnish with fresh cilantro leaves. Serve with warmed naan bread.

Slow Cooker Directions

Serves: 4   **Cooking Time:** 8 hours on LOW

Change Ingredients: Reduce the beef stock or water to ½ cup; Substitute frozen cauliflower for the fresh cauliflower

1. Pre-heat a 5-quart multi-function slow cooker using the BROWN or SAUTE setting. Add the oil and sauté the onion and cinnamon stick sauté gently for 5 minutes. Add the carrots, celery, garlic and ginger for another 5 minutes. Add the spices and cook for 2 minutes. Add the tomatoes and let the mixture simmer for at least 5 minutes. (If your cooker doesn't have a brown setting, use a Dutch oven or sauté pan on the stovetop for the steps above and transfer the contents to the cooker now.)

2. Add the lamb to the cooker and season with salt and freshly ground black pepper. Cover and slow cook on LOW for 8 hours (or 4 hours on HIGH).

3. Add the cauliflower and chickpeas and return the lid to the cooker. Let the curry sit for 10 minutes. This will be enough time to heat the cauliflower and chickpeas through and cool the curry to an edible temperature.

4. Sprinkle the toasted almonds on top and garnish with fresh cilantro leaves. Serve with warmed naan bread.

Deep Dish Prosciutto, Spinach and Mushroom Pizza

Possible Cooking Methods: Oven   Air Fryer

One of my favorite one-pan meals – pizza! This recipe can work as a template for any ingredient you love. Can't find prosciutto – substitute ham or par-cooked bacon, or omit it altogether for a vegetarian pie. Don't like spinach – try chopped broccoli florets instead. You see how that works?

4 ounces button mushrooms, sliced

1 tablespoon olive oil

¼ teaspoon Italian seasoning

¾ cup frozen spinach, thawed

1 pound pizza dough, homemade or frozen and thawed

1½ cups pizza sauce

2 cups grated mozzarella cheese

4 ounces thinly sliced prosciutto

*All quantities change for alternate method

Oven Directions

Serves: 4   **Cooking Time:** 35 minutes

1. Toss the mushrooms with the olive oil and Italian seasoning, and set aside to marinate for at least 15 minutes. Squeeze as much liquid as possible from the spinach and set the spinach aside as well.

2. Pre-heat the oven to 450⁰F.

3. Grease the inside of a 9-inch cake pan with olive oil, or use a pan with a non-stick surface. Roll or stretch the pizza dough out into a circle that is 11 inches in diameter and transfer it to the pan, pressing the crust up the sides of the pan.

4. Fill the inside of the pizza crust with the sauce and top with half of the mozzarella cheese. Layer half of the spinach and mushrooms over the cheese. Repeat with another layer of cheese and another layer of spinach and mushrooms. Tear the prosciutto up into pieces and scatter the pieces on top of the pizza. Transfer the pan to the oven.

5. Bake at 450⁰F for 30 to 35 minutes, until the crust is brown and the cheese has melted.

6. Serve with a nice salad and a glass of red wine!

You don't have to toss the pizza dough to make this recipe, but it sure is fun.

Deep Dish Prosciutto, Spinach & Mushroom Pizza

Air Fryer Directions

Serves: 2   **Cooking Time:** 22 minutes

Change Ingredients:
3 ounces button mushrooms, sliced
½ cup frozen spinach, thawed
1 tablespoon olive oil
¼ teaspoon Italian seasoning
12 ounces pizza dough
⅓ cup pizza sauce
1½ cups grated mozzarella cheese
3 ounces thinly sliced prosciutto

1. Toss the mushrooms with the olive oil and Italian seasoning, and set aside to marinate for at least 15 minutes. Squeeze as much liquid as possible from the spinach and set the spinach aside as well.

2. Pre-heat the air fryer to 370ºF.

3. Grease the inside of a 7-inch baking pan with olive oil, or use a pan with a non-stick surface. Roll or stretch the pizza dough out into a circle that is 8 to 9 inches in diameter and transfer it to the pan, pressing the crust up the sides of the pan. Dock the dough by piercing holes in the bottom crust with a fork. Transfer the pan to the air fryer basket.

4. Air-fry at 370ºF for 5 minutes. Remove the pan from the air fryer. Flip the crust over in the pan by inverting it onto a plate and sliding it back into the pan. (Yes, this seems counterintuitive and you will worry about the walls of the pizza collapsing, but they won't.) Return the pan to the air fryer and air-fry for 5 minutes to brown the bottom of the crust. Flip the crust back over in the pan.

5. Fill the inside of the pizza crust with the sauce and top with half of the mozzarella cheese. Layer half of the spinach and mushrooms over the cheese. Repeat with another layer of cheese and another layer of spinach and mushrooms. Tear the prosciutto up into pieces and scatter the pieces on top of the pizza. Return the pan to the air fryer.

6. Air-fry at 350ºF for 10 to 12 minutes until the crust is brown and the cheese has melted.

7. Serve with a nice salad and a glass of red wine!

Spicy Szechuan Pork and Jasmine Rice

Possible Cooking Methods: Stovetop Pressure Cooker

Szechuan dishes are generally bold and spicy, and this recipe is no exception. You can, however, control the spice level by adding less or more of the red chili sauce to suit your taste. Look in the ethnic aisle of your grocery store for all the ingredients listed below. While they may not be on your regular shopping list, they are all pretty widely available. For a quick shortcut, you could pick up a bottle of ready-made Szechuan sauce and use ½ cup of that instead. This delicious one-pot meal is better than take-out, and you won't have to tip the delivery person!

canola oil

1 (1-pound) pork tenderloin, cut in 2-inch strips

1 onion, sliced

2 cloves garlic, thinly sliced

2 carrots, julienned

1 red bell pepper, sliced

1½ cups jasmine rice

3 cups chicken stock*

1 (5-ounce) can bamboo shoots, drained

1 to 2 tablespoons red chili sauce

1 tablespoon soy sauce

1 tablespoon sesame oil

¼ cup oyster sauce

2 tablespoons water

5 scallions, cut into 2-inch pieces

Quantity changes for alternate methods

Stovetop Directions

Serves: 4   **Cooking Time:** 30 minutes

1. Pre-heat a large 12-inch skillet or wok over high heat. Add the oil and quickly sear the pork strips on both sides. Remove the seared pork from the pan and set it aside.

2. Add the onion to the skillet and sauté over high heat for 2 minutes. Add the garlic, carrots and red pepper, sautéing for another 2 minutes. Stir in the rice and sauté for a few minutes more. Add the chicken stock and bamboo shoots, cover, reduce the heat to low and simmer for 15 minutes. Do not stir or lift the lid during this time.

3. Combine the chili sauce, soy sauce, sesame oil, oyster sauce and water in a small bowl. (Remember to adjust the chili sauce to your taste for spice.) Add this sauce mixture and the scallions to the rice in the skillet. Return the pork to the pan, toss and simmer for a few more minutes, until everything is heated through and the sauce has thickened.

4. Serve the pork and rice in bowls with chopsticks and extra soy sauce and sesame oil at the table.

Spicy Szechuan Pork and Jasmine Rice

Pressure Cooker Directions

Serves: 4   **Cooking Time:** 14 minutes

Change Ingredients: Reduce chicken stock to 2½ cups

1. Pre-heat a 6-quart multi-function pressure cooker using the BROWN or SAUTE setting.

2. Add the oil and quickly sear the pork strips on both sides. Remove the seared pork from the cooker and set it aside.

3. Add the onions to the cooker and sauté for 2 minutes. Add the garlic, carrots, red pepper and rice, sautéing for another 2 minutes. (If your cooker doesn't have a brown setting, use a skillet on the stovetop for the steps above and transfer the contents to the cooker now.) Add the chicken stock and bamboo shoots, and return the seared pork to the cooker. Cover and lock the lid in place.

4. Pressure cook on HIGH for 5 minutes.

5. Combine the chili sauce (remember to adjust the chili sauce to your taste for spice), soy sauce, and sesame oil and oyster sauce in a small bowl.

6. Release the pressure using the QUICK-RELEASE method and carefully remove the lid. Stir the sauce and the scallions into the rice and serve with extra soy sauce and sesame oil at the table.

Tuscan Pork Sausage
with Kale, Butternut Squash and Toasted Bread

Possible Cooking Methods: Stovetop   Pressure Cooker   Slow Cooker

This is a dish that can be filled with any mixture of vegetables, really. I love kale and all its health benefits, but you could easily substitute any other dark leafy green. The butternut squash gives this a nice burst of color, but you could use potato or turnip instead if you prefer. Rustic torn fried bread croutons go on top, and while in some variations of this recipe making them will require using a second pan, I think they are well worth it.

olive oil

4 cups rustic Italian bread, crusts removed and torn into bite-sized pieces

salt and freshly ground black pepper

2 pounds Tuscan pork sausage, casings removed and broken into chunks

1 onion, finely chopped

¼ teaspoon crushed red pepper flakes

2 cups diced butternut squash, 1-inch dice

4 sprigs fresh thyme

1 teaspoon dried oregano

4 ounces (½ bunch) Lacinato kale, stems removed and rough chopped

2 tomatoes, chopped

½ cup white wine

4 cups chicken stock*

Parmesan cheese

*Quantity changes for alternate methods

Stovetop Directions

Serves: 4   **Cooking Time:** 65 minutes

1. Pre-heat a Dutch oven over medium-high heat.

2. Add a good coating of oil to the bottom of the pot and add the bread pieces. Season with salt and fry the bread in batches until browned and crispy. Set the browned bread pieces aside.

3. Add a little more oil to the pot and sauté the pork sausage for 5 or 6 minutes, until it has rendered out much of its fat and is nicely browned. Remove the browned sausage and set it aside.

4. Add the onion and crushed red pepper flakes to the pot and sauté until the onion starts to soften – about 5 minutes. Add the butternut squash, thyme and oregano, season with salt and continue to sauté for another 5 minutes. Stir in the kale and tomatoes and the pour in the wine. Bring the wine to a simmer for a minute or two and then add the chicken stock. Return the browned sausage to the pot, cover with the lid askew and lower the heat to medium-low. Simmer for 45 minutes.

5. Remove the lid and season to taste. Serve in deep bowls with several toasted pieces of bread and shavings of Parmesan cheese on top.

Tuscan Pork Sausage with Kale, Butternut Squash and Toasted Bread

Pressure Cooker Directions

Serves: 4   **Cooking Time:** 10 minutes

Change Ingredients: Reduce stock to 3 cups. While you can toast the bread pieces in a multi-cooker that has a brown setting, it could be time consuming. Toasting the bread on the stovetop, in the oven or in an air fryer is a great option.

1. Pre-heat a 6-quart multi-function pressure cooker using the BROWN or SAUTE setting.

2. Add the pork sausage and cook for 5 or 6 minutes, until it has rendered out much of its fat and is nicely browned. Remove the browned sausage and set aside. Add the white wine to the cooker and scrape up any brown bits on the bottom of the pot. (If your cooker doesn't have a brown setting, use a skillet on the stovetop for the steps above and transfer the contents to the cooker now.)

3. Add the onion, crushed red pepper flakes, butternut squash, thyme and oregano and stir well. Stir in the kale and tomatoes, season with salt and the pour in the chicken stock. Cover and lock the lid in place.

4. Pressure cook on HIGH for 10 minutes.

5. Release the pressure with the QUICK-RELEASE method and carefully remove the lid. Season to taste. Serve in deep bowls with several toasted pieces of bread and shavings of Parmesan cheese on top.

Slow Cooker Directions

Serves: 4   **Cooking Time:** 2 to 3 hours on LOW

Change Ingredients: Reduce stock to 3 cups. While you can toast the bread pieces in a multi-cooker that has a brown setting, it could be time consuming. Toasting the bread in the oven or in an air fryer is a great option.

1. Pre-heat a 5- to 6-quart multi-function slow cooker using the BROWN or SAUTE setting.

2. Add the pork sausage and cook for 5 or 6 minutes, until it has rendered out much of its fat and is nicely browned. Remove the browned sausage and set aside. Add the white wine to the cooker and scrape up any brown bits on the bottom of the pot. (If your cooker doesn't have a brown setting, use a skillet on the stovetop for the steps above and transfer the contents to the cooker now.)

3. Add the onion, crushed red pepper flakes, butternut squash, thyme and oregano and stir well. Stir in the kale and tomatoes and the pour in the chicken stock. Cover and slow cook on LOW for 2 to 3 hours (1½ hours on HIGH).

4. Season to taste. Serve in deep bowls with several toasted pieces of bread and shavings of Parmesan cheese on top.

Fruit and Nut Stuffed Pork Loin with Pineapple Glaze and Roasted Cauliflower and Broccoli

Possible Cooking Methods: Oven Air Fryer

Here's another elegant one-pan dinner worthy of a dinner party. The trickiest part is double-butterflying the pork loin (which you can see in photos on the next page). If that seems overwhelming to you, ask your butcher to prepare the pork loin before you leave the store. With that done, this recipe really is a breeze. The fruit and nut stuffing compliments the pork so nicely and the pineapple glaze will make you think of the tropics. If you can't find the sweet and tender King Hawaiian bread, try substituting brioche.*

4 cups cubed Hawaiian sweet bread

⅓ cup chicken stock, warmed

¼ cup grated onion

½ cup diced dried pineapple

½ cup diced dried mango

½ teaspoon dried sage

2 tablespoons chopped fresh parsley

1 egg, lightly beaten

⅓ cup chopped mixed nuts (pistachios, cashews, pecans, almonds, but no peanuts)

½ teaspoon salt

freshly ground black pepper

1 (1½-pound) pork loin roast, about 12 inches in length

8 ounces pineapple preserves

1 tablespoon brown sugar

1 tablespoon soy sauce

½ head broccoli florets

½ head cauliflower florets

olive oil

Oven Directions

Serves: 4   **Cooking Time:** 45 minutes

1. Pre-heat the oven to 425⁰F.

2. Make the stuffing by combining the bread cubes, warm chicken stock and grated onion together in a bowl. Stir in the dried pineapple, mango, sage, parsley, egg, chopped nuts, salt and freshly ground black pepper. Combine well.

3. Double butterfly the pork loin as follows. Place the pork loin on a cutting board with one end pointing towards you. Using a long slicing knife, make a slice into the side of the pork loin parallel to the cutting board and about one third of the way down from the top surface of the loin. Stop before you slice completely through the loin. Roll the pork loin over so that the cut side is away from your knife and what was the bottom of the loin becomes the top. Make another incision into the pork loin, parallel to the cutting board and one third of the way down from the top surface of the loin. Stop before you slice completely through the loin. Open the flaps of meat so that the pork loin is now a large rectangle three times its original width.

4. Cover the pork with a piece of plastic wrap and pound the meat lightly with a meat mallet to an even thickness.

5. Season the pork with salt and freshly ground black pepper. Spread the stuffing on top of the pork, leaving a 1-inch border on one short end. Starting from the other end roll the pork into a log, jelly-roll style. Tie the pork loin with kitchen twine in 3 to 4 places down the roast to secure it, rub the outside of the roast with olive oil and season it with salt and freshly ground black pepper. Transfer the pork to a large roasting pan.

6. Transfer the pan to the oven and roast at 425⁰F for 20 minutes.

7. While the meat is cooking, make the glaze by combining the pineapple preserves, brown sugar and soy sauce in a bowl. After 20 minutes of roasting, brush some of the glaze over the pork loin. Add the broccoli and cauliflower florets around the roast, drizzling with olive oil and seasoning with salt and freshly ground black pepper. Roast for an additional 20 minutes, glazing the pork two more times during the cooking process. The pork should reach an internal temperature of 155⁰F on an instant read thermometer inserted into the thickest part of the loin.

8. Transfer the pork to a cutting board and let it rest for 15 minutes. Continue to roast the vegetables for 5 more minutes, until the vegetables are cooked to your liking. Slice the pork into ½-inch slices and serve with the roasted vegetables.

Fruit and Nut Stuffed Pork Loin with Pineapple Glaze and Roasted Cauliflower and Broccoli

Air Fryer Directions

Serves: 4   **Cooking Time:** 47 minutes

1. Pre-heat the air fryer to 380°F.

2. Make the stuffing by combining the bread cubes, warm chicken stock and grated onion together in a bowl. Stir in the dried pineapple, mango, sage, parsley, egg, chopped nuts, salt and freshly ground black pepper. Combine well.

3. Double butterfly the pork loin as follows. Place the pork loin on a cutting board with one end pointing towards you. Using a long slicing knife, make a slice into the side of the pork loin parallel to the cutting board and about one third of the way down from the top surface of the loin. Stop before you slice completely through the loin. Roll the pork loin over so that the cut side is away from your knife and what was the bottom of the loin becomes the top. Make another incision into the pork loin, parallel to the cutting board and one third of the way down from the top surface of the loin. Stop before you slice completely through the loin. Open the flaps of meat so that the pork loin is now a large rectangle three times its original width.

4. Season the pork with salt and freshly ground black pepper. Spread the stuffing on top of the pork, leaving a 1-inch border on one short end. Starting from the other end roll the pork into a log, jelly-roll style. Tie the pork loin with kitchen twine in 3 to 4 places down the roast to secure it, rub the outside of the roast with olive oil and season it with salt and freshly ground black pepper.

5. Make the glaze by combining the pineapple preserves, brown sugar and soy sauce in a bowl.

6. Place the pork roast in the air fryer basket and air-fry at 380°F for 35 minutes, glazing the roast and rotating it every 8 to 10 minutes.

7. The pork should reach internal temperature of 155°F on an instant read thermometer inserted into the thickest part of the loin.

8. Transfer the pork to a cutting board and let it rest for 15 minutes. Add the cauliflower to the air fryer basket, drizzling with olive oil and seasoning with salt and freshly ground black pepper. Air-fry the cauliflower for 6 minutes. Add the broccoli to the cauliflower in the air fryer basket and air-fry for another 6 to 8 minutes, tossing halfway through the cooking process.

9. Slice the pork into ½-inch slices and serve with the roasted vegetables.

Kielbasa, Pierogies and Sauerkraut Bake

Possible Cooking Methods: Stovetop and Oven   Pressure Cooker

I am a sucker for pierogies. I think it started when I was young, growing up in Alberta where I had a friend of Ukranian heritage. We used to go visit her grandmother in Red Water and she would make homemade pierogies, which we would eat with reckless abandon. I think of my friend, Carolyn every time I eat pierogies to this day. This recipe combines pierogies with crispy fried Polish Kielbasa sausage, sautéed onions and tangy sauerkraut, all baked with cheese. It's over the top, but an indulgent treat for anyone who loves traditional eastern European foods.

1 (1-pound) bag of sauerkraut

1 teaspoon canola oil

1 pound Polish Kielbasa sausage, cut into 1-inch slices

½ onion, sliced

salt and freshly ground black pepper

½ teaspoon caraway seeds

1 tablespoon stone-ground mustard

1 cup chicken stock or beer*

1 (1-pound) bag frozen potato and cheese filled pierogies

1 cup grated white Cheddar cheese

1 cup grated Swiss cheese

chopped scallions

Quantity changes for alternate methods

Stovetop and Oven Directions

Serves: 4   **Cooking Time:** 35 minutes

1. Pre-heat the oven to 350⁰F.

2. Drain the sauerkraut, reserving the liquid.

3. Pre-heat a large 12-inch oven-proof skillet over medium-high heat. Add the oil and brown the Kielbasa sausage slices on both sides. Remove the browned sausage from the pan and set aside.

4. Add the onion to the skillet and season with salt and freshly ground black pepper. Sauté until the onion starts to brown – about 5 minutes. Add the drained sauerkraut and caraway seeds and continue to sauté for a few more minutes. Add the stock or beer, reserved sauerkraut liquid and stone-ground mustard. Bring the mixture to a boil and return the browned Kielbasa to the skillet.

5. Add the pierogies, nestling them into the sauerkraut and onions. Lower the heat under the pan and simmer for 5 minutes. Sprinkle the Cheddar and Swiss cheeses on top and transfer the pan to the oven.

6. Bake at 350⁰F for 10 to 12 minutes, until the pierogies are cooked through and the cheese has melted. Top with chopped scallions and enjoy!

Additional Cooking Directions for

Kielbasa, Pierogies and Sauerkraut Bake

Pressure Cooker Directions

Serves: 4   **Cooking Time:** 14 minutes

Change Ingredients: Add an additional ½ cup of chicken stock.

1. Pre-heat a 6-quart multi-function pressure cooker using the BROWN or SAUTE setting.

2. Add the oil and brown the kielbasa sausage slices on both sides. Remove the browned sausage from the cooker and set aside.

3. Add the onions to the cooker and season with salt and freshly ground black pepper. Sauté until they start to brown – about 5 minutes. (If your cooker doesn't have a brown setting, use a skillet on the stovetop for the steps above and transfer the contents to the cooker now.) Add the sauerkraut, caraway seeds, chicken stock or beer, reserved sauerkraut liquid, stone-ground mustard and browned kielbasa to the cooker and stir well. Add the pierogies, nestling them into the sauerkraut and onions. Cover and lock the lid in place.

4. Pressure cook on HIGH for 4 minutes.

5. Release the pressure using the QUICK-RELEASE method and carefully remove the lid. Transfer the mixture to a large serving dish and sprinkle the Cheddar and Swiss cheeses over the top. Cover with aluminum foil for a few minutes to melt the cheese. Top with the chopped scallions and enjoy!

Fish and Seafood

Lemon-Thyme Halibut en Papillote
with Roasted Fingerling Potatoes and Asparagus

Possible Cooking Methods: Oven Air Fryer

Cooking fish en papillote could become your favorite way to prepare fish. It is quick and easy, creates little to no mess or smell, and leaves you with a ready-made sauce in the end. What's not to love? This technique can be used on any number of fish, so feel free to mix it up. The only thing to take into consideration is the cooking time – the thicker the piece of fish in the paper package, the longer it will take. If you choose to make this recipe with halibut, remember to look for Pacific halibut. Atlantic halibut is currently on the "avoid" list with Seafood Watch since it is at risk of becoming endangered.

1 pound fingerling potatoes, halved lengthwise

olive oil

salt and freshly ground black pepper

2 teaspoons chopped fresh thyme leaves, plus 4 sprigs fresh thyme

4 (6-ounce) fillets of Pacific halibut

1 lemon, zest and juice

2 tablespoons butter, cut into 4 pieces

4 teaspoons white wine

1 bunch asparagus (about 8 ounces)

salt and freshly ground black pepper

*All quantities change for alternate methods

Oven Directions

Serves: 4   **Cooking Time:** 25 minutes

1. Pre-heat the oven to 425°F.

2. Toss the potatoes in a bowl with olive oil, salt, freshly ground black pepper and thyme leaves and place them on a large baking sheet. Transfer the sheet to the oven and roast for 10 minutes while you prepare the fish.

3. Cut out 4 large rectangles of parchment paper – about 10-inches by 15-inches each. Place a fillet of fish on one half of each rectangle and season with salt and freshly ground black pepper. Sprinkle the lemon zest on the fish and place a sprig of thyme and a piece of butter on top. Drizzle a teaspoon of wine on each of the four fillets.

4. Fold up each parchment rectangle by first folding the paper in half over the fish. Then starting at one corner, twist or fold the paper over on itself all the way around the fish. End by twisting the corner of the paper. The goal is to ensure that the package has become steam-proof and won't come unraveled in the oven. Push the potatoes aside to make room and place the packages of fish in the middle of the large sheet pan.

5. Toss the asparagus with olive oil, salt and freshly ground black pepper and place the spears on the other side of the fish. Return the pan to the oven and roast for another 15 minutes.

6. Remove the fish to four dinner plates, tear open the paper and squeeze a little lemon juice inside. Squeeze a little lemon juice over the vegetables and sprinkle with any extra lemon zest.

Lemon-Thyme Halibut en Papillote with Roasted Fingerling Potatoes and Asparagus

Air Fryer Directions

Serves: 2   **Cooking Time:** 25 minutes

Change Ingredients: Cut ALL ingredients in half.

1. Pre-heat the air fryer to 400ºF.

2. Toss the potatoes with olive oil, salt, freshly ground black pepper and thyme leaves and place them in the air fryer basket. Air-fry at 400ºF for 5 minutes, shaking the basket a few times during the cooking process. Toss the asparagus in the bowl with olive oil, salt and pepper and add them to the basket with the potatoes. Continue to air fry at 400ºF for another 5 minutes. When the potatoes and asparagus are tender, transfer them to a side plate and tent with aluminum foil while you cook the fish.

3. Meanwhile, prepare the fish. Cut out 2 large rectangles of parchment paper – about 10-inches by 15-inches each. Place a fillet of fish on one half of each rectangle and season with salt and freshly ground black pepper. Sprinkle the lemon zest on the fish and place a sprig of thyme and a piece of butter on top. Drizzle the wine on the fish, dividing it between the two fillets.

4. Fold up each parchment rectangle by first folding the paper in half over the fish. Then starting at one corner near the fold, twist or fold the paper over on itself all the way around the fish. End by twisting the corner of the paper. The goal is to ensure that the package has become steam proof and won't come unraveled in the air fryer. Transfer the packages of fish to the air fryer basket and cook at 400ºF for 10 minutes. Remove the fish from the air fryer basket and return the potatoes and asparagus to the air fryer. Air-fry at 400ºF for 3 to 5 minutes just to reheat. The fish will stay warm in the parchment paper.

5. Remove the fish to two dinner plates, tear open the paper and squeeze a little lemon juice inside. Squeeze a little lemon juice over the vegetables and sprinkle with any extra lemon zest.

Cod, Potato and Leek Casserole

Possible Cooking Methods: Oven

This is not the prettiest of dishes, but it might win the award for most satisfying and tastiest fish recipe in this book. It's very easy to make – simply layering raw cod with raw potatoes and raw leeks, covering with cream and baking just like a potato gratin – and the combination of potato, leek, cream and cod is beautiful. Just remember to keep the potato slices thin (½-inch) and consistent so that it bakes evenly and in the directed amount of time. I'd enjoy this on a winter evening with a glass of wine and a crisp green salad. Although I tested this recipe in the air fryer, it saved no time and the quality of the result just didn't measure up to the oven method – so my recommendation for this is to bake in a traditional oven.

1½ pounds Russet potatoes, thinly sliced (about ¼-inch)

1 large or 2 small leeks, cleaned, dark greens discarded and whites thinly sliced (about ¼-inch)

1 pound fresh cod, sliced ½-inch thick on the bias

salt and freshly ground black pepper

1 tablespoon fresh thyme leaves

1 cup heavy cream

⅓ cup grated Parmesan cheese

2 tablespoons butter, plus more for buttering the casserole dish

Oven Directions

Serves: 4   **Cooking Time:** 60 to 75 minutes

1. Pre-heat the oven to 400ºF.

2. Grease a 9-inch square casserole dish or baking pan with butter. Place a third of the potato slices on the bottom of the casserole dish in one layer, slightly overlapping as needed. Season with salt, freshly ground black pepper and fresh thyme leaves. Scatter a quarter of the leeks on top. Then, arrange half the cod on top and season with salt and freshly ground black pepper. Scatter another quarter of the leeks on the fish and top with another layer of potatoes. Repeat the leeks, cod, leeks and potatoes one more time, seasoning the potatoes and cod each time.

3. Pour the heavy cream over the layers, sprinkle the Parmesan cheese on top and dot the top of the potatoes with the butter. Cover with aluminum foil and transfer the pan to the oven to bake for 30 minutes. Remove the aluminum foil and continue to bake for another 30 to 45 minutes, or until the potatoes start to brown nicely on top and a paring knife inserted into the center feels little to no resistance.

4. Let the casserole cool for a few minutes before sprinkling a few more thyme leaves on top and serving with a crisp green salad (and that glass of wine!).

Baked Salmon
with Bacon, White Beans, Tomatoes and Arugula

Possible Cooking Methods: Oven Air Fryer

I didn't really like salmon when I was younger, but as an adult I've grown to love it. I do prefer Pacific Salmon most of the time, but more important to me than the species is the quality of the fish. Buy your fish from a trusted purveyor, whether that is your local fish market or an online source. This fish recipe is a sheet pan dinner or an air fryer meal that ends up with lots of color and lots of flavor. If you don't eat meat, leave out the bacon and add a little olive oil to the beans at the beginning.

4 slices bacon, chopped

2 (17-ounce) cans cannellini beans, drained and rinsed

1 clove garlic, thinly sliced

1 to 2 sprigs fresh rosemary

2 cups cherry tomatoes

1 tablespoon olive oil

salt and freshly ground black pepper

½ to 1 cup chicken stock*

4 (6-ounce) fillets salmon

2 ounces arugula

1 lemon

fresh parsley leaves

All quantities change for alternate methods

Oven Directions

Serves: 4   **Cooking Time:** 25 minutes

1. Pre-heat the oven to 425⁰F.

2. Place the chopped bacon on a large sheet pan and bake in the oven until almost crispy – 5 to 10 minutes. Remove the bacon with a slotted spoon and set aside. Drain away most of the grease from the sheet pan, but leave enough to coat the beans.

3. Toss the white beans, garlic, rosemary and tomatoes together in a bowl with olive oil, season with salt and freshly ground black pepper and transfer them to the sheet pan. Pour the chicken stock on top (enough to moisten all the beans) and return the sheet pan to the oven. Bake for 5 minutes.

4. Place the salmon fillets on top of the beans, spritz with olive oil, season with salt and freshly ground black pepper and bake for another 10 minutes.

5. Remove the salmon to serving plates. Transfer the warmed beans and tomatoes into a large bowl with the arugula and cooked bacon and toss. Season to taste with salt, freshly ground black pepper and a squeeze of lemon juice.

6. Serve the fish and beans with parsley leaves scattered on top and lemon wedges on the side.

Baked Salmon with Bacon, White Beans, Tomatoes and Arugula

Air Fryer Directions

Serves: 2   **Cooking Time:** 20 minutes

Change Ingredients: Cut ALL ingredients in half; use smaller quantity of stock

1. Pre-heat the air fryer to 400ºF.

2. Place the chopped bacon in the air fryer basket and air-fry at 400ºF for 5 minutes, until almost crispy. Remove the bacon with a slotted spoon and set aside.

3. Combine the white beans, garlic, rosemary and tomatoes together in a bowl, season with salt and freshly ground black pepper and pour some of the bacon fat from the bottom of the air fryer into the bowl. Toss and transfer the mixture to an 8-inch cake pan (one that will fit into your air fryer). Pour ¼ cup of chicken stock on top and air-fry for another 5 minutes.

4. Place the salmon fillets on top of the beans in the cake pan, spritz with olive oil, season with salt and freshly ground black pepper and air-fry at 400ºF for 10 minutes.

5. Remove the salmon to serving plates. Transfer the warmed beans and tomatoes into a large bowl with the arugula and cooked bacon and toss. Season to taste with salt, freshly ground black pepper and a squeeze of lemon juice.

6. Serve the fish and beans with parsley leaves scattered on top and lemon wedges on the side.

New England Fish Chowder

Possible Cooking Methods: Stovetop   Pressure Cooker   Slow Cooker

This is essentially a New England clam chowder, but with more to love – two different types of fish as well as shrimp are added with the clams at the end to give the soup more bulk and interest. This is more of a wintery soup that is finished at the end with heavy cream. As with all my recipes, think of this as a template for what you'd like to make. If you'd like it a little lighter, you could add half-and-half instead of cream. It won't be as rich, but it will still be a hearty meal. I think this is especially nice with fresh clams, but a good quality canned clam is an easy substitute. You can also substitute any fresh fish for the salmon and haddock – whatever floats your boat (so to speak!). Bottled clam juice can be found in the same aisle as the tuna in a grocery store – don't feel compelled to use the liquid from a can of clams or you'll end up buying more cans than you really need.

4 strips bacon, chopped

1 onion, finely chopped

2 ribs celery, finely chopped

3 cloves garlic, smashed

1 pound red potatoes, diced

4 sprigs fresh thyme

1 bay leaf

salt and freshly ground black pepper

2 cups chicken stock*

1 cup clam juice

½ cup clams (fresh, steamed and shelled are great, but frozen or canned is fine too)

8 to 10 ounces haddock, cut into 1-inch cubes

8 to 10 ounces salmon, cut into 1-inch cubes

6 ounces extra small shrimp

2 tablespoons cornstarch

1 cup heavy cream

1 to 2 teaspoons hot sauce (like Tabasco®) (optional)

mini oyster crackers

fresh dill weed

*Quantity changes for alternate methods

Stovetop Directions

Serves: 6 to 8   **Cooking Time:** 35 minutes

1. Pre-heat Dutch oven over medium-high heat.

2. Add the bacon and cook until the bacon is crispy and has rendered out most of its fat. Remove the bacon from the pot and set aside. Discard any excess fat, but leave at least 2 table-spoons in the pot. Add the onion and celery and sauté until the vegetables just start to soften – about 5 minutes. Add the garlic, potatoes, thyme and bay leaf and stir to coat with the fat. Cook for another minute or two and season with salt and freshly ground black pepper.

3. Pour in the chicken stock and clam juice and bring to a boil. Lower the heat to medium-low and simmer the chowder for 15 minutes, or until the potatoes are tender. Season to taste with salt and freshly ground black pepper.

4. Add the clams, fish and shrimp and simmer on low heat for another 5 minutes. While the fish is cooking, combine the cornstarch with 2 tablespoons of water. Stir the cornstarch slurry into the pot and bring the soup back to a boil to thicken. Stir in the heavy cream and season to taste with salt and hot sauce, if using.

5. Garnish the soup with the mini oyster crackers, some fresh dill weed and some of the chopped cooked bacon.

New England Fish Chowder

Pressure Cooker Directions

Serves: 6 to 8   **Cooking Time:** 25 minutes

Change Ingredients: Reduce stock to 1 cup

1. Pre-heat a 5- to 6-quart multi-function pressure cooker using the BROWN or SAUTE setting.

2. Add the bacon to the cooker and cook until the bacon is crispy and has rendered out most of its fat. Remove the bacon from the cooker and set aside. Discard any excess fat, but leave at least 2 tablespoons in the cooker. Add the onion and celery and sauté until the vegetables just start to soften – about 5 minutes. Add the garlic, potatoes, thyme and bay leaf and stir to coat with the fat. Cook for another minute or two and season with salt and freshly ground black pepper. (If your cooker doesn't have a brown setting, brown the bacon on the stovetop in a skillet. The rest of the ingredients can go into the cooker raw.)

3. Pour in the chicken stock and clam juice. Cover and lock the lid in place.

4. Pressure cook on HIGH for 5 minutes.

5. Release the pressure using the QUICK-RELEASE method and carefully remove the lid. Add the clams, fish and shrimp and return the cooker to the BROWN or SAUTE setting. Simmer the fish for 4 minutes.

6. While the fish is cooking, combine the cornstarch with 2 tablespoons of water. Stir the cornstarch slurry into the cooker and bring the soup back to a boil to thicken. Stir in the heavy cream and season to taste with salt and hot sauce, if using.

7. Garnish the soup with the mini oyster crackers, some fresh dill weed and some of the chopped cooked bacon.

Slow Cooker Directions

Serves: 6 to 8   **Cooking Time:** 4½ to 5½ hours on LOW

Change Ingredients: Reduce stock to 1 cup

1. Pre-heat a 6-quart multi-function slow cooker using the BROWN or SAUTE setting.

2. Add the bacon to the cooker and cook until the bacon is crispy and has rendered out most of its fat. Remove the bacon from the cooker and set aside. Discard any excess fat, but leave at least 2 tablespoons in the cooker. Add the onion and celery and sauté until the vegetables just start to soften – about 5 minutes. Add the garlic, potatoes, thyme and bay leaf and stir to coat with the fat. Cook for another minute or two. (If your cooker doesn't have a brown setting, brown the bacon on the stovetop in a skillet. The rest of the ingredients can go into the cooker raw.)

3. Pour in the chicken stock and clam juice. Cover and slow cook on LOW for 4 to 5 hours (2½ hours on HIGH).

4. Once the potatoes are tender, add the fish, shrimp and clams and slow cook on HIGH for 30 minutes, until the seafood is fully cooked.

5. Combine the cornstarch with 2 tablespoons of water. Stir the cornstarch slurry into the cooker and keep the cooker on HIGH for a few minutes to thicken the soup. Turn the cooker off and stir in the heavy cream. Season to taste with salt and hot sauce, if using.

6. Garnish the soup with the mini oyster crackers, some fresh dill weed and some of the chopped cooked bacon.

Seafood Stew
with Fennel, Tomatoes and Potatoes

Possible Cooking Methods: Stovetop   Pressure Cooker   Slow Cooker

This seafood stew is a contrast to the New England Fish Stew in this book because it is tomato based, rather than cream based. It's just as lovely and really enjoyable on a summer evening. In fact, I think it's a great meal for entertaining because it's a meal that you can easily have all prepared before your guests arrive, just adding the fish at the last minute. It is elegant and delicious and will impress dinner guests every time. The many subtle flavors of fennel, saffron and anise really compliment the fish and seafood in this dish. I recommend serving this stew with crusty bread and a glass of white or rosé wine.

2 tablespoons olive oil

1 leek, cleaned, white and light green parts thinly sliced

1 clove garlic, smashed

3 Yukon Gold potatoes, cut into 1-inch chunks (about 2½ cups)

1 bulb fennel, chopped

1 tablespoon tomato paste

½ cup white wine

1 (28-ounce) can chopped tomatoes

3 cups seafood stock (or chicken stock if you can't find seafood stock)*

4 sprigs fresh thyme

1 teaspoon saffron threads (optional)

1 pound white fish fillets (such as halibut, turbot, red snapper, striped bass, grouper or cod), cut into 2-inch pieces

12 mussels, scrubbed and de-bearded (discard any mussels that are open, broken or don't close their shells when tapped)

18 large raw shrimp, peeled and de-veined

3 tablespoons anise-flavored liqueur (Pernod, Pastis or Sambuca)

zest of one orange

salt and freshly ground black pepper

¼ cup chopped fresh parsley

Quantity changes for alternate methods

Stovetop Directions

Serves: 4 to 6   **Cooking Time:** 40 minutes

1. Pre-heat a large Dutch oven over medium heat. Add the olive oil and sauté the leek and garlic for 3 to 4 minutes. Add the potatoes and fennel and cook, stirring occasionally for about 10 minutes. Let the leek brown slightly, but do not let it burn. Stir in the tomato paste and continue to cook for a couple of minutes.

2. Deglaze the pot with the white wine, scraping any brown bits that may have formed on the bottom of the pan. Add the tomatoes, stock, thyme and saffron (if using), and let the mixture simmer over medium-low to low heat for about 10 to 15 minutes.

3. Stir in the fish and continue to simmer for 5 minutes. Add the mussels and shrimp, cover and simmer for another 5 minutes.

4. Remove the pan from the heat and stir in the anise-flavored liqueur and orange zest. Discard any mussels whose shells did not open. Season to taste with salt and freshly ground black pepper. Serve in bowls with the parsley sprinkled generously on top and serve with some crusty bread to soak up the remaining sauce.

Seafood Stew with Fennel, Tomatoes and Potatoes

Pressure Cooker Directions

Serves: 6 to 8   **Cooking Time:** 25 minutes

Change Ingredients: Reduce stock to 1 cup; add 1 (14-ounce) can tomato purée

1. Pre-heat a multi-function pressure cooker using the BROWN or SAUTE setting. Add the olive oil and cook the leek and garlic for a few minutes. Add the potatoes and fennel and cook, stirring occasionally for about 10 minutes. Stir in the tomato paste and continue to cook for a couple of minutes.

2. Add the white wine and saffron, crushing the saffron threads between your fingers as you add it. (If your cooker doesn't have a brown setting, use a skillet on the stovetop for the steps above and transfer the contents to the cooker now.) Stir in the tomatoes, tomato purée and stock and drop the white fish into the cooker. Add the mussels and lock the lid in place.

3. Pressure cook on HIGH for 4 minutes.

4. Let the pressure drop NATURALLY and carefully remove the lid.

5. Add the shrimp to the cooker, nestling them into the stew, and return the lid to the cooker. Let this sit for 3 minutes or until all the shrimp has cooked and turned bright pink.

6. Stir in the anise-flavored liqueur and orange zest. Discard any mussels whose shells did not open. Season to taste with salt and freshly ground black pepper. Serve in bowls with the parsley sprinkled generously on top and serve with some crusty bread to soak up the remaining sauce.

Slow Cooker Directions

Serves: 6 to 8   **Cooking Time:** 4 to 5 hours on LOW + 30 minutes on HIGH

Change Ingredients: Reduce stock to 1 cup; add 1 (14-ounce) can tomato purée

1. Pre-heat a multi-function slow cooker using the BROWN or SAUTE setting. Add the olive oil and cook the leek and garlic for a few minutes. Add the potatoes and fennel and cook, stirring occasionally for about 10 minutes. Stir in the tomato paste and continue to cook for a couple of minutes.

2. Add the white wine and saffron, crushing the saffron threads between your fingers as you add it. (If your cooker doesn't have a brown setting, use a skillet on the stovetop for the steps above and transfer the contents to the cooker now.) Stir in the tomatoes, tomato purée, stock and thyme and cover with the lid. Slow cook on LOW for 4 to 5 hours (or 2½ hours on HIGH).

3. When the potatoes are tender, add the fish, mussels, and shrimp to the cooker. Cover and cook on HIGH for 30 minutes.

4. Stir in the anise-flavored liqueur and orange zest. Discard any mussels whose shells did not open. Season to taste with salt and freshly ground black pepper. Serve in bowls with the parsley sprinkled generously on top and serve with some crusty bread to soak up the remaining sauce.

Steamed Mussels
with Chorizo, Tomato and Potato

Possible Cooking Methods: Stovetop   Pressure Cooker

Mussels are almost always a one-pot meal. They steam open over a broth and instantly add a natural saltiness and flavor, making the sauce almost more delicious than the mussels themselves! In this recipe, the addition of the Chorizo sausage, potatoes and tomatoes makes it more of a complete meal, but don't forget a nice piece of crusty French bread to soak up all of the flavor. A crisp and crunchy salad with frisée lettuce would be nice too.

2 pounds mussels

1 tablespoon olive oil

1 pound raw Chorizo sausage, removed from casing and crumbled

1 small onion, sliced (about 1 cup)

2 cloves garlic, minced

2 large Yukon Gold potatoes, diced ½-inch (about 2 cups)

3 tomatoes, chopped (about 2 to 2½ cups)

1½ cups white wine*

¼ cup chopped fresh parsley

2 tablespoons finely chopped orange zest

half an orange

freshly ground black pepper

2 tablespoons butter

*Quantity changes for alternate methods

Stovetop Directions

Serves: 4   **Cooking Time:** 20 minutes

1. Clean the mussels by scrubbing them with a brush under running water. Pull off the beard (the whiskery hairs protruding from the shell). Discard any mussels that are broken or won't close their shells when tapped.

2. Pre-heat a large 5-quart braiser pan (one that has a lid). Add the olive oil and sauté the Chorizo sausage until browned. Add the onion and garlic and sauté for a couple of minutes. Add the potatoes and continue to cook for 5 to 10 minutes, until the potatoes start to soften. Add the tomatoes and the wine, increase the heat to high and bring the liquid to a boil.

3. Add the mussels and cover the pan with the lid. Steam the mussels for roughly 5 minutes, until they open.

4. Remove the mussels from the pot with a slotted spoon and place in serving bowls, discarding any mussels whose shells did not open or are cracked and broken. Stir in the parsley, orange zest and black pepper. Remove the pan from the heat and swirl in the butter. Squeeze the half an orange into the sauce and pour the sauce over the mussels. Serve immediately with crusty bread or French fries to soak up the tasty liquid.

Steamed Mussels with Chorizo, Tomato and Potato

These are Cara Cara oranges, which are a type of navel orange with a pinky red and orange flesh. They are a little sweeter and less acidic than regular navel oranges and seedless too. You don't need to use Cara Cara oranges in this recipe, but they are nice if they are available.

Pressure Cooker Directions

Serves: 4 **Cooking Time:** 7 minutes

Change Ingredients: Reduce the wine to 1 cup

1. Clean the mussels by scrubbing them with a brush under running water. Pull off the beard (the whiskery hairs protruding from the shell). Discard any mussels that are open, broken or don't close their shells when tapped.

2. Pre-heat the pressure cooker using the BROWN setting. Add the olive oil and sauté the Chorizo sausage until browned. Add the onion and garlic and sauté for a couple of minutes. (If your cooker doesn't have a brown setting, use a pot on the stovetop for the steps above and transfer the contents to the cooker now.) Add the potatoes, tomatoes, wine and all the mussels. Lock the lid in place.

3. Pressure cook on HIGH for 4 minutes.

4. Reduce the pressure with the QUICK-RELEASE method and carefully remove the lid.

5. Remove the mussels from the pot with a slotted spoon and place in serving bowls, discarding any mussels whose shells did not open or are cracked and broken. Stir the parsley, orange zest and black pepper into the sauce. Remove the pan from the heat and swirl in the remaining butter. Squeeze the half an orange into the sauce and pour the sauce over the mussels. Serve immediately with crusty bread or French fries to soak up the tasty liquid.

One Pot Shrimp and Grits

Possible Cooking Methods: Stovetop Pressure Cooker Slow Cooker

Shrimp and grits used to be a morning meal in the Southern United States, but now you can find it on menus all hours of the day. Usually the grits are made in one pot and the shrimp is sautéed in another. Here, we make them all together in one pot and drizzle flavorful oil on at the end. I've made the smoked paprika optional here, but I think it does add a nice smoky essence to the dish and highly recommend it. You'll also see Cajun seasoning in the ingredient list. It's quite common in most grocery stores, but if you can't find it, check out the recipe on page 165 (see Cajun Shrimp and Rice).

2 tablespoons olive oil

1 teaspoon Cajun seasoning
(see note above)

¼ teaspoon smoked paprika (optional)

1 scallion, minced

2 cups coarse stone-ground corn grits
(not the instant variety)

8 cups water or chicken stock

2 teaspoons salt

20 to 24 large shrimp, peeled and deveined

2 to 4 tablespoons butter

8 ounces Cheddar cheese, grated

freshly ground black pepper

chopped fresh parsley

Stovetop Directions

Serves: 4   **Cooking Time:** 40 minutes

1. Combine the olive oil, Cajun seasoning, smoked paprika (if using) and scallion in a small bowl. Stir to combine and then let the mixture sit so the flavors can blend together.

2. Rinse the grits in a bowl of cold water, pouring off any husks that float to the surface. Drain as well as you can.

3. Bring the 8 cups of water to a boil and whisk in the grits. Whisk until the grits become suspended in the water rather than sinking to the bottom of the pot – about 3 to 5 minutes.

4. Once the grits come to a boil, reduce the heat to very low and season with salt. Cook, covered but stirring regularly (every 5 to 10 minutes), for 30 to 40 minutes. If the grits become too dry, whisk in a little more warm water and continue to cook. When the grits are almost tender, stir in the shrimp, cover and turn the heat to the lowest setting. Let the grits sit like this for 5 minutes to cook the shrimp.

5. Stir in the butter and cheese and season to taste with salt and lots of freshly ground black pepper. Thin the grits to the desired consistency with more water.

6. Serve in bowls and drizzle the Cajun seasoned oil on top in a zigzag design. Swirl the oil into the grits with a spoon and sprinkle the parsley on top.

One Pot Shrimp and Grits

Pressure Cooker Directions

Serves: 4   **Cooking Time:** 15 minutes

1. Combine the olive oil, Cajun seasoning, smoked paprika (if using) and scallion in a small bowl. Stir to combine and then let the mixture sit so the flavors can blend together.

2. Rinse the grits in a bowl of cold water, pouring off any husks that float to the surface. Drain as well as you can.

3. Pre-heat a 6-quart multi-function pressure cooker using the BROWN or SAUTE setting. Add the butter, water and salt and bring the mixture to a boil. (If your cooker doesn't have a brown setting, use a kettle to boil the water and add the water, butter and salt to the cooker now.) Whisk the grits into the water, whisking for a full minute so the grits become suspended in the water rather than sinking to the bottom of the pot. Cover and lock the lid in place.

4. Pressure cook on HIGH for 10 minutes.

5. Let the pressure drop NATURALLY and carefully remove the lid. Give the grits a good stir – they may have settled somewhat on the bottom of the cooker. Once you've stirred the grits, immediately stir in the shrimp. Return the lid to the cooker and let the grits sit for 5 minutes to cook the shrimp.

6. Stir in the butter and cheese and season to taste with salt and lots of freshly ground black pepper. Thin the grits to the desired consistency with more water.

7. Serve in bowls and drizzle the Cajun seasoned oil on top in a zigzag design. Swirl the oil into the grits with a spoon and sprinkle the parsley on top.

Slow Cooker Directions

Serves: 4   **Cooking Time:** 6½ to 8 hours on LOW

1. Pre-heat a 4-to 6-quart multi-function slow cooker using the BROWN or SAUTE setting, or using the HIGH slow cook function to warm up the cooker.

2. Combine the olive oil, Cajun seasoning, smoked paprika (if using) and scallion in a small bowl. Stir to combine and then let the mixture sit so the flavors can blend together.

3. Rinse the grits in a bowl of cold water, pouring off any husks that float to the surface. Drain as well as you can. Add the grits, water, salt and butter to the cooker and stir well. Turn the multi-cooker or slow cooker to the LOW setting, cover and slow cook for 6 to 7 hours.

4. Thirty minutes before you are ready to serve, stir in the shrimp and continue to slow cook on LOW for 30 to 60 minutes. Stir in the cheese and season to taste with salt and lots of freshly ground black pepper. Thin the grits to the desired consistency with more water. They should be creamy and smooth, but still have a toothsome quality to each grain.

5. Serve in bowls and drizzle the Cajun seasoned oil on top in a zigzag design. Swirl the oil into the grits with a spoon and sprinkle the parsley on top.

Cajun Shrimp and Rice

Possible Cooking Methods: Stovetop   Pressure Cooker

This recipe takes your average rice dish and spices it up in a jiffy. That spice will come from the Cajun seasoning and from the Andouille sausage. Make sure you get raw Andouille, rather than pre-cooked sausage. Raw Andouille sausage will add more flavor to the rest of the dish, as its spices will spread in the fat that renders out of it. If you are tailoring the spice level of the dish to suit milder tastes, try sweet Italian sausage instead of the Andouille and reduce the Cajun seasoning to taste. Fire-roasted tomatoes add a nice smoky note to the dish, but if you can't find fire-roasted tomatoes, don't sweat it. Regular canned tomatoes will be fine.

1 tablespoon olive oil

12 ounces raw Andouille sausage, sliced 1-inch thick

1 pound large shrimp, peeled and deveined

½ onion, chopped

2 ribs celery, chopped

2 cloves garlic, minced

½ red bell pepper, chopped

½ green bell pepper, chopped

1 to 2 tablespoons Cajun seasoning

1½ cups long-grain white rice

1 (14-ounce) can fire-roasted diced tomatoes

3½ cups chicken stock*

1 teaspoon salt

freshly ground black pepper

3 scallions, thinly sliced

*Quantity changes for alternate methods

Stovetop Directions

Serves: 4 to 6   **Cooking Time:** 45 minutes

1. Pre-heat a large 12-inch sauté pan over medium heat. Add the olive oil and brown the Andouille sausage on all sides. Transfer the browned sausage to a bowl and set aside.

2. Add the shrimp to the sauté pan and sear quickly on both sides. Set the shrimp aside with the sausage.

3. Add the onion and celery to the pan and sauté for a couple of minutes. Add the garlic and peppers and sauté for another couple of minutes. Stir in the Cajun seasoning and rice and continue to cook to toast the rice. Add the tomatoes, chicken stock and salt. Cover, reduce the heat and simmer for 20 minutes.

4. Return the browned sausage and shrimp back to the pot and cook covered for 5 to 10 minutes, until the rice is tender. Season to taste, stir in the sliced scallions and serve.

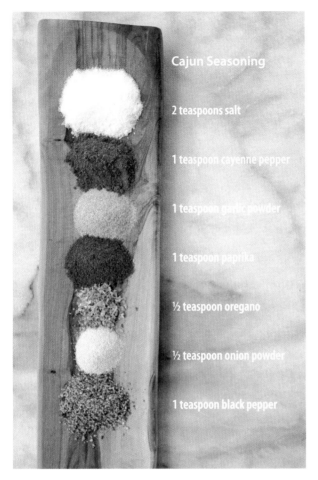

Cajun Seasoning

2 teaspoons salt

1 teaspoon cayenne pepper

1 teaspoon garlic powder

1 teaspoon paprika

½ teaspoon oregano

½ teaspoon onion powder

1 teaspoon black pepper

Pressure Cooker Directions

Serves: 4 to 6   **Cooking Time:** 18 minutes

Change Ingredients: Reduce the chicken stock to 3 cups

1. Pre-heat a 6-quart multi-function pressure cooker using the BROWN or SAUTE setting.

2. Add the sliced Andouille sausage and brown on all sides. Transfer the browned sausage to a bowl and set aside.

3. Add the onions, celery and garlic and sauté for a couple of minutes. Stir in the Cajun seasoning and rice and continue to cook to toast the rice. (If your cooker doesn't have a brown setting, use a skillet on the stovetop for the steps above and transfer the contents to the cooker now.) Add the shrimp, peppers, diced tomatoes, chicken stock and salt and return the browned sausage to the cooker. Cover and lock the lid in place.

4. Pressure cook on HIGH for 6 minutes.

5. Release the pressure using the QUICK-RELEASE method and carefully remove the lid.

6. Season to taste, stir in the sliced scallions and serve.

Garlic Shrimp and Crab Garganelli

Possible Cooking Methods: Stovetop   Pressure Cooker

If you can't find garganelli pasta (hand-rolled penne), you can use another pasta shape like gemelli, bow-ties, rotini or penne rigate. Just follow the cooking time listed on the box for stovetop cooking. When cooking pasta in a pressure cooker, cook for roughly half the time listed on the box, plus one minute. That usually yields properly cooked pasta and the shrimp will cook in the residual heat from the dish so they won't interfere with the cooking time.

1 tablespoon olive oil	pinch crushed red pepper flakes	8 ounces medium or large shrimp, peeled and deveined
1 tablespoon butter	1 (14-ounce) can tomatoes, chopped	6 ounces jumbo lump crabmeat
½ large onion, finely chopped	2 cups chicken stock	½ cup chopped fresh basil leaves
3 cloves garlic, minced	12 ounces dried garganelli pasta (or other shape if you prefer) (about 4 cups)	1 lemon
3 sprigs fresh thyme	salt and freshly ground black pepper	

Stovetop Directions

Serves: 2 to 4   **Cooking Time:** 22 minutes

1. Pre-heat a large 12-inch sauté pan over medium-high heat. Add the oil and butter and sauté the onion until it just starts to soften – about 5 minutes. Add the garlic, thyme and crushed red pepper flakes, and continue to cook for another minute. Add the tomatoes and chicken stock and bring the mixture to a boil.

2. Stir in the pasta, ensuring that all the pasta is submerged in the liquid. Season with salt and freshly ground black pepper, cover and lower the heat to simmer. Simmer for 14 minutes, or until the pasta is almost al dente.

3. Add the shrimp and continue to simmer for another 2 to 3 minutes, until the shrimp turn bright pink and are cooked through. Remove the sprigs of thyme, stir in the crabmeat and chopped fresh basil and squeeze the lemon over everything. Stir to combine well and serve immediately with a leafy green salad and some bread to mop up the sauce.

Garlic Shrimp and Crab Garganelli

Pressure Cooker Directions

Serves: 2 to 4   **Cooking Time:** 18 minutes

1. Pre-heat a 6-quart multi-function pressure cooker using the BROWN or SAUTE setting.

2. Add the oil and butter and sauté the onion until it just starts to soften – about 5 minutes. Add the garlic, thyme and crushed red pepper flakes and continue to cook for another minute. (If your cooker doesn't have a brown setting, use a sauté pan on the stovetop for the steps above and transfer the contents to the cooker now.) Add the tomatoes and chicken stock, season with salt and freshly ground black pepper and mix well.

3. Stir in the pasta, ensuring that all the pasta is submerged in the liquid. Cover and lock the lid in place.

4. Pressure cook on HIGH for 6 minutes.

5. Release the pressure using the QUICK-RELEASE method and carefully remove the lid. Immediately add the shrimp and cover for 5 to 6 minutes, until the shrimp turn bright pink and are cooked through. Remove the sprigs of thyme, stir in the crabmeat and chopped fresh basil and squeeze lemon over everything to taste. Stir to combine well and serve immediately with a leafy green salad and some bread to mop up the sauce.

Garganelli is like a little square of pasta that has been hand-rolled to look like penne. It is both elegant and rustic at the same time. If you can't find garganelli, you can use penne rigate, bow-ties, gemelli or rotini.

Crab Macaroni and Cheese
with Peas and Cherry Tomatoes

Possible Cooking Methods: Stovetop and Oven   Pressure Cooker

There are so many macaroni and cheese recipes out in the world and here's one more. This one is a little different in that you don't have to use a pot to cook the pasta, a pan to make the cheese sauce and another dish in which to bake the cheesy casserole. Instead, you'll make the sauce in the same pan that you use to cook the pasta and then pop the whole pan into the oven to toast the crunchy topping at the end. Three different cheeses make this mac and cheese super creamy, the crab gives it a rich flavor that is livened up with the peas and cherry tomatoes and the crunchy topping is well, as they say, the cherry on top.

4 tablespoons butter

2 shallots, diced

2 tablespoons all-purpose flour*

½ cup dry sherry

4 cups whole milk*

1 cup water*

⅛ teaspoon ground nutmeg

1 teaspoon salt

freshly ground white pepper (or black pepper)

12 ounces dried large shell pasta

1 tablespoon fresh thyme leaves

1 cup grated Monterey Jack cheese

1 cup grated sharp white Cheddar cheese

1 cup grated mozzarella cheese

1 pound jumbo lump crab meat

1 cup frozen peas

2 cups sliced cherry tomatoes

Topping:

1½ cups crushed oyster crackers

1 cup grated Monterey Jack cheese

5 tablespoons melted butter

2 teaspoons Old Bay® Seasoning

Quantity changes for alternate methods

Stovetop and Oven Directions

Serves: 6   **Cooking Time:** 50 minutes

1.   Pre-heat the oven to 375°F.

2.   Melt the butter in a 4- or 5-quart oven-safe Dutch oven over medium heat. Add the shallots and sauté for a couple of minutes. Stir in the flour and cook for another couple of minutes. Pour in the sherry, milk and water and bring the mixture to a simmer. Season with the nutmeg, salt and white pepper.

3.   Add the dried pasta and simmer uncovered for 15 minutes, stirring occasionally. While the pasta is cooking prepare the topping. Combine the crushed oyster crackers, Monterey Jack cheese, melted butter and Old Bay® Seasoning in a bowl..

4.   When the pasta is cooked al dente, add the thyme leaves, Monterey Jack, Cheddar and mozzarella cheeses. Stir until all the cheese has melted.

5.   Fold in the jumbo lump crab, peas and cherry tomatoes. Sprinkle the oyster cracker topping on top of the pasta and transfer the pan to the oven. Bake at 375°F for 25 to 30 minutes. Remove the pan from the oven and let it cool for just a few minutes. Serve with a butter lettuce salad.

Crab Macaroni and Cheese with Peas and Cherry Tomatoes

Pressure Cooker Directions

Serves: 6 **Cooking Time:** 8 minutes

Change Ingredients: Omit flour and milk; add a total of 2 cups of water and 1 cup heavy cream; make the topping on the stovetop

1. Pre-heat a 6-quart multi-function pressure cooker using the BROWN or SAUTE setting.

2. Add the butter and shallots and sauté for 2 minutes. Add the dried pasta and stir to coat. Pour in the sherry, water and heavy cream and try to push the pasta down to submerge it completely. Cover and lock the lid in place.

3. Pressure cook on HIGH for 6 minutes.

4. While the pasta cooks, make the crunchy oyster cracker topping on the stovetop. Heat a small skillet over medium heat. Melt the butter and add the oyster crackers and Old Bay® Seasoning. Sauté, tossing regularly until the cracker crumbs are nicely browned and toasted. Set aside.

5. Release the pressure using the QUICK-RELEASE method and carefully remove the lid. Season the pasta with salt, white pepper, thyme leaves and Monterey Jack, Cheddar and mozzarella cheeses. Stir until all the cheeses have melted. Fold in the crab, thawed peas and cherry tomatoes.

6. Transfer the pasta to a serving bowl and sprinkle the remaining Monterey Jack cheese on top. Loosely tent with foil and let sit for a few minutes – the sauce will thicken and the cheese will melt. Remove the foil, add the toasted crushed oyster cracker topping and serve with a butter lettuce salad.

Creamy Braised Halibut
with Spinach and Mushrooms

Possible Cooking Methods: Stovetop   Pressure Cooker   Slow Cooker

I'm very fond of fish with mushrooms, especially halibut. I love the earthy flavor of the mushrooms with the firm white flakes of fish. This creamy braised halibut also incorporates spinach and toma-toes for a very colorful, tasty and complete meal. You could serve it with rice or mashed potatoes, but I really enjoy it with just a salad and piece of crusty bread to soak up all the sauce. If you'd prefer a non-creamy version of this dish, you can replace the cream with chicken stock, but make sure it's a good quality stock with lots of flavor. When making this dish in the pressure cooker, skip the searing step. Most cookers are round and deep and that makes it hard to get at the fish to flip it over, plus the fish can easily over cook if you are following the sear with intense pressure-cooking. Finally, remember to look for Pacific halibut when shopping for this recipe. Atlantic halibut is currently on the "avoid" list with Seafood Watch since it is at risk of becoming endangered.

---

2 tablespoons olive oil, divided

4 (6-ounce) fillets Pacific halibut, skin removed

salt and freshly ground black pepper

1 shallot, finely chopped

1 clove garlic, smashed

1 pound brown mushrooms, thinly sliced

2 teaspoons fresh thyme leaves

¾ cup white wine*

½ to 1 cup heavy cream

8 ounces baby spinach

1 cup cherry tomatoes, halved

Quantity changes for alternate methods

Stovetop Directions

Serves: 4   **Cooking Time:** 25 minutes

1. Pre-heat a large 12-inch sauté pan over medium-high heat.

2. Add 1 tablespoon of olive oil to the pan, season the halibut with salt and freshly ground black pepper and sear the halibut flesh side down for 4 to 5 minutes. Remove the seared fillets and set them aside.

3. Add the second tablespoon of olive oil and sauté the shallot, garlic and mushrooms until the mushrooms soften – about 6 minutes. Season with salt and freshly ground black pepper and add the thyme leaves, cooking for another minute. Deglaze with the white wine and let it come to a simmer for a minute or two. Pour in the heavy cream and return the fish to the pan with the seared flesh side up, nestling it down into the sauce. Cover with a lid and lower the heat to medium-low. Simmer for 5 minutes.

4. Add the spinach to the pan, nestling it down around the fish (but it's ok if some rests on top) and toss in the cherry tomatoes. Cover and let the dish continue to simmer gently for another 5 minutes.

5. Remove the fish from the pan and stir to incorporate the wilted spinach and tomatoes into the sauce. Season to taste and serve in shallow bowls with crusty French bread to sop up the sauce.

Creamy Braised Halibut with Spinach and Mushrooms

Pressure Cooker Directions

Serves: 4   **Cooking Time:** 10 minutes

Change Ingredients: Reduce white wine to ½ cup

1. Pre-heat a 6-quart multi-function pressure cooker using the BROWN or SAUTE setting.

2. Add the olive oil to the cooker and sauté the shallot, garlic and mushrooms until the mushrooms soften. Add the thyme leaves and continue to sauté for another minute. Deglaze with the white wine and let it come to a simmer for a minute or two. Pour in the heavy cream and season to taste with salt and freshly ground black pepper. (If your cooker doesn't have a brown setting, use a skillet on the stovetop for the steps above and transfer the contents to the cooker now.)

3. Add the fish fillets to the cooker, nestling them down into the sauce gently. Season with salt and freshly ground black pepper. Cover and lock the lid in place.

4. Pressure cook on HIGH for 2 minutes.

5. Release the pressure with the QUICK-RELEASE method and carefully remove the lid. Remove the fish to a side plate and tent with foil. Add the spinach and tomatoes to the cooker and replace the lid. Let the cooker sit powered off for 4 to 5 minutes. This will wilt the spinach, warm the tomatoes through and let the food cool to an edible temperature.

6. Remove the lid and stir to incorporate the spinach into the sauce. Season one last time to taste. Return the fish to the sauce, just to reheat and coat. Then, serve in shallow bowls with crusty French bread to sop up the sauce.

Slow Cooker Directions

Serves: 4   **Cooking Time:** 1 hour on LOW

Change Ingredients: Reduce white wine to ½ cup

1. Pre-heat a 6-quart multi-function slow cooker using the BROWN or SAUTE setting.

2. Add the olive oil to the cooker and sauté the shallot, garlic and mushrooms until the mushrooms soften. Add the thyme leaves and continue to sauté for another minute. Deglaze with the white wine and let it come to a simmer for a minute or two. (If your cooker doesn't have a brown setting, use a skillet on the stovetop for the steps above and transfer the contents to the cooker now.) Pour in the heavy cream, stir in the spinach and tomatoes and season to taste with salt and freshly ground black pepper.

3. Add the fish fillets to the cooker, nestling them down into the sauce gently. Season with salt and freshly ground black pepper. Cover and slow cook on LOW for 1 hour, or until the fish is flaky but does not fall apart.

4. Remove the lid and season one last time to taste. Then, serve in shallow bowls with crusty French bread to sop up the sauce.

Risotto with Shrimp, Asparagus and Lemon

Possible Cooking Methods: Stovetop   Pressure Cooker

This is a beautiful risotto for the spring, when asparagus is in season. This recipe bends my one pot rule a little because you do have to heat your stock in a separate saucepan, but the majority of your cooking is done in one sauté pan or skillet. On the stovetop this recipe takes about 30 minutes of your time and attention, but it is well worth it and can be quite relaxing and enjoyable to make. If you don't have that time, don't have that attention span or don't need to relax, making it in the pressure cooker will cut the cooking time to 15 minutes and you don't even have to watch it.

4 cups chicken stock*

1 tablespoon butter (plus more at the end of cooking optionally)

1 tablespoon olive oil

1 large shallot, finely chopped (or ½ white onion)

1 clove garlic, minced

1½ cups Arborio or Carnaroli rice

½ cup dry white wine (optional)

12 large shrimp, peeled and deveined

8 ounces asparagus, sliced on the bias, ¼-inch slices

1 lemon, 4 teaspoons zest and 1 tablespoon juice

2 tablespoons butter

2 tablespoons chopped fresh parsley

salt and freshly ground black pepper

*Quantity changes for alternate methods

Stovetop Directions

Serves: 2 to 4   **Cooking Time:** 20 to 30 minutes

1. Pour the chicken stock into a saucepan and bring it to a boil. Reduce the heat to its lowest setting and keep warm.

2. Heat a large sauté pan or skillet over medium heat. Add the butter and olive oil to the pan. Cook the shallot until it is translucent and tender – about 2 minutes. Add the garlic and cook for 30 seconds.

3. Stir in the rice and coat each kernel well with the butter and olive oil. Add the white wine (if using) and stir until the wine has almost disappeared. Add a ladle of hot chicken stock to the pan and stir until almost all the liquid has disappeared again. Then, add another ladle of stock and continue to stir. Continue in this manner until the rice reaches the desired tenderness, adding one ladle of stock at a time. If you run out of stock before the rice has cooked to your satisfaction, simply continue using water instead of stock. Before you add your last ladle or two of stock, stir in the shrimp and asparagus. Continue to cook until the asparagus is tender and the shrimp are pink and cooked through – about 5 minutes.

4. When the rice is tender, remove the pan from the heat and add the lemon zest and juice, butter and parsley. Season to taste with salt and freshly ground black pepper and serve with a side salad of mixed greens with a citrus vinaigrette.

Risotto with Shrimp, Asparagus and Lemon

Whenever a recipe calls for lemon zest AND juice, remember to zest the lemon first. It's very hard to zest a lemon once you've cut it in half, let alone squeezed the juice out.

Pressure Cooker Directions

Serves: 4 to 6   **Cooking Time:** 15 minutes

Change Ingredients: Reduce stock to 3½ cups

1. Pre-heat a 6-quart multi-function pressure cooker pressure cooker using the BROWN or SAUTE setting.

2. Add the butter and olive oil and sauté the shallot until translucent and tender – about 4 minutes. Add the garlic and cook for an additional minute. (If your cooker doesn't have a brown setting, do this step on your stovetop with a skillet and transfer the contents to the cooker now.)

3. Stir in the rice and coat with the butter and oil. Add the white wine (if using) and stock, cover and lock the lid in place.

4. Pressure cook on HIGH for 7 minutes.

5. Release the pressure using the QUICK-RELEASE method and carefully remove the lid. Stir in another ladle full of stock and add the shrimp and asparagus to the cooker. Cover and let the risotto cook the shrimp and cool to an edible temperature.

6. Finally, add the lemon zest and juice, butter and parsley. Season to taste with salt and freshly ground black pepper and serve with a side salad of mixed greens with a citrus vinaigrette.

Salmon with Potatoes and Peas in a Ginger Broth

Possible Cooking Methods: Stovetop   Pressure Cooker   Slow Cooker

This dish borders on being a soup. What sets it apart from soups is that the salmon is kept in a whole piece, rather than being broken up. The rich, flavored broth is filled with potatoes and peas and spiced with a little chili pepper. The presentation can be really beautiful if you pick the right fillets. Choose wider fillets of salmon, rather than narrow pieces. When I'm shopping for multiple servings of fish, I prefer to buy a very large piece (equal to all four portions put together) and cut it up myself into the size and shape I need for my recipe. I highly recommend that strategy here if you are lucky enough to have a good fish market near you.

4 (6-ounce) salmon fillets

salt and freshly ground black pepper, to taste

1 tablespoon olive oil

2 cloves garlic, sliced

¼ teaspoon hot red pepper flakes

2 inches fresh gingerroot, peeled and thinly sliced

4 cups rich chicken broth

10 to 12 small yellow potatoes, sliced ¼-inch thick

2 cups frozen peas

soy sauce or salt, to taste

3 scallions, sliced

1 hot red chili pepper, thinly sliced

Stovetop Directions

Serves: 4   **Cooking Time:** 20 minutes

1. Pre-heat a 10-inch sauté pan over medium-high heat. Season the salmon fillets with salt and freshly ground black pepper. Add the olive oil to the pan and sear the salmon really well, flesh side down – about 4 minutes. Remove the fillets to a side plate and set aside. Add the garlic, red pepper flakes and gingerroot to the pan and sauté for just a minute. Add the chicken broth and bring the mixture to a gentle simmer.

2. Add the potatoes and simmer for 10 minutes, or until the potatoes are barely tender to a knifepoint. Place the salmon, seared side up, into the pan with the potatoes and cover. Simmer for just 5 minutes and then turn off the heat.

3. Add the peas to the broth and season the broth with soy sauce or salt to taste. (The soy sauce does a nice job of darkening the broth to an appealing color.) Transfer the salmon, potatoes, peas and broth into four shallow bowls and sprinkle the scallions and hot red chili pepper on top.

Salmon with Potatoes and Peas in a Ginger Broth

Pressure Cooker Directions

Serves: 4   **Cooking Time:** 4 minutes

1. Pre-heat a 6-quart multi-function pressure cooker using the BROWN or SAUTE setting.

2. Add the olive oil to the cooker and lightly sauté the garlic, red pepper flakes and gingerroot for just a minute or two. Add the chicken broth and bring the mixture to a simmer. (If your cooker doesn't have a brown setting, use a skillet on the stovetop for the steps above and transfer the contents to the cooker now.)

3. Add the potatoes, season the salmon and place the salmon into the cooker on top of the potatoes. Cover and lock the lid in place.

4. Pressure cook on HIGH for 2 minutes.

5. Release the pressure using the QUICK-RELEASE method and carefully remove the lid.

6. Add the peas to the broth and season the broth with soy sauce or salt to taste. Transfer the salmon, potatoes, peas and broth into four shallow bowls and sprinkle the scallions and hot red chili pepper on top.

Slow Cooker Directions

Serves: 4   **Cooking Time:** 1½ hours on HIGH

1. Pre-heat a 6-quart multi-function slow cooker using the BROWN or SAUTE setting.

2. Add the olive oil to the cooker and lightly sauté the garlic, red pepper flakes and gingerroot for just a minute or two. Add the chicken broth and bring the mixture to a simmer. (If your cooker doesn't have a brown setting, use a skillet on the stovetop for the steps above and transfer the contents to the cooker now.)

3. Add the potatoes, cover and slow cook on HIGH for 1 hour.

4. When the potatoes are tender, season the salmon and nestle it into the cooker with the potatoes. Cover and slow cook on HIGH for 30 minutes or LOW for 1 hour.

5. Add the peas to the broth and season the broth with soy sauce or salt to taste. Transfer the salmon, potatoes, peas and broth into four shallow bowls and sprinkle the scallions and hot red chili pepper on top.

Sheet Pan Fish and Chips

Possible Cooking Methods: Oven   Air Fryer

Regardless of whether you make this recipe in the oven or the air fryer, this version of fish and chips is much better for you and a lot less messy to prepare than the deep fried version. I really enjoy these out of the air fryer, even though you do have to make the French fries and fish in separate batches. Just remember to cook up some extra fries because you know you will sneak some while the fish cooks. 😜 If you can't find seasoned salt for the chips, you could certainly use regular kosher salt or you could make your own seasoned salt. Just mix 1 part of each of the following – chili powder, paprika, dried parsley, cayenne pepper and ground cumin – with 2 parts of the following – kosher salt, freshly ground black pepper, onion powder and garlic powder. The seasoned salt along with some malt vinegar will really give you that traditional "fish and chips" taste.

3 large Russet potatoes, peeled and cut into ½-inch sticks

canola oil

seasoned salt

¼ cup all-purpose flour

2 tablespoons Dijon mustard

2 eggs

¾ cup seasoned breadcrumbs

zest of 1 lemon

1 tablespoon paprika

1 tablespoon salt

1½ pounds cod fillets cut into 4-inch pieces

malt vinegar

tartar sauce

lemon wedges

Cooking Directions for
Sheet Pan Fish and Chips

Oven Directions

Serves: 4   **Cooking Time:** 40 minutes

1. Soak the potato sticks in a bowl of cold water for 30 minutes. Strain the potatoes and pat them dry with a clean kitchen towel.

2. Pre-heat the oven to 450ºF.

3. Toss the potato sticks with some canola oil and a sprinkling of seasoned salt, place them on a large sheet pan in a single layer and transfer the pan to the oven. Bake at 450ºF for 25 minutes.

4. While the potatoes are cooking, set up a dredging station with three shallow dishes. Add the flour to the first shallow dish. In a second dish, whisk the Dijon mustard and eggs together. In the third dish, combine the breadcrumbs, lemon zest, paprika and salt. Dredge the chunks of fish in the flour first. Then dip them into the egg mixture, allowing any excess to drip off, and finally coat them with the breadcrumb mixture. Pat the bread-crumbs on lightly to make sure the crumbs adhere to the fish.

5. After 25 minutes of baking time, remove the pan from the oven and turn the potatoes over, pushing them to one side of the sheet pan. Spritz the coated fish fillets generously with canola oil on all sides and add them to the sheet pan. Bake at 450ºF for 15 minutes. The fish should be crispy on top and flaky on the inside.

6. Serve the fish and chips with malt vinegar, tartar sauce and lemon wedges, and a little coleslaw on the side.

Air Fryer Directions

Serves: 4   **Cooking Time:** 35 minutes

1. Soak the potato sticks in a bowl of cold water for 30 minutes. Strain the potatoes and pat them dry with a clean kitchen towel.

2. Pre-heat the air fryer to 400ºF.

3. Toss the potato sticks with some canola oil and a sprinkling of seasoned salt, and air-fry at 400ºF for 22 minutes, shaking the basket a few times during the cooking process.

4. While the potatoes are air-frying, set up a dredging station with three shallow dishes. Add the flour to the first shallow dish. In a second dish, whisk the Dijon mustard and eggs together. In the third dish, combine the breadcrumbs, lemon zest, paprika and salt. Dredge the chunks of fish in the flour first. Then dip them into the egg mixture, allowing any excess to drip off, and finally coat them with the breadcrumb mixture. Pat the bread-crumbs on lightly to make sure the crumbs adhere to the fish.

5. When the potatoes have finished air-frying, remove them from the air fryer and transfer them to a bowl, leaving them uncovered. Spritz the coated fish fillets generously with canola oil on all sides and transfer them to the air fryer basket. Air-fry at 400ºF for 10 to 12 minutes, flipping the fillets over halfway through the cooking process. The fish should be crispy on top and flaky on the inside.

6. Remove the fish from the air fryer. Give the air fryer basket a quick wipe and return the potatoes to the air fryer. Air-fry at 400ºF for 3 minutes, just to heat up the chips.

7. Serve the fish and chips with malt vinegar, tartar sauce and lemon wedges, and a little coleslaw on the side.

Vegetarian

Stir Fried Zoodles and Vegetables
with Tofu

Possible Cooking Methods: Stovetop   Air Fryer

Zoodles (zucchini noodles) have become all the rage and are especially popular with those looking to curb their carb intake. So popular in fact, that you can buy zoodles in most grocery stores and don't need to have your own spiralizer at home. This recipe can be made on top of your stovetop or in your air fryer. Although there are no required ingredient changes for the air fryer version, you will find that you'll use a lot less oil when you make this in your air fryer and I've never known a better way to cook tofu!

1 tablespoon canola oil

2 tablespoons rice wine vinegar

2 tablespoons brown rice syrup or honey

2 tablespoons sriracha chili sauce

2 tablespoons soy sauce

1 tablespoon sesame oil

1 teaspoon minced fresh ginger

1 pound extra firm tofu, cubed

½ onion, sliced

2 carrots, sliced

1 red bell pepper, sliced

1 cup snow peas, sliced into 1-inch pieces on the bias

1 can baby corn, drained and cut into 1-inch pieces

8 ounces spiralized zucchini (zoodles)

fresh cilantro leaves

Stovetop Directions

Serves: 4   **Cooking Time:** 15 minutes

1. Combine the canola oil, rice wine vinegar, brown rice syrup, sriracha chili sauce, soy sauce, sesame oil, and ginger in a bowl. Add the tofu and let it marinate for 15 minutes.

2. Pre-heat a large 12-inch skillet over medium-high heat. Remove the tofu cubes from the marinade with a slotted spoon and dry them lightly with a clean paper towel. Reserve the marinade. Pour enough oil into the pan to coat the bottom and fry the tofu until it is nicely browned and crispy. Remove it from the pan and set it aside.

3. Add the onion and carrots to the pan and stir-fry for a few minutes, until they start to soften. Add the red pepper, snow peas and baby corn and continue to stir-fry for a few more minutes. Then add the zucchini noodles and toss the zoodles as they cook. When the zoodles start to soften, return the tofu to the pan and add the reserved marinade. Stir-fry for a few more minutes, until the vegetables are tender and heated through. Serve in bowls with fresh cilantro leaves on top.

Stir Fried Zoodles and Vegetables with Tofu

Air Fryer Directions

Serves: 4 **Cooking Time:** 30 minutes

1. Combine the canola oil, rice wine vinegar, brown rice syrup, sriracha chili sauce, soy sauce, sesame oil, and ginger in a bowl. Add the tofu and let it marinate for 15 minutes.

2. Pre-heat the air fryer to 400ºF.

3. Remove the tofu from the marinade with a slotted spoon and transfer it to the air fryer basket. Reserve the marinade. Air-fry the tofu at 400ºF for 15 minutes, until the tofu is nicely browned and crispy, shaking the basket a few times during the cooking process. Remove it from the air fryer and set it aside.

4. Add the onion and carrots to the air fryer and air-fry at 400ºF for 5 minutes. Add the red pepper, snow peas and baby corn and continue to air-fry for another 5 minutes. Then toss in the zucchini and air-fry for another 5 minutes, shaking the basket once during the cooking process.

5. Return the tofu to the air fryer basket with the vegetables and pour the reserved marinade over the top. Toss everything to coat with the sauce. Air-fry for just a few more minutes, until the vegetables are tender and heated through.

6. Transfer everything to serving bowls and pour any marinade from the air fryer drawer on top. Serve in bowls and scatter a few fresh cilantro leaves on top.

Spaghetti Caprese

Possible Cooking Methods: Stovetop

The easiest of pastas! Because there are so few ingredients in this recipe, it's really important that those ingredients be the best quality you can find. The tomatoes must be super ripe and in season, so make this pasta at the end of summer when tomatoes and basil are abundant and full of flavor. Use your best extra virgin olive oil – the one you reserve for salads. With the best ingredients, spaghetti caprese is a crowd-pleaser. This recipe cooks so quickly that there's really no advantage to using a pressure cooker and on top of that, spaghetti won't fit into most pressure cookers because the majority of them are round. If, however, you want to use a pasta of a different shape in your pressure cooker, cover the pasta with water by at least 2 inches and pressure cook on HIGH for half the time indicated on the pasta package plus 1 minute. Use the quick-release method to release the pressure and follow steps 3 and 4 below.

1 pound dried spaghetti	1 to 2 cups fresh bocconcini mozzarella balls, halved	½ cup torn fresh basil leaves
salt		freshly ground black pepper
	2 cups chopped ripe tomatoes or halved cherry tomatoes	¼ to ½ cup extra virgin olive oil

Stovetop Directions

Serves: 4   **Cooking Time:** 12 minutes

1. Bring a large stockpot of water to a boil. Season the water generously with salt. Add the pasta and boil until it is cooked al dente (according to package instructions).

2. While the pasta is cooking, combine the mozzarella, tomatoes and basil in a large bowl. Season with salt and freshly ground black pepper and add the olive oil.

3. Scoop out one cup of pasta water and set it aside. Drain the pasta and add the hot pasta to the bowl with the tomatoes and mozzarella. Toss well, season to taste again with salt and pepper, and loosen with some of the reserved pasta water if desired. (As the pasta sits, it will continue to absorb water and might need a little loosening. Keep that in mind if you go back for second helpings.) Serve with a light mixed green salad and piece of crusty baguette.

Vegetarian Skillet Moussaka

Possible Cooking Methods: Stovetop and Oven   Slow Cooker

This moussaka is one of my favorite vegetarian meals and is also a favorite of my vegetarian neighbor, who eagerly received the recipe testing samples. Although I tested this in the pressure cooker, the end result was just not good enough to qualify for a recipe in this book. My recommendation is to use the traditional stovetop and oven or the slow cooker cooking methods for this variation on the Greek classic. While there is no beef or potato in this non-traditional moussaka, it still has the Greek flavors of oregano and cinnamon, and ingredients of eggplant, tomatoes, and feta cheese.

Sauce:

2 tablespoons olive oil

1 large eggplant, cut into 1-inch cubes

1 onion, finely diced

2 carrots, finely diced

2 ribs celery, finely diced

2 cloves garlic, minced

12 ounces crimini or portobello mushrooms, chopped

1 teaspoon dried oregano OR 3 tablespoons chopped fresh oregano leaves

1 teaspoon ground cinnamon

1 teaspoon salt

½ teaspoon crushed red pepper flakes

¼ cup white wine (optional)

1 (28-ounce) can crushed tomatoes

Topping:

3 cups (1½-pounds) ricotta cheese

3 eggs

1½ cups grated Parmesan cheese (about 4 ounces)

1 tablespoon fresh oregano leaves

salt and freshly ground black pepper

½ cup crumbled feta cheese

Stovetop and Oven Directions

Serves: 4   **Cooking Time:** 65 minutes

1. Pre-heat the oven to 375ºF.

2. Pre-heat a large oven-safe 12-inch sauté pan over medium-high heat. Add the olive oil and sauté the eggplant cubes until nicely browned and starting to become tender. Remove the browned eggplant from the pan and set it aside. Add the onion, carrots and celery to the pan and sauté until tender – about 10 minutes. Add the garlic, mushrooms and dried spices and cook for another 10 minutes. Add the white wine (if using) and crushed tomatoes. Return the eggplant to the pan and cook until the sauce thickens slightly and all the vegetables are tender – about 15 minutes.

3. Combine the ricotta cheese, eggs, Parmesan cheese and oregano in a large bowl. Season with salt and freshly ground black pepper.

4. Remove the sauté pan from the heat and spread or dollop the ricotta mixture on top. Smooth the cheese mixture out as well as you can and sprinkle the crumbled feta cheese on top. Transfer the pan to the oven and bake for 30 minutes or until the top has puffed slightly and is nicely browned.

Vegetarian Skillet Moussaka

Slow Cooker Directions

Serves: 4 **Cooking Time: 4 to 5 hours on HIGH**

1. Add all the sauce ingredients to a 5-quart slow-cooker and stir well. Cover and slow cook for 3 to 4 hours on HIGH.

2. While the sauce cooks, combine the ricotta cheese, eggs, Parmesan cheese and oregano in a large bowl. Season with salt and freshly ground black pepper.

3. When the vegetables in the sauce are tender, give them a good stir and spread the cheese mixture on top. Smooth the cheese layer out as well as you can. Return the lid to the cooker and slow cook on HIGH for another hour, until the cheese has melted and the topping has set up.

4. Serve with the feta cheese sprinkled on top.

Savory Spinach and Mushroom Bread Pudding

Possible Cooking Methods: Stovetop and Oven

This recipe cheats just a little bit from my one-pot rule – for the tastiest result, you need to toast the bread cubes and for that step, you'll need a baking sheet or your air fryer. I hope you forgive me. I'm confident that you will after you taste this delicious savory pudding. Try to get a great loaf of bread for this recipe since it is the main ingredient. I really prefer rustic levain or sourdough bread, one that is not sliced so you can cut it into the cube size you want. You need bread that can hold its own with the flavors of the mushroom and Gruyère cheese, so if you can't find a levain loaf, go with a multi-grain loaf that you can slice yourself.

1½ pounds rustic levain or sourdough bread, cut into 1½- to 2-inch cubes

olive oil

salt and freshly ground black pepper

4 large onions, sliced

½ teaspoon dried oregano

½ teaspoon dried thyme

8 ounces brown mushrooms, thinly sliced

8 ounces spinach

½ cup white wine or dry vermouth

½ cup grated Parmesan cheese

1½ cups grated Gruyère cheese (4 ounces)

4 to 5 cups vegetable stock

Stovetop and Oven Directions

Serves: 4   **Cooking Time:** 1 hour 15 minutes

1. Pre-heat the oven to 350ºF.

2. Toss the bread cubes with olive oil and a good sprinkling of salt and toast on a baking sheet until nicely browned and crispy – about 15 minutes. Set the bread cubes aside.

3. Pre-heat a 4-quart Dutch oven over medium heat. Add 1 to 2 tablespoons of olive oil, onions, oregano and thyme and cook the onions over medium to medium-low heat for 25 minutes or so (stirring occasionally and scraping up any brown bits on the bottom of the pot) until the onions have browned and caramelized. Season the onions with salt and freshly ground black pepper, remove the onions from the pot and set aside.

4. Add another tablespoon of olive oil to the pot and increase the heat to medium-high. Add the mushrooms and sauté until browned and tender – about 6 minutes. Add the spinach and let it wilt into the mushrooms. Deglaze the pot with the white wine and bring the mixture to a simmer. Simmer until the wine has almost evaporated. Then, remove the spinach and mushrooms from the pot and set them aside with the onions, mixing all the vegetables together.

5. Combine the cheeses together in a bowl.

6. Build the bread pudding by layering the ingredients back into the Dutch oven: a third of the vegetables, a third of the bread cubes, a third of the cheese. Create three layers like this, ending with a layer of cheese. Pour the vegetable stock over the entire pudding, letting the bread cubes soak up as much of the stock as they can. If necessary, wait for the bread to soak up the liquid and then add more. Push down on the bread cubes slightly to help them absorb the liquid. Cover with a lid and transfer the pot to the oven.

7. Bake for 30 minutes. Remove the lid and continue to bake for another 15 minutes, until the top is nicely browned and the edges of the bread are crispy. Remove and let the pudding cool for 10 to 15 minutes before serving with a lightly dressed mixed green salad and a glass of wine.

Mulligatawny

Possible Cooking Methods: Stovetop   Pressure Cooker   Slow Cooker

Mulligatawny is a traditional Indian curry soup and there are many variations. Some versions have meat in them; others do not. I prefer a mulligatawny made with red lentils, vegetables and coconut milk, so that is what you have here. It's most definitely a full meal with a piece of bread or a salad. Don't be daunted by the list of ingredients here – look how short the directions are. Once you've measured the spices, your 90% done!

1 tablespoon vegetable or coconut oil	1 teaspoon ground cumin	5 cups vegetable stock or water*
1 onion, finely chopped	1 teaspoon ground cinnamon	1 (15-ounce) can coconut milk (not lite)
2 carrots, finely chopped	½ teaspoon crushed red pepper flakes (optional)	lime juice, to taste
2 ribs celery, finely chopped	2 teaspoons salt	fresh cilantro, chopped
2 cloves garlic, minced	1 large ripe tomato, chopped	roasted cashews, almonds or peanuts, for garnish
2 tablespoons minced fresh gingerroot	2 apples, peeled and diced	*Quantity changes for alternate methods*
2 tablespoons curry powder	1½ cups red lentils	

Stovetop Directions

Serves: 4   **Cooking Time:** 35 minutes

1. Pre-heat a large 6-quart Dutch oven over medium heat.

2. Add the oil and sauté the onion, carrots and celery until they start to become tender – about 5 minutes. Add the garlic, ginger, spices and salt and stir well. Sauté for a minute or two. Stir in the tomato, apples and lentils and add the stock or water. Bring the mixture to a simmer for 30 minutes.

3. Purée roughly half the mixture in a blender or food processor and return it to the pot. Stir in the coconut milk and season to taste with salt, freshly ground black pepper and a squeeze of lime. Thin the soup to your desired consistency with water.

4. Serve with fresh cilantro and roasted nuts on top.

Mulligatawny

Pressure Cooker Directions

Serves: 4   **Cooking Time:** 17 minutes

Change Ingredients: Reduce water or stock to 4½ cups

1. Pre-heat a 6-quart multi-function pressure cooker using the BROWN or SAUTE setting.

2. Add the oil and sauté the onion, carrots and celery until they start to become tender – about 5 minutes. Add the garlic, ginger, spices and salt and stir well. Sauté for a minute or two. (If your cooker doesn't have a brown setting, use a skillet on the stovetop for the steps above and transfer the contents to the cooker now.) Stir in the tomato, apples and lentils and add the stock or water. Cover and lock the lid in place.

3. Pressure cook on HIGH for 10 minutes.

4. Release the pressure with the QUICK-RELEASE method and carefully remove the lid. Purée roughly half the mixture in a blender or food processor and return it to the pot. Stir in the coconut milk and season to taste with salt, pepper and a squeeze of lime. Thin the soup to your desired consistency with water.

5. Serve with fresh cilantro and roasted nuts on top.

Slow Cooker Directions

Serves: 4   **Cooking Time:** 4 hours on HIGH

Change Ingredients: Reduce water or stock to 4½ cups

1. Pre-heat a 6-quart multi-function slow cooker using the BROWN or SAUTE setting.

2. Add the oil and sauté the onion, carrots and celery until they start to become tender – about 5 minutes. Add the garlic, ginger, spices and salt and stir well. Sauté for a minute or two. (If your cooker doesn't have a brown setting, use a skillet on the stovetop for the steps above and transfer the contents to the cooker now.) Stir in the tomato, apples and lentils and add the stock or water. Cover and slow cook on HIGH for 4 hours (or 8 hours on LOW).

3. Purée roughly half the mixture in a blender or food processor and return it to the pot. Stir in the coconut milk and season to taste with salt, pepper and a squeeze of lime. Thin the soup to your desired consistency with water.

4. Serve with fresh cilantro and roasted nuts on top.

Parmesan Cauliflower Steaks
with Roasted Tomato Sauce

Possible Cooking Methods: Oven   Air Fryer

This is a light and easy recipe for a quick supper. In my opinion, the star of this dish is actually the tomato sauce. For many, making a tomato sauce requires a big pot and a long simmer, but not here. The ingredients for the sauce roast on the sheet pan for just 20 minutes (or in the air fryer for just 10 minutes) before being blended into a sauce. The result is a bright and fresh sauce with vibrant flavors. You might even want to fill your sheet pan with the sauce ingredients and make a big batch of sauce for another occasion.

2 cups cherry tomatoes

1 clove garlic, peeled

¼ red onion, cut into large chunks and layers separated

olive oil

salt and freshly ground black pepper

1 large head cauliflower

½ teaspoon chopped fresh thyme leaves

¼ cup grated Parmigiano-Reggiano cheese

2 tablespoons chopped fresh parsley

Oven Directions

Serves: 2   **Cooking Time:** 20 minutes

1. Pre-heat the oven to 425°F.

2. Place the cherry tomatoes, garlic clove and red onion on a baking sheet. Drizzle olive oil, salt and pepper all over and mix well with your hands so that all the vegetables are coated. Move the vegetables to one side of the sheet.

3. Cut two steaks out of the center of the head of cauliflower. To do this, cut the cauliflower in half and then cut one slice about 1-inch thick off each half. The rest of the cauliflower will fall apart into florets, which you can roast on their own or save for another meal. Brush both sides of the cauliflower steaks with olive oil and season generously with salt, freshly ground black pepper and fresh thyme. Place the cauliflower steaks on the other side of the baking sheet.

4. Transfer the baking sheet to the oven and roast for 20 minutes.

5. When the cauliflower is tender to a knifepoint, the sauce ingredients are tender and the tomatoes have cracked, transfer all the sauce ingredients (including any juices on the baking sheet) to a blender or food processor. Sprinkle the Parmesan cheese on the cauliflower steaks and return the baking sheet to the oven for 5 minutes.

6. Blend or pulse the sauce ingredients to a chunky sauce. Add a little warm water if necessary to get the desired consistency. Season to taste with salt and add the parsley.

7. Remove the cauliflower steaks from the baking sheet and place them on serving plates and pour the sauce over the top, or pool the sauce on the plate and serve the cauliflower steak on top. Sprinkle parsley and serve with a hearty salad.

Parmesan Cauliflower Steaks with Roasted Tomato Sauce

Air Fryer Directions

Serves: 2   **Cooking Time:** 23 minutes

1. Pre-heat the air fryer to 400ºF.

2. Start by making the roasted tomato sauce. Place the cherry tomatoes, garlic clove and red onion into the air fryer basket and air-fry at 400ºF for 10 minutes, shaking the basket to turn the ingredients over halfway through the cooking time. When the sauce ingredients have finished air-frying, transfer everything to a blender or food processor and blend or process to a smooth sauce, adding a little warm water to get the desired consistency. Season to taste with salt, add the parsley and set aside.

3. Pre-heat the air fryer to 370ºF.

4. Cut two steaks out of the center of the cauliflower. To do this, cut the cauliflower in half and then cut one slice about 1-inch thick off each half. The rest of the cauliflower will fall apart into florets, which you can roast on their own or save for another meal.

5. Brush both sides of the cauliflower steaks with olive oil and season with salt, freshly ground black pepper and fresh thyme. Place the cauliflower steaks into the air fryer basket and air-fry for 6 minutes. Turn the steaks over and air-fry for another 4 minutes. Sprinkle the Parmesan cheese on top of both steaks and air-fry for another 3 minutes until the cheese has melted. Serve the cauliflower steaks on serving plates and pour the sauce over the top, or pool the sauce on the plate and serve the cauliflower steak on top. Sprinkle parsley and serve with a hearty salad.

Fettuccine
with Creamy Wild Mushroom Sauce

Possible Cooking Methods: Stovetop   Pressure Cooker

This is a pasta recipe for those times when you feel decadent. It's rich and fulfilling and is sure to warm you up on a cool fall or winter evening. What type of wild mushrooms you use is completely up to you and depends on what is available. I'm particularly fond of chanterelles and porcini mushrooms, but they can be expensive and hard to find. Most grocery stores have a pre-mixed package of wild mushrooms or packaged shiitake mushrooms that will work perfectly here. The key to this recipe is to resist the urge to shake or stir the mushrooms while they are cooking. Let them sit in the pan for a few minutes and don't season them with salt right away. The salt will draw out the moisture and inhibit any browning. Once they have some color on them, then you can toss them around. The fettuccine cooks right in the pot with the sauce, which lets it take on the earthy mushroom flavor. The cream and Parmesan cheese adds the luxury to the meal, and who doesn't like luxury?

1 tablespoon butter	salt and freshly ground black pepper	2 cups heavy cream
1 shallot, finely chopped	½ cup dry sherry	$1/3$ cup grated Parmesan cheese
16 ounces assorted wild mushrooms, sliced	3½ cups vegetable or chicken stock	1 tablespoon chopped fresh parsley
1 clove garlic, minced	1 pound dried fettucine*	*Quantity changes for alternate methods*

Stovetop Directions

Serves: 4   **Cooking Time:** 25 minutes

1. Pre-heat a large 12-inch skillet over medium-high heat. Add the butter and sauté the shallot for a minute. Add the mushrooms and continue to sauté without stirring or shaking the pan. Don't toss the mushrooms in the pan until they start to brown on one side. Then, toss the mushrooms to flip them over, add the garlic and season with salt and freshly ground black pepper. Continue to cook until the mushrooms are evenly browned.

2. Deglaze the skillet with the sherry, scraping up any brown bits on the bottom of the pan. Bring the liquid to a boil for a minute or two. Add the stock and once it has returned to a boil, add the dried pasta and simmer uncovered for 10 minutes, stirring occasionally.

3. Add the heavy cream and simmer for another 5 minutes.

4. Remove the skillet from the heat and stir in the Parmesan cheese. Let the pasta sit for a few minutes and then stir in parsley and serve with more Parmesan cheese to sprinkle on top.

Fettuccine with Creamy Wild Mushroom Sauce

Pressure Cooker Directions

Serves: 4   **Cooking Time:** 6 minutes

Change Ingredients: Use nests of fettuccine egg noodles or break long noodles in half

1. Pre-heat a 6-quart multi-function pressure cooker using the BROWN or SAUTE setting.

2. Add the butter and sauté the shallot for a minute. Add the mushrooms and continue to sauté without stirring. Don't stir the mushrooms in the cooker until they start to brown on one side. Then, stir the mushrooms to flip them over, add the garlic and season with salt and freshly ground black pepper. Continue to cook until the mushrooms are evenly browned.

3. Deglaze the cooker with the sherry, scraping up any brown bits on bottom of the cooker. Bring the liquid to a boil for a minute or two. (If your cooker doesn't have a brown setting, use a skillet on the stovetop for the steps above and transfer the contents to the cooker now.) Add the stock and heavy cream. Add the nests of dried fettuccine or break long fettuccine noodles in half. Stir to cover the pasta with the liquid. Cover and lock the lid in place.

4. Pressure cook on HIGH for 6 minutes.

5. Release the pressure using with the QUICK-RELEASE method and carefully remove the lid. Stir in the Parmesan cheese. Let the pasta sit for a few minutes and then stir in parsley and serve with more Parmesan cheese to sprinkle on top.

Spring Green Vegetable Quiche

Possible Cooking Methods: Oven   Air Fryer

This quiche showcases everything about spring, but it's the herbed pastry crust that makes it special and gives it so much flavor. You could put any mix of spring vegetables inside and pour the egg custard over the top, but if you alter the crust, you'll break my heart. The herbs really shine and give it a fresh "green" flavor and it's pretty too. Whether you choose to make this dish in the oven or in the air fryer, use the air fryer to re-heat it – it does such a good job of keeping the crust crisp while making sure the inside is completely heated through. Plus, it's easier and faster than re-heating in the oven.

Herb Crust*:

2 cups all-purpose flour

1 tablespoon sugar

1 teaspoon salt

1 cup cold butter, cut into cubes

1 tablespoon chopped fresh parsley

1 tablespoon chopped fresh basil

1 tablespoon chopped fresh rosemary

3 to 4 tablespoons cold ice water

Quiche*:

2 cups chopped fresh spinach

¾ cup fresh or frozen and thawed peas

1 cup sliced asparagus

2 scallions, sliced

6 eggs

1½ cups heavy cream

1 teaspoon salt

freshly ground black pepper

3 ounces goat cheese, crumbled

*All quantities changes for alternate methods

Spring Green Vegetable Quiche

Oven Directions

Serves: 6 **Cooking Time:** 45 minutes

1. Make the pastry. Place the flour, sugar and salt in a food processor. Add the butter and pulse until the mixture forms coarse crumbles. Add the fresh herbs. Slowly add the cold water by the tablespoon and process until the pastry comes together in a ball. Remove the dough from the food processer onto a floured surface and shape it into a disk with your hands. Wrap the disk in plastic wrap and chill it in the refrigerator for at least 30 minutes.

2. Pre-heat the oven to 375ºF.

3. Roll the dough out into a 10-inch circle and transfer it to a 9-inch deep pie pan. Crimp the edges of the pastry to form a pretty crust around the outside and transfer the pie pan to the freezer for 30 minutes.

4. Scatter the chopped spinach, peas, asparagus, and scallions in the pie crust. Combine the eggs, heavy cream, salt and freshly ground black pepper in a bowl, whisking well. Pour the egg mixture into the pie crust. Top with crumbles of goat cheese.

5. Bake for 40 to 45 minutes until the quiche has set. If the crust starts to get too dark, cover the perimeter of the quiche with a ring of aluminum foil. Let it rest for 20 minutes before serving. Cut it into wedges and serve with a side salad.

Air Fryer Directions

Serves: 4 **Cooking Time:** 60 minutes

Change Ingredients: Cut the crust ingredients in half; decrease quiche ingredients as follows:

Quiche:
1 cup chopped fresh spinach
½ cup fresh or thawed peas
½ cup sliced asparagus
1 scallion, sliced
4 eggs
1 cup heavy cream
½ teaspoon salt
freshly ground black pepper
2 ounces goat cheese, crumbled

1. Make the pastry. Place the flour, sugar and salt in a food processor. Add the butter and pulse until the mixture forms coarse crumbles. Add the fresh herbs. Slowly add the cold water by the tablespoon and process until the pastry comes together in a ball. Remove the dough from the food processer onto a floured surface and shape it into a disk with your hands. Wrap the disk in plastic wrap and chill in the refrigerator for at least 30 minutes.

2. Roll the dough out into an 8-inch circle and transfer it to a 7-inch cake pan. Crimp the edges of the pastry to form a pretty crust around the outside and transfer the cake pan to the freezer for 30 minutes.

3. Pre-heat the air fryer to 370ºF.

4. Transfer the cake pan to the air fryer basket and air-fry at 370ºF for 10 minutes.

5. Scatter the chopped spinach, peas, asparagus, and scallions in the pie crust. Combine the eggs, heavy cream, salt and freshly ground black pepper in a bowl, whisking well. Pour the egg mixture into the pie crust. Top with crumbles of goat cheese.

6. Return the pan to the air fryer and air-fry at 350ºF for 10 minutes. Cover the quiche with aluminum foil, tucking the ends underneath the pie pan so it doesn't blow off, and air-fry for an additional 35 to 40 minutes, until the quiche has set. Let the quiche rest for 20 minutes before serving. Cut it into wedges and serve with a side salad.

Portobello Mushroom Fajitas

Possible Cooking Methods: Stovetop   Air Fryer

Portobello mushrooms are often a vegetarian go-to ingredient because of their substantial hearty texture. Vegetarians rarely miss meat, but this is a good vegetarian meal when serving those who do not usually opt for vegetarian meals. You will need to cook the vegetables in this dish in stages, not only because they are plentiful in quantity, but also because they have different cooking times. Serve the vegetables with warmed up soft tortillas or heat some oil in a skillet and fry the tortillas for a few minutes on each side to add a crispy texture. Fajitas are a great option for picky eaters because everyone can build and top their own meal.

1 pound portobello mushrooms (4 to 5)	1 teaspoon canola oil	*Fajita toppings:*
1 tablespoon chili powder	1 large onion, sliced	salsa
1 teaspoon ground cumin	1 orange bell pepper, sliced	shredded lettuce
1 teaspoon smoked paprika	1 yellow bell pepper, sliced	black olives
½ teaspoon garlic powder	1 green bell pepper, sliced	guacamole
⅛ teaspoon cayenne pepper	1 red bell pepper, sliced	grated Cheddar cheese
½ tablespoon all-purpose flour	¾ cup water	sour cream
1 teaspoon salt	8 (8-inch) flour tortillas	
freshly ground black pepper		

Stovetop Directions

Serves: 4 to 6   **Cooking Time:** 25 minutes

1. Remove the stems from the portobello mushrooms and scrape out the dark gills on the inside with a spoon. Slice the portobello mushrooms into ½-inch thick slices.

2. Combine the chili powder, cumin, smoked paprika, garlic powder, cayenne pepper, flour, salt and freshly ground black pepper in a small bowl.

3. Pre-heat a large 12-inch skillet over medium-high heat. Add the oil and sear the portobello mushroom slices, browning them well. Remove the mushrooms from the pan and set aside. Add the onion to the pan, along with some additional oil if needed. Sauté for a few minutes, until the onion starts to brown, and then add the peppers and the spice mixture. Continue to sauté for another 3 minutes, until the peppers start to soften. Add the water and cook for a few more minutes, until everything is tender. Return the portobello mushrooms to the pan for a couple of minutes.

4. Warm the tortillas. You can do this by wrapping them in damp paper towels and popping them into the microwave on high for 1 to 2 minutes, or wrapping them in aluminum foil and placing them in a 350ºF oven for 5 minutes.

5. Transfer the vegetables to a serving dish. Serve the vegetables with the warm flour tortillas and various fajita toppings, letting everyone make their own fajita at the table.

Additional Cooking Directions for

Portobello Mushroom Fajitas

Air Fryer Directions

Serves: 4   **Cooking Time:** 20 minutes

Change Ingredients: Omit water

1. Pre-heat the air fryer to 400ºF.

2. Remove the stems from the portobello mushrooms and scrape out the dark gills on the inside with a spoon. Slice the portobello mushrooms into ½-inch thick slices.

3. Combine the chili powder, cumin, smoked paprika, garlic powder, cayenne pepper, flour, salt and freshly ground black pepper in a small bowl.

4. Place the portobello mushrooms into the air fryer basket. Drizzle or spray with canola oil and sprinkle one third of the spice mix on top, tossing to coat well. Air-fry for 4 minutes, flipping the mushroom slices over halfway through the cooking process. Remove the mushrooms from the air fryer and set aside.

5. Add the onion to the air fryer, drizzle or spray with oil and toss with half of the remaining spice mix. Air-fry at 400ºF for 5 minutes, shaking the basket a couple of times during the cooking process. Add the peppers and the rest of the spice mixture and continue to air-fry for an additional 4 to 5 minutes, until the vegetables are soft.

6. Return the portobello mushrooms to the air fryer and toss together. Air-fry for 2 more minutes. Transfer all the vegetables to a serving dish.

7. Warm the tortillas. Stack the tortillas and wrap them first in damp paper towels and then in aluminum foil. Air-fry at 380ºF for 4 minutes, flipping the package over halfway through the cooking time.

8. Serve the vegetables with the warm tortillas and various fajita toppings, letting everyone make their own fajita at the table.

Pasta e Fagioli

Possible Cooking Methods: Stovetop   Pressure Cooker

Pasta e Fagioli literally translates as "pasta and beans." That really sums up this soup, although with the vegetables, tomatoes and kale mixed in, it really is a meal all by itself. I always save the rinds from my wedges of Parmigiano-Reggiano. They are, after all, just as expensive as the cheese itself. Wrap them in plastic and store them in the freezer. They are a perfect way to season this soup (and others too). In my neck of the woods, Pasta e Fagioli is pronounced "pasta fazool" which actually stems from the Neapolitan name "Pasta e Fasule." I just call it dinner.

1 tablespoon olive oil	½ teaspoon dried thyme	2 (14-ounce) cans cannellini beans, drained and rinsed
1 tablespoon butter	½ teaspoon dried rosemary	4-inch Parmesan cheese rind (optional)
½ onion, diced	1 bay leaf	1½ cups dried ditalini pasta (or other small shape)
2 carrots, diced	1 teaspoon salt	4 cups coarsely chopped kale
2 stalks celery, diced	freshly ground black pepper	grated Parmesan cheese
1 clove garlic, minced	1 (28-ounce) can diced tomatoes	
	6 cups vegetable or chicken stock	

Stovetop Directions

Serves: 6 to 8   **Cooking Time:** 55 minutes

1. Pre-heat a 6-quart Dutch oven or stockpot over medium-high heat. Add the olive oil and butter and sauté the onion, carrots and celery until they start to soften – about 5 minutes. Add the garlic, thyme, rosemary, bay leaf, salt and freshly ground black pepper and continue to sauté for a few more minutes.

2. Add the diced tomatoes, stock, cannellini beans and the Parmesan cheese rind. Cover and simmer for 40 minutes. Add the ditalini pasta and simmer, uncovered, for another 15 minutes. Stir in the kale and season with salt and freshly ground black pepper.

3. Serve in large bowls with warm crusty bread and extra Parmesan cheese grated on top.

Pressure Cooker Directions

Serves: 6 to 8   **Cooking Time:** 12 minutes

1. Pre-heat a 6-quart multi-function pressure cooker using the BROWN or SAUTE setting.

2. Add the olive oil and butter to the cooker and sauté the onions, carrots and celery until they start to soften – about 5 minutes. Add the garlic, thyme, rosemary, bay leaf, salt and freshly ground black pepper and continue to sauté for a few more minutes. (If your cooker doesn't have a brown setting, use a skillet on the stovetop for the steps above and transfer the contents to the cooker now.) Add the diced tomatoes, stock, cannellini beans, Parmesan cheese rind and dried pasta. Cover and lock the lid in place.

3. Pressure cook on HIGH for 6 minutes.

4. Release the pressure using the QUICK-RELEASE method and carefully remove the lid. Stir in the kale and season with salt and freshly ground black pepper.

5. Serve in large bowls with warm crusty bread and extra Parmesan cheese grated on top.

Eggplant and Zucchini Lasagna

Possible Cooking Methods: Oven **GF**

This lasagna recipe is a low-carb option for people who crave the classic Italian pasta dish. Instead of using sheets of pasta to create the layers in this lasagna, you'll use eggplant and zucchini slices. There's no cooking needed ahead of time and it's all made in one easy baking pan. Remember to leave time for the lasagna to set up before you try to slice into it. In fact, this recipe sets up perfectly in the refrigerator overnight and re-heats extremely well the following day. So why not make it ahead of time and take tomorrow off? Sadly, this recipe does not translate easily to your pressure cooker or slow cooker, so stick with the oven version.

1 small eggplant, peeled and sliced lengthwise ¼-inch thick

2 zucchini, sliced lengthwise ¼-inch thick

salt

1¼ cups ricotta cheese

1½ cups grated mozzarella cheese, divided

¾ cup grated Parmesan cheese, divided

1 egg

2 tablespoons chopped fresh parsley

½ teaspoon salt

freshly ground black pepper

1¼ cups marinara sauce

½ teaspoon dried oregano

Oven Directions

Serves: 6 to 8   **Cooking Time:** 45 minutes

1. Pre-heat the oven to 375⁰F.

2. Lay the eggplant and zucchini slices out in a single layer on a cutting board or sheet pan. Sprinkle both sides with salt and let them sit for 15 minutes. Rinse and pat with paper towels until the vegetables are completely dry.

3. Combine the ricotta cheese, 1 cup of the mozzarella cheese, ½ cup of the Parmesan cheese, egg, parsley, salt and freshly ground black pepper in a bowl. Stir well to combine.

4. Build the lasagna. Spoon a thin layer of sauce on the bottom of an 8-inch by 8-inch baking pan. Layer half of the zucchini slices over the sauce. Spread half of the ricotta cheese mixture over the zucchini and top with a thin layer of sauce. Place the eggplant slices on the sauce and top with the remaining ricotta cheese. Then create more layers with the remaining zucchini, more sauce and remaining cheeses. Sprinkle a little dried oregano on top and cover with aluminum foil. Transfer the pan to the oven.

5. Bake at 375⁰F for 30 minutes. Remove the foil and bake for another 10 to 15 minutes, until the cheese has melted and browned around the edges and the vegetables are tender. Let the lasagna rest for at least 30 minutes before serving.

Caramelized Onion and Mushroom Tarte Tatin

Possible Cooking Methods: Stovetop and Oven   Air Fryer

This rich and decadent savory tart is especially nice with a mixed green salad for a meatless meal, but can also be served in smaller wedges as an elegant first course or appetizer. It is a twist on the classic apple Tarte Tatin, where the pastry bakes on top of the filling, rather than the other way around. With the pastry baking on top, you're sure to get a crispy result, which can be a challenge when making a regular tart. Using puff pastry also helps with this since the delicious flaky layers of pastry separate slightly in baking.

1½ tablespoons butter, divided*	salt and freshly ground black pepper	4 ounces grated Swiss or Fontina cheese
½ Vidalia (or other sweet) onion, sliced	8 ounces cremini mushrooms, sliced	1 sheet frozen puff pastry, thawed
½ tablespoon sugar	1 teaspoon fresh thyme leaves	*Quantity changes for alternate methods*

Stovetop and Oven Directions

Serves: 2   **Cooking Time:** 40 minutes

1. Pre-heat the oven to 400ºF.

2. Melt 1 tablespoon of the butter in a 10-inch sauté pan over medium heat. Add the sliced onions and sauté until they start to soften. Add the sugar, season with salt and freshly ground black pepper and continue to cook on medium-low heat until the onions start to brown, stirring occasionally. Remove the onions from the pan and set them aside.

3. Add ½ tablespoon of the remaining butter to the pan and sauté the mushrooms over medium-high heat until they start to brown. Return the onions to the pan and sauté the vegetables together for another minute. Do not let them get too dark because they will have more cooking time in the oven later on. Remove the pan from the heat and sprinkle the thyme leaves and grated cheese on top to cover.

4. Cut a 12-inch circle out of the puff pastry sheet. Place the circle of puff pastry over the cheese and tuck the edges into the pan. Pierce a few holes in the puff pastry to create steam vents and transfer the pan to the oven.

5. Bake the tart in the oven for 20 to 25 minutes, until the pastry is golden brown and cooked through. Remove the pan from the oven and let it sit for 5 minutes. Place a plate over the puff pastry and carefully invert the tart onto the plate.

6. Cut the tart into wedges and garnish with sprigs of thyme. Serve warm with a simple mixed green salad.

Air Fryer Directions

Serves: 2 **Cooking Time:** 25 minutes

Change Ingredients: Replace 1½ tablespoons of butter with 3 tablespoons melted butter, divided

1. Pre-heat the air fryer to 400°F.

2. Toss the onions with half of the melted butter, season with salt and freshly ground black pepper and air-fry for 7 minutes, tossing several times. Transfer the onions from the air fryer to a bowl and set them aside.

3. Toss the mushrooms with the remaining melted butter and air-fry for 5 minutes, shaking the basket a few times during the cooking process. Add the mushrooms to the onions in the bowl.

4. Line a 7-inch cake pan with aluminum foil. Arrange the onions and mushrooms in the bottom of the pan and sprinkle the thyme leaves and grated cheese on top to cover.

5. Cut a 9-inch circle out of the puff pastry sheet. Place the circle of puff pastry over the cheese and tuck the edges into the pan. Pierce a few holes in the puff pastry to create steam vents. Transfer the cake pan to the air fryer basket. (You can use an aluminum foil sling to help with this by taking a long piece of aluminum foil, folding it in half lengthwise twice until it looks like it is about 26-inches by 3-inches. Place this under the cake pan and hold the ends of the foil to move the cake pan into and out of the air fryer basket.) Air-fry at 350°F for 10 to 12 minutes, until the puff pastry has browned and is cooked through. Remove the tart from the air fryer. Place a plate over the puff pastry and carefully invert the tart onto the plate.

6. Cut the tart into wedges and garnish with sprigs of thyme. Serve warm with a simple mixed green salad.

Pad Thai

Possible Cooking Methods: Stovetop

This is another super quick meal that really should only be made on the stovetop. The pressure cooker won't save you any time and the slow cooker won't give you good results. The only appliance you might consider involving is the air fryer, and that would be just for the tofu. Tofu crisps up so nicely in the air fryer that you could cook it by itself and just toss it in at the end. That would be delicious, but alas… it wouldn't be using just one pan.

12 ounces pad thai rice noodles	2 tablespoons canola oil	*Garnish:*
2 tablespoons fish sauce	2 large shallots, sliced	½ cup chopped roasted peanuts
6 tablespoons brown sugar	1 red bell pepper, thinly sliced	¼ cup fresh cilantro leaves
¼ cup fresh lime juice	1 large carrot, julienned	2 cups bean sprouts
2 tablespoons rice wine vinegar	2 cloves garlic, sliced	4 lime wedges
2 tablespoons soy sauce	6 ounces extra firm tofu, cut into 1-inch cubes	
1 serrano or red Jalapeño chili pepper, thinly sliced	2 eggs, lightly beaten	
2 to 3 tablespoons water	4 green onions, whites thinly sliced and greens sliced 2-inches long	

Stovetop Directions

Serves: 4   **Cooking Time:** 10 minutes

1. Bring a kettle to a boil and pour boiling water over the pad thai rice noodles in a bowl. Let them sit for 5 minutes and then drain them and set them aside.

2. Combine the fish sauce, brown sugar, lime juice, rice wine vinegar, soy sauce, chili pepper and water in a bowl and set aside.

3. Pre-heat a large 12-inch skillet or wok over medium-high to high heat. When the pan is hot, add the oil and quickly stir-fry the shallots, pepper, carrot and garlic for just a couple of minutes tossing the food around regularly. Add the tofu and continue to stir-fry until the tofu has browned a little. Move the tofu and vegetables over to one side of the pan, add a little oil to the empty side and pour in the egg. Break up the egg as it cooks with a wooden spatula. When the egg has fully cooked, add the drained noodles and sauce ingredients to the pan and toss everything together. Scatter in the green onions (both whites and greens) and toss, cooking for just another minute or two.

4. Serve the pad thai in bowls with the roasted peanuts, cilantro and bean sprouts on top and a wedge of lime on the side.

Strawberry Rhubarb Slab Pie

Possible Cooking Methods: Oven

A slab pie is a great way to serve dessert to a crowd. You can feed 15 to 20 people with this pie! It's made in a sheet pan, which means there's more pastry for everyone. Of course, because this is a sheet pan dessert, there's no air fryer option to make it with these quantities, but you can make a mini pie with a pie pan. While you do have the option of buying frozen pre-made pastry, this pastry recipe is super easy and will give you enough pastry to easily roll it out to fit a half sheet pan – not the case with most store-bought pastry. In addition, the sour cream in this pastry gives it a nice tang next to the strawberry-rhubarb filling. Just remember to make the pastry twice.

Pastry (make this twice):

3 cups all-purpose flour, plus more for dusting the work surface

1 teaspoon salt

1 tablespoon sugar

12 ounces unsalted butter, cut into cubes and well-chilled

¾ cup sour cream

Filling:

7 cups sliced rhubarb (½-inch slices)

8 cups sliced hulled strawberries

1½ cups sugar

¼ teaspoon salt

¼ cup cornstarch

1 egg, lightly beaten

sanding sugar

Strawberry Rhubarb Slab Pie

Oven Directions

Serves: 15 to 20 **Cooking Time:** 60 minutes

1. Make the pastry by hand: Mix the flour, salt and sugar together in a bowl. Use a pastry cutter to cut the cold butter into the flour, or pinch the butter in the flour with your fingers, until it has the consistency of coarse meal.

2. Add the sour cream, pouring it over the flour as evenly as possible. Fold the dough together with your hands or a wooden spoon until you are able to collect it into a dough ball. You may need to add a little water in order to get to this stage, or if the pastry is too wet, add a little flour.

3. Shape the dough into a large rectangle. Wrap with plastic wrap and refrigerate for at least 30 minutes before proceeding with the slab pie.

1. Make the pastry using a food processor: Blend the flour, salt, and sugar together in the food processor bowl. Add the butter cubes and pulse together with the flour until the butter chunks in the flour are about the size of peas.

2. Add the sour cream, pouring it over the flour as evenly as possible, and pulse the mixture again to get the dough to come together. You may need to add a little water in order to get to this stage, or if the pastry is too wet, add a little flour.

3. Transfer the dough to a counter lined with plastic wrap, and shape the dough into a large rectangle. Refrigerate the dough for at least thirty minutes before proceeding with the slab pie.

4. Pre-heat the oven to 425ºF.

5. Combine the fruit, sugar, salt and cornstarch in a large bowl and toss together. Let this mixture sit while the oven pre-heats and you roll out the pastry.

6. Roll out one batch of pastry into a rectangle a little bigger than a half sheet pan (18-inches by 13-inches), remembering that it needs to be long and wide enough to come up and over the sides of the pan. Transfer the rolled out pastry to the half sheet pan. Allow the edges of the pastry to hang over the sides of the pan and trim to one inch bigger than the pan.

7. Roll out the second batch of pastry into another rectangle about 18-inches by 13-inches in size. Trim this rectangle so that it fits inside the pan perfectly. (If you want to cut a decoration in this top crust, do so now before you place the pastry on top of the fruit.)

8. Stir the fruit again to coat it evenly in the sugar mixture and pour the fruit onto the pastry in the sheet pan, spreading it out evenly. Top the fruit with the second rolled out pastry rectangle. Brush the pastry with egg wash (lightly beaten egg) and fold the bottom crust over the top crust, sealing the edges together by pushing lightly. Brush the pastry edges with more egg wash.

9. Pierce the pastry with a paring knife, making a few small diagonal slits across the pastry dough to allow steam to escape during cooking. You will have extra pastry left over from what you've made (it's much more convenient to have too much pastry than too little!) so decorate the pie by cutting shapes out of the extra pastry and gluing them on top with egg wash. Sprinkle the surface all over with sanding sugar (or granulated sugar if you can't find sanding sugar). Transfer the pan to the oven.

10. Bake at 425ºF for 15 minutes. Reduce the heat to 350ºF and continue to bake for another 45 minutes. If at any point the edges of the crust are getting too dark, cover the edges with aluminum foil. The pie is finished when nicely browned on top. Allow the pie to cool for 30 minutes and then cut it into squares and serve.

Mixed Berry Steamed Pudding

Possible Cooking Methods: Stovetop Pressure Cooker Slow Cooker

A steamed pudding is simply a rich cake batter made in a pudding basin or bowl and cooked in a bain marie, or water bath. The result is a moist but crumbly cake that is delicious just served with a little whipped cream. Traditionally, self-rising flour is used in a steamed pudding and this recipe follows that tradition. If you can't find self-rising flour (although it is very common in grocery stores these days), you can substitute 1 cup of all-purpose flour, ½ teaspoon of salt and 1½ teaspoons of baking powder. I put half the mixed berry mixture in the bottom of the pudding basin and swirl the remaining half into the batter because I like the way that looks in the end, with a mass of berries on top and beautiful deep purple swirls in the white cake. You could choose to do the same, or swirl the entire berry mix into the batter instead. Feel free to use a single berry, rather than a berry mix. It's your pudding!

1 cup frozen berry mix	½ cup sugar	4 teaspoons milk
2 tablespoons sugar	2 eggs	1 teaspoon vanilla extract
½ cup unsalted butter, room temperature	1 cup self-rising flour	heavy cream, for whipping

Stovetop Directions

Serves: 4   **Cooking Time:** 1½ hours

1. Combine the berries and 2 tablespoons of sugar in a food processor and pulse into a chunky mixture. Transfer half of this mixture to the bottom of a buttered 1- to 1½-quart round pudding bowl (or any round oven-safe bowl that will fit into your large stockpot or Dutch oven). Reserve the remaining berry mixture.

2. Wash the food processor bowl. Place the butter and ½ cup of sugar in the food processor and process until light and fluffy (you will need to scrape down the bowl several times). Add the eggs one at a time and continue to process. Add the flour, milk and vanilla extract and pulse into the egg mixture until no more streaks of white are visible. Add the remaining berry mixture to the processor and pulse only two or three times to create a swirl of berries in the white pudding batter. Transfer this batter to the pudding bowl on top of the berry mixture. Cover the pudding bowl with parchment paper and then aluminum foil, tightly tying the two around the bowl with kitchen twine.

3. Boil a kettle full of water. Place a small rack in the bottom of a large stockpot. Place the bowl on the rack and add enough boiling water to the stockpot to come halfway up the side of the bowl. Return the water to a boil over high heat. Once at a boil, lower the heat to a strong simmer, cover the stockpot and steam the pudding for 1½ hours. The pudding is done when a skewer inserted into the middle of the pudding (poked through the aluminum foil) comes out clean.

4. Transfer the pudding bowl to a wire rack to cool for 10 to 15 minutes. Invert the pudding onto a serving plate. Serve warm with whipped cream on the side.

Mixed Berry Steamed Pudding

Pressure Cooker Directions

Serves: 4   **Cooking Time:** 40 minutes

1. Combine the berries and 2 tablespoons of sugar in a food processor and pulse into a chunky mixture. Transfer half of this mixture to the bottom of a buttered 1- to 1½-quart round pudding bowl (or any round oven-safe bowl that will fit into your cooker). Reserve the remaining berry mixture.

2. Wash the food processor bowl. Place the butter and ½ cup of sugar in the food processor and process until light and fluffy (you will need to scrape down the bowl several times). Add the eggs one at a time and continue to process. Add the flour, milk and vanilla extract and pulse into the egg mixture until no more streaks of white are visible. Add the remaining berry mixture to the processor and pulse only two or three times to create a swirl of berries in the white pudding batter. Transfer this batter to the pudding bowl on top of the berry mixture. Cover the pudding bowl with parchment paper and then aluminum foil, tightly tying the two around the bowl with kitchen twine.

3. Boil a kettle full of water. Place a small rack in the bottom of a 6-quart pressure cooker. Place the bowl on the rack and add enough boiling water to the cooker to come halfway up the side of the bowl. Cover the cooker with a regular glass lid (or leave the pressure valve open on your pressure cooker lid) and steam the pudding for 20 minutes (with steam escaping from the valve). Then, close the pressure lid valve and pressure cook on HIGH for another 20 minutes.

4. Let the pressure drop NATURALLY and carefully remove the lid. The pudding is done when a skewer inserted into the middle of the pudding (poked through the aluminum foil) comes out clean.

5. Transfer the pudding bowl to a wire rack to cool for 10 to 15 minutes. Invert the pudding onto a serving plate. Serve warm with whipped cream on the side.

Slow Cooker Directions

Serves: 4   **Cooking Time:** 5 hours on HIGH

1. Combine the berries and sugar in a food processor and pulse into a chunky mixture. Transfer half of this mixture to the bottom of a buttered 1- to 1½-quart round pudding bowl (or any round oven-safe bowl that will fit into your slow cooker). Reserve the remaining berry mixture.

2. Wash the food processor bowl. Place the butter and sugar in the food processor and process until light and fluffy (you will need to scrape down the bowl several times). Add the eggs one at a time and continue to process. Add the flour, milk and vanilla extract and pulse into the egg mixture until no more streaks of white are visible. Add the remaining berry mixture to the processor and pulse only two or three times to create a swirl of berries in the white pudding batter. Transfer this batter to the pudding bowl on top of the berry mixture. Cover the pudding bowl with parchment paper and then aluminum foil, tightly tying the two around the bowl with kitchen twine.

3. Boil a kettle full of water. Place a small rack in the bottom of a 6-quart slow cooker. Place the bowl on the rack and add enough boiling water to the cooker to come halfway up the side of the bowl. Cover and slow cook on HIGH for 5 hours.

4. The pudding is done when a skewer inserted into the middle of the pudding (poked through the aluminum foil) comes out clean.

5. Transfer the pudding bowl to a wire rack to cool for 10 to 15 minutes. Invert the pudding onto a serving plate. Serve warm with whipped cream on the side.

Peach and Blueberry Cobbler

Possible Cooking Methods: Oven   Air Fryer

A cobbler is so named because the batter baked on top of the fruit below should look like a cobbled street. I've found the best batter for that result is similar to a biscuit batter. When I make biscuits I use a hand grater to grate the cold butter into the flour mixture. This is the easiest way to incorporate the butter into the flour and it leaves the butter pieces the perfect size, resulting in a flaky biscuit topping. You are welcome to vary the fruit in this cobbler – you really can't go wrong.

1/3 cup sugar

3 tablespoons cornstarch

pinch of salt

6 cups sliced, peeled peaches*
(fresh or frozen and thawed)

2 cups blueberries
(fresh or frozen and thawed)

juice of half a lemon

Topping:

1 cup all-purpose flour*

1½ teaspoons baking powder*

½ teaspoon salt*

6 tablespoons sugar*

¼ cup unsalted butter, cold*

¾ cup buttermilk*

Turbinado sugar

Quantity changes for alternate methods

Oven Directions

Serves: 6 to 8   **Cooking Time:** 50 minutes

1. Pre-heat the oven to 400ºF.

2. Combine the sugar, cornstarch and a pinch of salt in a large bowl. Add the peaches, blueberries and lemon juice and toss the fruit so that everything is coated with the sugar mixture. Transfer the fruit to a 9-inch by 9-inch baking dish or a 10-inch oven-safe skillet.

3. In a large mixing bowl, stir together the flour, baking powder, salt and sugar. Grate the butter into the flour and stir it in to coat evenly. Gently stir in the buttermilk. The dough should be quite wet.

4. Dollop the batter on top of the fruit, leaving some of the fruit uncovered. Sprinkle the Turbinado sugar over the batter – this will form a crunchy texture on top of the dough.

5. Transfer the baking dish to the oven and bake for 50 minutes, until the fruit is bubbling and the topping is lightly browned.

6. Let the cobbler stand for at least 10 minutes and then serve warm with vanilla ice cream.

Peach and Blueberry Cobbler

Air Fryer Directions

Serves: 4 to 6   **Cooking Time:** 50 minutes

Change Ingredients: Reduce peach quantity to 3 cups.
Reduce topping as follows:
¾ cup all-purpose flour
1 teaspoon baking powder
¼ teaspoon salt
4 tablespoons sugar
3 tablespoons butter, cold
²/₃ cup buttermilk

1. Combine the sugar, cornstarch and a pinch of salt in a large bowl. Add the peaches, blueberries and lemon juice and toss the fruit so that everything is coated with the sugar mixture. Transfer the fruit to an 7-inch baking dish or cake pan – one that will fit into your air fryer.

2. In a large mixing bowl, stir together the flour, baking powder, salt and sugar. Grate the butter into the flour and stir it in to coat evenly. Gently stir in the buttermilk. The dough should be quite wet.

3. Pre-heat the air-fryer to 380⁰F.

4. Dollop the batter on top of the fruit, leaving some of the fruit uncovered. Sprinkle the Turbinado sugar over the batter – this will form a crunchy texture on top of the dough. Wrap the cake pan with aluminum foil, leaving a dome on the top so that the foil doesn't touch the dollops of batter and lower it into the air fryer basket.

5. Air-fry at 380⁰F for 65 minutes. Remove the aluminum foil and air-fry at 330⁰F for another 15 minutes or until the dough on top is nicely browned and the fruit is bubbling.

6. Let the cobbler stand for at least 10 minutes and then serve warm with vanilla ice cream.

Pistachio Pavlova
with Strawberries

Possible Cooking Methods: Oven   Air Fryer

Pavlovas have fascinated me for some time. They are quite something to present at a dining room table and yet they are really very easy to prepare and can be decorated in any number of ways. I love that there is a deliberate inelegance about a pavlova that gives the cook the freedom to err. It doesn't have to be perfectly round, you don't have to take great care to ice it properly or decorate it meticulously. It's fancy-free and footloose! This pavlova is flavored delicately with pistachio crumbs and then decorated with more pistachios and strawberries.

½ cup roasted, salted and shelled pistachios	1 tablespoon cornstarch	1 cup heavy cream
4 egg whites	1 teaspoon white vinegar	2 cups sliced strawberries
1 cup sugar	1 teaspoon vanilla extract	*All quantities change for alternate method*

Oven Directions

Serves: 4 to 6   **Cooking Time:** 1 to 1½ hours

1. Pre-heat the oven to 350ºF.

2. Put the pistachios in a mini chopper, food processor or clean spice grinder. Pulse the nuts until you have some larger chunks as well as some fine crumbs. Set this aside.

3. Using a stand mixer with the whisk attachment or a hand mixer, beat the egg whites until fluffy. Add the sugar one table-spoon at a time and continue to beat the egg whites until they are glossy and stiff. Pour the pistachios into a coarse strainer over the bowl of beaten egg whites, letting the fine crumbs fall through into the whites. Set the coarser chunks aside for later. Gently fold the fine crumbs into the egg whites along with the cornstarch, vinegar and vanilla.

4. Line a baking sheet with parchment paper and spread the egg white mixture on top in a circle about 10-inches in diameter. Transfer the pan to the oven and lower the heat to 275ºF for 1 hour. When the pavlova has finished baking, let it sit in a turned off oven for at least an hour. Then remove it from the oven and let it cool completely on a wire rack.

5. When you are ready to serve, beat the heavy cream until soft peaks form. Spread the cream on top of the pavlova and then scatter the strawberries on top randomly. Sprinkle the large chunks of pistachio on top and slice into wedges at the table.

Pistachio Pavlova with Strawberries

Air Fryer Directions

Serves: 4 to 6   **Cooking Time:** 30 minutes

Change Ingredients: Cut ALL ingredient quantities in half. This is a recipe for a 5- quart air fryer. While you might be able to fit the pavlova into a 3-quart air fryer, it can be a little challenging with a smaller unit. If you have a 3-quart air fryer, you're up for a challenge and aren't set on the pavlova looking like a perfect circle, give it a try.

1. Put the pistachios in a mini chopper, food processor or clean spice grinder. Pulse the nuts until you have some larger chunks as well as some fine crumbs. Set this aside.

2. Using a stand mixer with the whisk attachment or a hand mixer, beat the egg whites until fluffy. Add the sugar one tablespoon at a time and continue to beat the egg whites until they are glossy and stiff. Pour the pistachios into a coarse strainer over the bowl of beaten egg whites, letting the fine crumbs fall through into the whites. Set the coarser chunks aside for later. Gently fold the fine crumbs into the egg whites along with the cornstarch, vinegar and vanilla. Pre-heat the air fryer to 350ºF.

3. Cut a circle of parchment paper that is roughly 8-inches in diameter. Spread half the egg white mixture onto the parchment paper, leaving a 1-inch border around the edge of the paper circle. Lower the parchment paper into the basket of the air fryer. (You can use an aluminum foil sling to help with this by taking a long piece of aluminum foil, folding it in half lengthwise twice until it looks like it is about 26-inches by 3-inches. Place this under the raw pavlova and hold the ends of the foil to move the parchment circle into and out of the air fryer.)

4. Air-fry at 250ºF for 30 minutes. When the pavlova has finished baking, let it sit in the turned off air fryer for another 30 minutes. Then remove it from the air fryer basket and let it cool on a wire rack.

5. Repeat with the remaining pavlova batter.

6. When you are ready to serve, beat the heavy cream until soft peaks form. Spread the cream on top of the two pavlova circles and then scatter the strawberries on top randomly or in a decorative manner. Sprinkle the large chunks of pistachio on top.

7. You can choose to serve two smaller pavlovas or you can make a double decker pavlova by stacking one circle on top of the other and pressing down gently. Slice into wedges to serve.

Apple Blackberry Pecan Crisp

Possible Cooking Methods: Oven   Air Fryer

There are few desserts easier than a crisp. You simply mix fruit together, adding sugar to taste, and top with a simple streusel topping. Feel free to mix up the fruit in this recipe and you can also vary what nuts you use in the topping. Make it your own! If you're in the mood for apple crisp, however, the best apples to use would be Granny Smith, Pink Lady, Honey Crisp, Empire or Braeburn – any apple that can hold its shape when baked.

6 apples, peeled, cored and diced (about 2 pounds; ½-inch dice)*

3 cups blackberries*

½ cup sugar, plus more for sprinkling on top*

1 teaspoon ground cinnamon*

¼ teaspoon ground nutmeg* (or preferably freshly grated nutmeg)

¼ teaspoon allspice*

¼ teaspoon salt*

4 teaspoons cornstarch*

Topping:

½ cup brown sugar

½ cup chopped pecans

1 cup rolled oats

½ cup all-purpose flour

¾ cup unsalted butter, divided*

*Quantity changes for alternate methods

Oven Directions

Serves: 8   **Cooking Time:** 60 minutes

1. Pre-heat the oven to 375°F.

2. Combine the apples and blackberries in a large bowl. In a separate smaller bowl, combine the sugar, spices, salt and cornstarch, breaking up any lumps of cornstarch. Toss the spices over the fruit and mix well. Transfer to a 9-inch square baking pan.

3. Using the same large bowl, combine the brown sugar, pecans, rolled oats and flour. Reserve 2 tablespoons of the butter and melt the remaining butter. Pour the melted butter into the topping mixture and combine well with a fork until the mixture looks crumbly. Scatter the topping mix on top of the apples and blackberries. Cut the remaining 2 tablespoons of butter into small pieces and dot the top of the crisp.

4. Transfer the baking pan to the oven and bake for 60 minutes, or until the top is nicely browned and the fruit is tender and bubbling. Let the crisp cool before serving with some ice cream or whipped cream.

Apple Blackberry Pecan Crisp

Air Fryer Directions

Serves: 4 to 6   **Cooking Time:** 45 minutes

Change Ingredients: Cut all the filling ingredients in half; keep the topping ingredients the same, but use ½ cup + 2 tablespoons of butter

1. Pre-heat the air fryer to 380ºF.

2. Combine the apples and blackberries in a large bowl. In a separate smaller bowl, combine the sugar, spices, salt and cornstarch, breaking up any lumps of cornstarch. Toss the spices over the fruit and mix well. Transfer to a 7-inch round baking pan (one that will fit into your air fryer).

3. Using the same large bowl, combine the brown sugar, pecans, rolled oats and flour. Melt the butter and pour it into the topping mixture. Combine well with a fork until the mixture looks crumbly. Scatter the topping mix on top of the apples and blackberries. Cover the pan with aluminum foil.

4. Transfer the baking pan to the oven and air-fry at 380ºF for 25 minutes. Remove the aluminum foil and continue to air-fry uncovered at 320ºF for another 20 minutes, or until the top is nicely browned and the fruit is tender and bubbling. Let the crisp cool before serving with some ice cream or whipped cream.

Chocolate Mousse Cake

Possible Cooking Methods: Oven   Pressure Cooker   Slow Cooker   **GF**

This is a one-dish dessert, although you will need three bowls to prepare the ingredients. The results are worth those few extra dishes because this flourless dessert will make you wonder if you're eating a piece of chocolate cake, or a forkful of chocolate mousse. You might just need another bite to figure it out. *This recipe calls for a 9-inch or 7-inch springform pan. If you don't have one, you can substitute a regular round cake pan lined with parchment paper. After baking, you will need to run a knife around the edges before unmolding the cake. There are three different cooking methods available to you when making this dessert, but they do have different outcomes. The regular oven method results in a rich, moist cake that doesn't need icing – a dollop of whipped cream or a dusting of powdered sugar will do the trick. The pressure cooker method will deliver a more dense result and I encourage you to serve it with some poured heavy cream. The slow cooker gives you the opposite result – a cake that is more airy and light. It would be delicious with a scoop of ice cream.*

butter, for greasing the pan

4 cups semi-sweet chocolate chips*

6 eggs, separated into yolks and whites*

¾ cup sugar*

1¼ cups sour cream*

⅛ teaspoon salt*

whipped cream or powdered sugar, for serving

fresh raspberries, for serving

Quantity changes for alternate methods

Oven Directions

Serves: 6 to 8   **Cooking Time:** 50 minutes

1. Pre-heat the oven to 325ºF. Line a 9-inch springform pan with a circle of parchment paper and grease the bottom and sides of the pan (and paper) with butter.

2. Melt the chocolate chips in the microwave or in a double boiler and let the melted chocolate cool for a few minutes. In a separate bowl, beat the egg yolks and sugar together until light and smooth. Stir the eggs and sugar into the melted chocolate, whisking to combine. Fold in the sour cream and salt.

3. In another clean bowl, whip the egg whites to soft peak stage. Fold the whipped whites into the chocolate mixture and pour the batter into the prepared springform pan.

4. Transfer the pan to the oven and bake at 325ºF for 40 to 50 minutes, until the cake is set. A toothpick inserted into the center of the cake should come out clean. Cool the cake completely and then refrigerate it for at least 2 hours before serving.

5. To serve, unmold the cake and transfer it to a plate. Sift some powdered sugar or dollop some whipped cream on top and garnish with the fresh raspberries.

Pressure Cooker Directions

Serves: 6   **Cooking Time:** 35 minutes

Change Ingredients: Reduce the ingredient quantities as follows:
3 cups semi-sweet chocolate chips
5 eggs, separated into whites and yolks
½ cup sugar
1 cup sour cream
pinch of salt

1. Line a 7-inch springform pan with a circle of parchment paper and grease the bottom and sides of the pan (and paper) with butter.

2. Melt the chocolate chips in the microwave or in a double boiler and let the melted chocolate cool for a few minutes. In a separate bowl, beat the egg yolks and sugar together until light and smooth. Stir the eggs and sugar into the melted chocolate, whisking to combine. Fold in the sour cream and salt.

3. In another clean bowl, whip the egg whites to soft peak stage. Fold the whipped whites into the chocolate mixture and pour the batter into the prepared springform pan. Wrap the pan completely with aluminum foil.

4. Place a rack in a pressure cooker big enough to hold the springform pan. Add 1 cup of water to the cooker and place the cake pan on the rack in the pressure cooker. (You can use an aluminum foil sling to help with this by taking a long piece of aluminum foil, folding it in half lengthwise twice until it looks like it is about 26-inches by 3-inches. Place this under the cake pan and hold the ends of the foil to move the cake pan into and out of the pressure cooker.)

5. Pressure cook on HIGH for 35 minutes.

6. Release the pressure using the QUICK-RELEASE method and carefully remove the lid. Let the cake cool completely and then refrigerate for at least 2 hours before serving.

7. To serve, unmold the cake and transfer it to a plate. Sift some powdered sugar on top and garnish with the fresh raspberries. Serve with heavy cream to pour over at the table.

Slow Cooker Directions

Serves: 6   **Cooking Time:** 2½ to 3 hours on HIGH

Change Ingredients: Reduce the ingredient quantities as follows:
3 cups semi-sweet chocolate chips
5 eggs, separated into eggs and yolks
½ cup sugar
1 cup sour cream
pinch of salt

1. Pre-heat a 6-quart slow cooker on HIGH for at least 20 minutes.

2. Line a 7-inch springform pan with a circle of parchment paper and grease the bottom and sides of the pan (and paper) with butter.

3. Melt the chocolate chips in the microwave or in a double boiler and let the melted chocolate cool for a few minutes. In a separate bowl, beat the egg yolks and sugar together until light and smooth. Stir the eggs and sugar into the melted chocolate, whisking to combine. Fold in the sour cream and salt.

4. In another clean bowl, whip the egg whites to soft peak stage. Fold the whipped whites into the chocolate mixture and pour the batter into the prepared springform pan. Wrap the pan completely with aluminum foil.

5. Lower the cake pan into the slow cooker. (You can use an aluminum foil sling to help with this by taking a long piece of aluminum foil, folding it in half lengthwise twice until it looks like it is about 26-inches by 3-inches. Place this under the cake pan and hold the ends of the foil to move the cake pan into and out of the slow cooker.) Add enough water to submerge 1 inch of the cake pan. Place a clean kitchen towel over the cooker and put the lid on top of the towel. Slow Cook on HIGH for 2½ to 3 hours (or 5 to 6 hours on LOW).

6. Cool the cake completely and then refrigerate for at least 2 hours before serving.

7. To serve, unmold the cake and transfer it to plate. Serve with a scoop of vanilla ice cream and garnish with fresh raspberries.

Pear and Ginger Tart
with Ginger Whipped Cream

Possible Cooking Methods: Oven   Air Fryer

To make this tart as beautiful as the ones you see in pastry shops, take your time as you shingle the pear slices. Look for like-sized slices and shingle them next to each other. The oven version of this tart is a rectangular shape and will feed 6 to 8 people, but the air fryer version is round and serves 4 people. If you're only serving 4 people, there's no reason why you couldn't make the circular tart and bake it in the oven if that is your preference.

2 pears, peeled and sliced into ¼-inch slices*

2 tablespoons sugar*

1 tablespoon all-purpose flour*

½ teaspoon ground cinnamon*

1 teaspoon fresh grated ginger *

1 sheet frozen puff pastry, thawed

2 tablespoons unsalted butter, melted*

2 tablespoons apricot jam, melted*

Ginger Whipped Cream:

1½ cups heavy cream*

1 teaspoon fresh grated ginger*

¹/₃ cup sugar*

Quantity changes for alternate methods

Oven Directions

Serves: 6 to 8   **Cooking Time:** 35 minutes

1. Pre-heat the oven to 400°F and line a baking sheet with parchment paper.

2. Toss the pears with the sugar, flour, cinnamon and grated ginger in a bowl and set aside.

3. On a lightly floured surface, roll the puff pastry out into a 14-inch by 8-inch rectangle. Place the pastry on the baking sheet. Fold up one inch of pastry all the way around the perimeter to form a "crust" for your tart. Press a fork around the edges to seal the crust shut.

4. Shingle the pears in three rows inside the puff pastry. Do not place any pears on the 1-inch crust of the pastry. Brush the melted butter over the pastry and pears. Transfer the pan to the center rack of the oven.

5. Bake at 400°F for 30 to 35 minutes, until the pears are soft and the pastry is golden brown.

6. While the tart is baking, make the ginger whipped cream. Combine the heavy cream with 1 teaspoon of fresh ginger in a chilled bowl. Use an electric mixer to whip the heavy cream.

When the cream starts to thicken, slowly add the sugar. Whip the cream into smooth stiff peaks.

7. Once the tart has cooled, brush the pears with the melted apricot jam and let it set to a shine. Serve the pear tart with the ginger whipped cream and garnish the cream with a dusting of ground cinnamon.

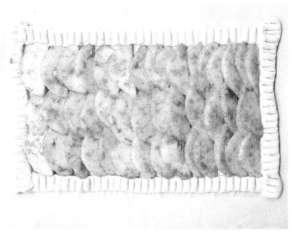

Air Fryer Directions

Serves: 4   **Cooking Time:** 30 minutes

Change Ingredients: Divide all the ingredients in half, except for the puff pastry – you will still need one sheet of pastry to make the tart, but you'll probably have some left over scraps that you could bake and toss with sugar for a little snack.

1. Toss the pears with the sugar, flour, cinnamon and grated ginger in a bowl and set aside.

2. On a lightly floured surface, roll the puff pastry out and cut it into a 7- or 8-inch circle (whatever will fit easily into your air fryer). Place the pastry on a 10-inch circle of aluminum foil. Roll up one inch of pastry all the way around the perimeter of the dough to form a "crust" for your tart. Press a fork around the edges to seal the crust shut and pierce the center of the pastry circle several times with a fork.

3. Working from the outside in, shingle the pears in concentric circles inside the puff pastry tart, leaving the crust bare. Brush the pastry and pears with the melted butter. Using the aluminum foil to carry it, transfer the tart (along with the foil) to the air fryer basket.

4. Air-fry at 350°F for 20 minutes, until the pears are soft and the pastry is golden.

5. While the tart is air-frying, make the ginger whipped cream. Combine the heavy cream with 1 teaspoon of fresh ginger in a chilled bowl. Use an electric mixer to whip the heavy cream. When the cream starts to thicken, slowly add the sugar. Whip the cream into smooth stiff peaks.

6. After 20 minutes, remove the tart from the air fryer and invert the tart onto a second circle of aluminum foil. (Don't worry, the pears will not fall out of the tart.) Return the tart to the air fryer, upside down and air-fry for an additional 5 minutes to finish cooking the bottom crust. Remove the tart from the air fryer and invert it onto a cooling rack.

7. Once the tart is cool, brush the pears with the melted apricot jam and let it set to a shine. Serve the pear tart with the ginger whipped cream and garnish the cream with a dusting of ground cinnamon.

Chocolate Butterscotch Cake

Possible Cooking Methods: Oven

When I was a kid, I always had a favorite chocolate bar and would immediately spend my weekly allowance on whatever was my current chocolate infatuation. For a while, that favorite was Hershey's SKOR® bar – a thin slab of butter toffee coated with milk chocolate. These days, SKOR® is not as easy to find as it used to be. The good news is that the Heath® bar is very similar, just a little thicker, so you can use either for the cake topping. This recipe takes my favorite flavors of my childhood chocolate dreams and puts them together in a cake that will feed a crowd AND travels well, making it a great dessert to take to a party. You can also make it a day ahead of time, but remember to let it sit at room temperature for 30 minutes before serving. It's what is known as a "poke" cake – holes are poked into the cake layer and butterscotch sauce is poured into those holes to keep the cake moist and delicious. It's easy to make your own butterscotch sauce instead of buying it, should you be so inclined. Simply combine 1 stick of butter, 1 cup of dark brown sugar, 1 cup of heavy cream and a teaspoon of salt. Bring the mixture to a boil and then simmer it for 5 minutes. You'll even impress yourself!

2¼ cups all-purpose flour	1 (3.4-ounce) box chocolate pudding mix	1 (3.4-ounce) box butterscotch instant pudding mix
1¾ cups sugar	2¼ cups milk	1 cup milk
1¼ cups cocoa powder	3 eggs, lightly beaten	1 cup heavy cream
¾ teaspoon baking soda	6 tablespoons unsalted butter, melted	1 cup chopped SKOR® bars OR Heath bars® or toffee chips, for garnish
1¼ teaspoons baking powder	1½ teaspoons vanilla	
½ teaspoon salt	12 ounces butterscotch sauce	

Oven Directions

Serves: 8 to 10   **Cooking Time:** 50 minutes

1. Pre-heat the oven to 350ºF and grease a 13-inch by 9-inch cake pan with butter.

2. Combine the flour, sugar, cocoa powder, baking soda, baking powder, salt and chocolate pudding mix together in a large bowl. Pour in the milk, eggs, melted butter and vanilla and beat with an electric mixer for 2 minutes on medium speed. Pour the batter into the prepared pan and transfer the pan to the oven.

3. Bake for 45 to 50 minutes, until a toothpick inserted into the center of the cake comes out clean.

4. Remove the cake from the oven and let it cool for 10 minutes. Poke holes all over cake with a skewer, wiggling the skewer slightly to make the holes a little bigger. Pour the butterscotch sauce over the warm cake, spreading it evenly with a spatula so that the cake can absorb the sauce. Continue to let the cake cool completely.

5. Use an electric mixer to whip the butterscotch pudding mix and milk together for a few minutes. In a separate clean bowl, whip the heavy cream into stiff peaks. Gently fold the whipped cream into the butterscotch pudding until no streaks of white remain. Spread the whipped butterscotch topping over the cooled cake.

6. Garnish with chopped SKOR® bars, Heath® bars or toffee chips. Refrigerate the cake until you are ready to serve.

Citrus Tea Cake

Possible Cooking Methods: Oven   Slow Cooker

This cake doesn't need any frosting – it's a light and airy sponge cake that is delicately sweet and perfect for a brunch or afternoon tea. It's baked in a water bath, which produces a thin layer of custard on the bottom of the cake (which becomes the top once you've inverted it out of the pan). Simply decorate it with some orange segments or some canned mandarin orange segments if you like things on the sweeter side.

butter, softened (for greasing the pan)	¼ cup fresh orange juice	1 teaspoon vanilla extract
3 eggs, separated into whites and yolks	zest of 1 orange	$1/3$ cup all-purpose flour
½ cup sugar	zest of 1 lemon	$1/8$ teaspoon salt
½ cup whole milk	zest of 1 lime	orange segments, to garnish

Oven Directions

Serves: 6   **Cooking Time:** 35 minutes

1. Pre-heat the oven to 350ºF. Line the bottom of a 9-inch cake pan with aluminum foil and grease the pan (and the foil) with butter.

2. Whisk the egg yolks and sugar together until they are light in color and fall from the whisk in thick continuous ribbons. Add the milk, orange juice, orange zest, lemon zest, lime zest and vanilla extract and whisk until smooth. Stir in the flour and salt.

3. Whip the egg whites into stiff peaks. Gently fold the egg whites into the yolk mixture and pour the batter into the prepared cake pan. Bring a kettle full of water to a boil. Place the cake pan in a roasting pan and pour enough boiling water into the roasting pan to come 1 inch up the outside of the cake pan. Transfer the roasting pan to the oven.

4. Bake at 350ºF for 30 to 35 minutes, until golden brown. Let the cake cool for 10 minutes and then run a knife around the edges of the pan before inverting it onto a serving dish. Peel the aluminum foil off the top of the cake. If any of the custard sticks to the foil, simply spread it back onto the cake with a knife. Cool completely to room temperature.

5. Top the cake with orange segments just before serving and then cut into wedges and enjoy with a cup of tea.

Slow Cooker Directions

Serves: 6   **Cooking Time:** 3 hours on HIGH

1. Pre-heat a 6-quart slow cooker on HIGH for at least 20 minutes. Line the bottom of a 7-inch cake pan with aluminum foil and grease the pan (and the foil) with butter.

2. Whisk the egg yolks and sugar together until they are light in color and fall from the whisk in thick continuous ribbons. Add the milk, orange juice, orange zest, lemon zest, lime zest and vanilla extract and whisk until smooth. Stir in the flour and salt.

3. Whip the egg whites into stiff peaks. Gently fold the egg whites into the yolk mixture and pour the batter into the prepared cake pan.

4. Fill the bottom of the slow cooker with 1 inch of hot water. Place the cake pan into the cooker. (You can use an aluminum foil sling to help with this by taking a long piece of aluminum foil, folding it in half lengthwise twice until it looks like it is about 26-inches by 3-inches. Place this under the cake pan and hold the ends of the foil to move the cake pan into and out of the slow cooker.) Place a clean kitchen towel over the cooker and cover with the lid – the towel will absorb the condensation and prevent it from falling on the cake. Slow cook on HIGH for 3 hours (or 6 hours on LOW).

5. Remove the pan from the cooker and let the cake cool for 10 minutes. Run a knife around the edges of the pan before inverting it onto a serving dish. Peel the aluminum foil off the top of the cake. If any of the custard sticks to the foil, simply spread it back onto the cake with a knife. Cool completely to room temperature.

6. Top the cake with orange segments just before serving and then cut into wedges and enjoy with a cup of tea.

Coconut Macaroon Brownies

Possible Cooking Methods: Oven   Air Fryer

A brownie is the quintessential one-dish dessert and if you like coconut and you like chocolate, there's no reason why you won't LOVE these brownies. The layers of chocolate and macaroon not only make this sweet treat delicious, but also very pretty and interesting to look at. This is an incredibly moist brownie, however, so to get a cleaner edge to each brownie, refrigerate the pan for an hour before you attempt to cut them. Use a serrated knife to saw across the macaroon on top, being sure not to push it into the brownie below.

Brownie Layer*:
3 eggs
¾ cup vegetable oil
1½ cups sugar
¾ cup cocoa powder
¾ cup all-purpose flour

½ teaspoon baking powder
¼ teaspoon salt*

Macaroon Layer*:
4 egg whites
½ cup sugar

1 teaspoon pure vanilla extract
14 ounces sweetened shredded coconut
2 tablespoons all-purpose flour
1 cup semi-sweet chocolate chips
1 tablespoon heavy cream

*All quantities change for alternate methods

Oven Directions

Serves: 18 brownie squares   **Cooking Time:** 45 minutes

1. Pre-heat the oven to 350ºF. Line a 9-inch by 13-inch cake pan with parchment paper, leaving 1-inch of the parchment paper extending over the sides of the pan.

2. Combine the eggs, oil and sugar in a bowl. In a second bowl, combine the cocoa powder, flour, baking powder and salt. Add the dry ingredients to the wet ingredients and stir until just combined, but do not over mix. Pour the brownie batter into the prepared cake pan.

3. To make the macaroon layer, whip the egg whites until frothy. Add the sugar and vanilla and whip into soft peaks. Fold the coconut and flour into the whites. Sprinkle the macaroon mixture over the brownie batter to cover it. Your hands are the best tools for this job – roll up your sleeves and drop the macaroon batter on top as evenly as you can, making sure not to push it into the brownie layer.

4. Transfer the cake pan to the oven and bake for 40 to 45 minutes, until the batter is set and the top layer is light brown. Transfer the pan to a cooling rack and cool for 15 minutes. Pull the brownies out of the pan using the parchment paper that extends over the side of the cake pan and cool completely. Cut the brownies into 18 squares and place the squares on the cooling rack to finish cooling.

5. Place the chocolate chips in a glass bowl with the heavy cream. Microwave together for 30 seconds. Stir to melt the chocolate chips and microwave for additional 10 seconds if needed. Transfer the melted chocolate to a pastry bag or zipper sealable plastic bag, cutting off one of the corners. Place a piece of parchment paper or a baking sheet under the brownies on the cooling rack. Drizzle the melted chocolate over the brownies. Allow the chocolate to set on the brownies before serving.

Coconut Macaroon Brownies

Air Fryer Directions

Serves: 8 brownie wedges   **Cooking Time:** 35 to 40 minutes

Change Ingredients: Reduce the quantities as follows:

Brownie Layer:
2 eggs
½ cup vegetable oil
1 cup sugar
½ cup cocoa powder
½ cup all-purpose flour
¼ teaspoon baking powder
¼ teaspoon salt

Macaroon Layer: (cut in half)
2 egg whites
¼ cup sugar
½ teaspoon vanilla extract
7 ounces sweetened shredded coconut
1 tablespoon all-purpose flour
½ cup semi-sweet chocolate chips
1½ teaspoons heavy cream

1.   Pre-heat the air fryer to 350ºF

2.   Line a 7-inch cake pan with parchment paper or aluminum foil. Spray the inside of the pan (and the parchment or foil) with oil or grease with butter.

3.   Combine the eggs, oil and sugar in a bowl. In a second bowl, combine the cocoa powder, flour, baking powder and salt. Add the dry ingredients to the wet ingredients and stir until just combined, but do not over mix. Pour the brownie batter into the cake pan and transfer the pan to the air fryer basket. (You can use an aluminum foil sling to help with this by taking a long piece of aluminum foil, folding in half lengthwise twice until it is roughly 26-inches by 3-inches. Place this under the pan and lower it into the air fryer basket.)

4.   Air-fry at 350ºF for 15 minutes.

5.   To make the macaroon layer, whip the egg whites until frothy. Add the sugar and vanilla and whip into soft peaks. Fold the coconut and flour into the whites. Sprinkle the macaroon mixture over the brownie batter to cover it. Your hands are the best tools for this job – roll up your sleeves and drop the macaroon batter on top as evenly as you can, making sure not to push it into the brownie layer. Cover the pan with aluminum foil and return the cake pan to the air fryer basket.

6.   Air-fry at 350ºF for 20 minutes. Remove the foil and air-fry at 330°F for an additional 5 minutes until the top layer is light brown.

7.   Cool the brownie in the pan for 20 minutes. Then remove the brownie from the pan and let it cool completely. Cut the brownies into squares or wedges and place them on a cooling rack.

8.   Place the chocolate chips in a glass bowl with the heavy cream. Microwave together for 30 seconds. Stir to melt the chocolate chips and microwave for additional 10 seconds if needed. Transfer the melted chocolate to a pastry bag or zipper sealable plastic bag, cutting off one of the corners. Place a piece of parchment paper or a baking sheet under the brownies on the cooling rack. Drizzle the melted chocolate over the brownies. Allow the chocolate to set on the brownies before serving.

Raspberry Almond Fruit Squares

Possible Cooking Methods: Oven   Air Fryer

This dessert is cut into squares but don't let that fool you into thinking this is not an elegant dessert. The almond paste in this recipe makes these bars creamy with a nice mellow almond flavor. The crust on these squares softens over time, but that's not necessarily a bad thing. Serve them the day you make them for a firmer cookie-like crust, or the next day for a softer cake-like crust. Any combination of fruit and jam can be used to make this dessert. This is a great use for seasonal fruit so feel free to get creative.

½ cup almond paste (about 5 ounces)

¾ cup unsalted butter, room temperature

1 cup sugar

1 egg

2 cups all-purpose flour

½ teaspoon baking powder

½ teaspoon baking soda

¼ teaspoon salt

1 cup seedless raspberry jam

4 cups raspberries

Crumb topping layer:

¾ cup all-purpose flour

¾ cup oatmeal

¾ cup brown sugar

¾ cup sliced almonds

½ cup unsalted butter, melted

All quantities change for alternate method.

Oven Directions

Serves: 20 to 24 squares   **Cooking Time:** 40 to 45 minutes

1. Pre-heat the oven to 350°F. Place a 15-inch long piece of parchment paper in a 9-inch by 13-inch baking pan so the ends extend over the sides of the pan.

2. Combine the almond paste and butter in a food processor, and pulse until combined. Add the sugar and egg and process until the mixture is smooth. Add the flour, baking powder, baking soda and salt. Process until the dough comes together. Press the mixture into the bottom of the prepared baking pan.

3. Whisk the jam until it is smooth. Gently fold in the raspberries to coat them with the jam and spoon the raspberry filling over the crust layer.

4. Make the crumb topping. Combine the flour, oatmeal, brown sugar and almonds in a bowl and toss to combine. Pour the melted butter on top and blend the ingredients with a fork to form coarse crumbles. Sprinkle the crumb topping over the fruit filling. Transfer the pan to the oven.

5. Bake at 350ºF for 40 to 45 minutes, until the top is light brown. Remove the pan from the oven and let it cool completely on a wire rack. Lift the parchment paper to remove the baked raspberry and almond out of the pan and transfer it to a cutting board. Cut into 20 to 24 squares.

Additional Cooking Directions for

Raspberry Almond Fruit Squares

Air Fryer Directions

Serves: 6 to 8   **Cooking Time:** 10 + 20 = 30

Change Ingredients: Reduce the quantities as follows:
2 ounces almond paste
¼ cup unsalted butter, room temperature
⅓ cup sugar
1 egg
1 cup all-purpose flour
¼ teaspoon baking powder
¼ teaspoon baking soda
⅛ teaspoon salt
⅓ cup seedless raspberry jam
2 cups raspberries

Crumb topping layer:
⅓ cup all-purpose flour
⅓ cup oatmeal
⅓ cup brown sugar
⅓ cup sliced almonds
3 tablespoons unsalted butter, melted

1. Pre-heat the air fryer to 350°F. Line a 7-inch cake pan with a circle of parchment paper.

2. Combine the almond paste and butter in a food processor, and pulse until combined. Add the sugar and egg and process until the mixture is smooth. Add the flour, baking powder, baking soda, and salt. Process until the dough comes together. Press the mixture into the bottom of the prepared baking pan.

3. Transfer the pan to the air fryer basket. You can use an aluminum foil sling to help with this by taking a long piece of aluminum foil, folding it in half lengthwise twice until it is roughly 26-inches by 3-inches. Place this under the pan and lower it into the air fryer basket. Air-fry for 10 minutes.

4. While the crust is cooking, prepare the filling. Whisk the jam until it is smooth and gently fold in the raspberries to coat them with the jam. Once the crust has baked for 10 minutes, spoon the raspberry filling on top of the crust layer.

5. Make the crumb topping. Combine the flour, oatmeal, brown sugar and almonds in a bowl and toss to combine. Pour the melted butter on top and blend the ingredients with a fork to form coarse crumbles. Sprinkle the crumb topping over the fruit filling. Cover the pan with aluminum foil and transfer the pan back to the air fryer basket.

6. Air-fry at 350°F for 10 minutes. Remove the foil and air-fry for an additional 10 minutes, until the top is golden brown. Remove the pan from the oven and let it cool completely on a wire rack. Invert the pan to remove the baked raspberry and almond out of the pan and transfer it to a cutting board. Cut into wedges and serve.

Chocolate Amaretto Budino
with Whipped Cream

Possible Cooking Methods: Stovetop

It only takes one pot to make these little puddings, but you will need 4 (8-ounce) jars, glasses or dishes for the individual desserts. It's so quick and deceptively easy that there is really no alternative method to making these – you won't save any time and there's no benefit to the final product in doing it a different way. Just enjoy the 5 minutes of stirring on the stovetop and the look of wonder on the faces of your guests when they marvel at how clever you are.

1½ cups whole milk	¼ cup sugar	1 cup heavy cream
12 ounces bittersweet chocolate, chopped	¼ cup amaretto liqueur	2 tablespoons sugar
5 egg yolks	2 cups crushed Amaretti or almond cookies	

Stovetop Directions

Serves: 4   **Cooking Time:** 20 minutes

1. Heat the milk in a 4-quart saucepan until it is almost at a simmer. Turn off the heat, add the chocolate and stir until it has completely melted into the milk. Whisk the egg yolks and sugar together in a bowl until the mixture falls from the whisk in thick continuous ribbons. Stir about a cup of the melted chocolate mixture into the egg yolks to temper the eggs, whisking constantly. Then pour the egg mixture into the saucepan with the remaining chocolate, stir in the amaretto liqueur and whisk well to combine.

2. Return the pan to low heat and simmer for 5 minutes until the mixture thickens, stirring constantly. Remove the pan from the heat. Strain the mixture through a fine mesh strainer and pour it into individual 8-ounce jars, glasses or dessert dishes. Top the chocolate pudding with crushed Amaretti cookies.

3. Whip the heavy cream to stiff peaks, adding the sugar for the last few minutes of beating. Top the cookie layer with a dollop of whipped cream and refrigerate for at least 2 hours before serving.

Nana's Trifle

Possible Cooking Methods: Stovetop

One of my favorite memories of my British maternal grandmother was her trifle. Every trip I made to England to see Nana, I was sure she would make a trifle for me (at least I thought it was especially for me – my cousins might have had other ideas). It was hands down my favorite dessert. Nana wasn't a prolific cook, but she had a sweet tooth like no other and I think she enjoyed how much I loved her trifle. While I personally like to stick to Nana's version of trifle, a trifle is certainly a recipe that is very easy to modify to suit different tastes. One option would be to use only fresh fruit. That would probably be my first inclination, but Nana always used canned fruit and for me the taste of the canned fruit really brings back childhood memories. So, this recipe uses a combination of the two. You can choose to do whichever suits you. Nana also always used Swiss Roll (a sponge cake rolled up with raspberry jam inside). If you can't find Swiss Roll, soft sponge ladyfingers with raspberry jam in between will work just fine. For the custard, Nana probably used Bird's® Custard Powder, and you are welcome to do that. I, however, prefer homemade custard and since there's no other cooking involved in the recipe, AND it's super easy, I think that's the way to go. There's only one pot used in preparing this dessert (the one to make the custard) and one bowl to serve it in, but there will be lots of smiles around the table.

Custard:	Fruit:	Cake:
2 cups milk	1 cup canned pears	3 cups cubed Swiss Roll (one large loaf) OR
2 cups heavy cream	1 cup canned peaches	12 ladyfinger sponge cakes
1 vanilla bean	2 cups fresh strawberries, hulled and sliced	3 tablespoons raspberry jam
½ cup sugar		
¼ cup cornstarch	1 cup fresh raspberries, plus a few extra for garnish	¼ cup dry sherry
6 egg yolks		1½ cups heavy cream
		½ cup sliced almonds, lightly toasted

Nana's Trifle

Stovetop Directions

Serves: 8 to 10   **Cooking Time:** 15 minutes

1. Start by making the custard at least 3 hours to as much as two days ahead of time. Combine the milk and heavy cream in a 3-quart saucepan. Split open the vanilla bean and scrape the seeds into the milk and cream mixture. Add the vanilla pod to the pan as well. Bring the mixture to a bare simmer and then turn off the heat. Let the cream sit while you prepare the remaining ingredients.

2. Combine the sugar and cornstarch in a large bowl, whisking to break up the lumps of cornstarch. Add the egg yolks and beat together until light in color and smooth so that it falls from your whisk in thick continuous ribbons (rather than drops). Temper the eggs into the cream by whisking a ladleful of the warm milk and cream mixture into the eggs. Add another ladleful, whisking constantly. Then pour the lightened egg mixture into the saucepan with the remaining milk and cream, whisking as you do so. Continue to whisk as you bring the entire mixture back to a bare simmer. Just before the mixture boils, it will thicken. If it boils, only let it do so for a few seconds before removing the pan from the heat. Should you end up with any lumps in the cream, simply strain the custard through a fine strainer. Otherwise, transfer the custard to a dish and cover with plastic wrap pressed right down on the surface of the custard (this will prevent a skin from forming). Refrigerate to cool completely.

3. Combine all the fruit in a bowl and taste for sweetness. If you are using some canned fruit, it should be sweet enough. If you choose to use all fresh fruit, sweeten the fruit to taste with a little sugar. Set the fruit aside.

4. Start to assemble the trifle. If you are using Swiss Roll, simply cut the roll into cubes or slices. If you can't find Swiss Roll and are using ladyfingers, split the ladyfingers and spread the jam inside, making little jam sandwiches. Then, cut the jam sandwiches in half. Cover the bottom of your 3-quart trifle bowl with the sponge cake cubes or slices.

5. Drizzle the sherry on top of the cake layer, attempting to soak all of the sponge cubes or slices.

6. Toss the fruit on top of the cake layer. (If you want the trifle to really look spectacular, arrange the fruit on the sides of the bowl carefully so that the presentation will be pretty.)

7. Give the cooled custard a good whisk and spread it on top of the fruit layer. You should have about 1 to 1½-inches of custard on top. Spread it out in a smooth layer and then refrigerate the trifle until you are ready to serve.

8. Just before you are ready to serve, whip the heavy cream until it is at stiff peak stage, but don't over-whip. Spread the whipped cream on top of the custard layer and use the back of a spoon to make light-hearted wispy peaks of cream on top. Arrange the raspberries and sliced almonds on top of the trifle. Serve to happy grandchildren to make them feel special (and others too!).

My maternal grandmother, who always made me feel special in her own quiet way.

Index

stovetop and oven

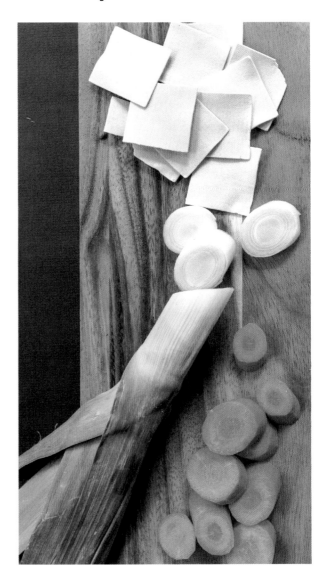

Meredith's Cookbooks

Make it Sous Vide

Take the worry out of under- or over-cooked dishes with Blue Jean Chef's sous vide eBook! *Make It Sous Vide* contains over thirty easy recipes along with tips, techniques and cooking time charts to guide you through the exciting world of sous vide cooking. Create perfectly cooked mouth-watering steak, juicy chicken, succulent fish and seafood, tender veggies plus incredible egg bites, customized yogurt, individual cheesecakes and more. From healthy to decadent, the choice is yours.

Air Fry Genius

Whether you're a novice in the kitchen or a more experienced chef, *Air Fry Genius* takes home cooks beyond air-frying as a trend, teaching you how to use any air fryer to create easy, delicious meals with less guilt than traditional frying. With over 100 recipes—from wholesome breakfasts to decadent desserts, and each paired with a color photo and nutritional information —*Air Fry Genius* also includes Meredith's signature tips and tricks for getting the most out of your air fryer to make foods that will impress your family and friends.

Air Fry Everything!

Air Fry Everything! is Meredith's first air fryer cookbook, which has sold over 200,000 copies. This cookbook will take your air-frying to the next level, creating delicious food and quick meals that burst with flavor, texture and color without the added calories and fat. *Air Fry Everything!* offers 140 all new recipes for both novices and experts, along with air-frying tips, tricks and techniques showing you that there's more to air-frying than fried foods!

Fast Favorites Under Pressure

Fast Favorites Under Pressure does all the work for you, with every recipe guaranteed to work in a 4-quart pressure cooker. However, all of these recipes double easily, so if you're cooking in an 8-quart cooker, you'll have no trouble making twice as many "fast favorites". *Fast Favorites Under Pressure* offers more tips and tricks plus 100+ flavorful recipes – even light versions – to be even more successful with your pressure cooker. From soups to pasta, meat to seafood, grains, vegetarian and dessert, all types of eaters will be able to get a meal on the table in a fraction of the time.

Delicious Under Pressure

Delicious Under Pressure is Meredith's second pressure cooker cookbook that is full of easy, flavorful and unexpected pressure cooker recipes. With 131 recipes, over 110 photos and all new chapters on Vegetarian Main Courses and Breakfast Dishes, it's a must-have cookbook for pressure-cooking at any level.

Comfortable Under Pressure

If your pressure cooker has been collecting dust, then you need to get *Comfortable Under Pressure!* With 125 recipes and over 100 tips and explanations, *Blue Jean Chef: Comfortable Under Pressure* will help you create delicious meals while becoming more versatile and at ease with your pressure cooker. Don't let the pressure get to you! Get *Comfortable Under Pressure!*

Comfortable in the Kitchen

Are you as comfortable in the kitchen as you are in your blue jeans? In *Blue Jean Chef: Comfortable in the Kitchen*, Meredith helps you settle into your comfort zone in the kitchen with tips, tricks and explanations of cooking techniques. Offering 200 kitchen-tested recipes, each chapter contains basic recipes that will give you a solid understanding of how the dish works, and four other recipes that build on that technique, but use different ingredients to create a unique and delicious meal. We spend a lot of time in the kitchen. You might as well get comfortable!

Air Fryer Cooking Chart

NOTE: All times and temperatures below assume that the food is flipped over half way through the cooking time or the basket is shaken to redistribute ingredients once or twice.

	Temperature (°F)	Time (min)		Temperature (°F)	Time (min)
Vegetables					
Asparagus (sliced 1-inch)	400°F	5	Onions (sliced)	400°F	15
Beets (whole)	400°F	40	Parsnips (½-inch chunks)	380°F	15
Broccoli (florets)	400°F	6	Peppers (1-inch chunks)	400°F	15
Brussels Sprouts (halved)	380°F	15	Potatoes (small baby, 1½ lbs)	400°F	15
Carrots (sliced ½-inch)	380°F	15	Potatoes (1-inch chunks)	400°F	12
Cauliflower (florets)	400°F	12	Potatoes (baked whole)	400°F	40
Corn on the cob	390°F	6	Spaghetti Squash (halved)	370°F	30
Eggplant (1½-inch cubes)	400°F	15	Squash (½-inch chunks)	400°F	12
Fennel (quartered)	370°F	15	Sweet Potato (baked)	380°F	30 to 35
Green Beans	400°F	5	Sweet Potato (1-inch chunks)	400°F	20
Kale leaves	250°F	12	Tomatoes (cherry)	400°F	4
Mushrooms (sliced ¼-inch)	400°F	5	Tomatoes (halves)	350°F	10
Onions (pearl)	400°F	10	Zucchini (½-inch sticks)	400°F	12

	Temperature (°F)	Time (min)		Temperature (°F)	Time (min)
Chicken					
Breasts, bone in (1¼ lbs.)	370°F	25	Legs, bone in (1¾ lbs.)	380°F	30
Breasts, boneless (4 oz.)	380°F	12	Wings (2 lbs.)	400°F	12
Breasts, stuffed	350°F	14	Game Hen (halved - 2 lbs.)	390°F	20
Drumsticks (2½ lbs.)	370°F	20	Whole Chicken (6½ lbs.)	360°F	75
Thighs, bone in (2 lbs.)	380°F	22	Tenders	360°F	8 to 10
Thighs, boneless (1½ lbs.)	380°F	18 to 20	Turkey Breast (whole, bone-in, 3 lbs.)	350°F	35 to 45

	Temperature (°F)	Time (min)		Temperature (°F)	Time (min)
Beef					
Burger (4 oz.)	370°F	16 to 20	Meatloaf (3 lbs.)	350°F	45 to 50
Filet Mignon (8 oz.)	400°F	18	Ribeye, bone in (1-inch, 8 oz.)	400°F	10 to15
Flank Steak (1½ lbs.)	400°F	12	Sirloin steaks (1-inch, 12 oz.)	400°F	9 to 14
London Broil (2 lbs.)	400°F	20 to 28	Beef Eye Round Roast (4 lbs.)	390°F	45 to 55
Meatballs (1-inch)	380°F	7	Veal Chops (bone-in, 6 oz.)	400°F	10 to 15
Meatballs (3-inch)	380°F	10			
Pork and Lamb					
Loin (2 lbs.)	360°F	55	Bacon (thick cut)	400°F	6 to 10
Pork Chops, bone in (1-inch, 6 oz.)	400°F	12	Sausages	380°F	15
Pork Chops, boneless (1-inch)	400°F	12	Lamb Loin Chops (1-inch thick)	400°F	8 to 12
Tenderloin (1 lb.)	370°F	15	Lollipop Lamb Chops	400°F	7
Bacon (regular)	400°F	5 to 7	Rack of lamb (1½ - 2 lbs.)	380°F	22
Fish and Seafood					
Calamari (8 oz.)	400°F	4	Tuna steak	400°F	7 to 10
Fish Fillet (1-inch, 8 oz.)	400°F	10	Crab Cake (4 oz.)	400°F	10
Salmon, fillet (6 oz.)	380°F	12	Lobster Tail (6 oz.)	370°F	5
Swordfish steak	400°F	10	Scallops	400°F	5 to 7
			Shrimp	400°F	5
Frozen Foods					
Onion Rings (12 oz.)	400°F	8	Egg rolls	400°F	12
Thin French Fries (20 oz.)	400°F	14	Fish Sticks (10 oz.)	400°F	10
Thick French Fries (17 oz.)	400°F	18	Fish Fillets (½-inch, 10 oz.)	400°F	14
Mozzarella Sticks (11 oz.)	400°F	8	Chicken Nuggets (12 oz.)	400°F	10
Pot Stickers (10 oz.)	400°F	8	Breaded Shrimp	400°F	9

Pressure Cooker Cooking Charts

	Cooking Time HIGH pressure (minutes)	Liquid Needed	Release Method		Cooking Time HIGH pressure (minutes)	Liquid Needed	Release Method
Poultry							
Chicken Bones for stock	40	6 cups	NATURAL	Chicken Thigh (boneless)	4	1 cup	QUICK
Chicken Breast (bone in)	6	1 cup	QUICK	Chicken, Whole	20	1½ cups	NATURAL
Chicken Breast (boneless)	4	1 cup	QUICK	Cornish Game Hen (1 to 1½ pounds)	8	1 cup	NATURAL
Chicken Thigh (bone in)	7	1 cup	QUICK	Turkey Breast (boneless, 2 to 3 pounds)	20 to 25	1½ cups	NATURAL
Beef							
Beef Bones for stock	40	6 cups	NATURAL	Meatloaf	35	1½ cups	NATURAL
Brisket (3½ to 4 pounds)	55 to 65	1½ cups	NATURAL	Pot Roast (3½ to 4 pounds)	55 to 65	2 cups	NATURAL
Corned Beef Brisket	55	covered	NATURAL	Short Ribs	55	1½ cups	NATURAL
Flank Steak (1 pound)	25	1 cup	NATURAL	Stew Meat (1-inch cubes)	15 to 20	1 cup	NATURAL
Ground Beef	5	1 cup	QUICK	Veal Shanks	20 to 25	1½ cups	NATURAL
Meatballs	5	1 cup	NATURAL	Veal Stew Meat (1-inch cubes)	10	1 cup	NATURAL
Pork							
Baby Back Ribs	30	1 cup	NATURAL	Pork Chops (boneless, 1-inch)	4 to 5	1½ cups	NATURAL
Country Style Ribs	20 to 25	1½ cups	NATURAL	Pork Loin (2 to 2½ pounds)	25	1½ cups	NATURAL
Ground Pork	5	1 cup	QUICK	Pork Shoulder (3 pounds)	55	1½ cups	NATURAL
Ham (bone in, 5 pounds, pre-cooked)	25 to 30	1½ cups	NATURAL	Sausages	10 to 15	1½ cups	QUICK
Meatballs	5	1 cup	NATURAL	Spare Ribs	45	1 cup	NATURAL
Pork Chops (bone in, 1-inch)	6	1½ cups	NATURAL	Stew Meat (1-inch cubes)	15 to 20	1 cup	NATURAL
Lamb							
Ground Lamb	5	1 cup	QUICK	Leg of Lamb (boneless, 3½ to 4 pounds)	35 to 45	1½ cups	NATURAL
Lamb Shanks	30	1½ cups	NATURAL	Stew Meat (1-inch cubes)	15 to 20	1 cup	NATURAL
Meatballs	5	1 cup	NATURAL				
Fish and Seafood							
Calamari	20	5 cup	QUICK	Mussels	4	2 cup	QUICK
Clams	4	1 cup	QUICK	Salmon	5	4 cup	QUICK
Crab Legs	4	1 cup	QUICK	Shrimp	2	3 cup	QUICK
Fish Fillet (1-inch thick)	5	6 cup	QUICK				

	Cooking Time HIGH pressure (minutes)	Liquid Needed	Release Method
Grains (1 cup)			
Barley (pearled)	20 to 25	3 cups	QUICK
Brown Rice	20	2 cups	NATURAL
Bulgur	6	2 cups	QUICK
Farro (pearled)	8	2 cups	QUICK
Farro (whole grain)	18	3 cups	QUICK
Polenta (coarse, not instant)	8 to 10	4 cups	QUICK
Polenta (fine, not instant)	5	4 cups	QUICK
Quinoa	5	1½ cups	QUICK
Steel Cut Oats	5	3 cups	NATURAL
White Rice, long-grain	4 to 6	1½ cups	QUICK
White Rice, short-grain	7	$2\frac{2}{3}$ cups	QUICK
Wild Rice	22	3 to 4 cups	QUICK

Beans and Legumes

	Un-Soaked	Soaked or Quick-Soaked	Release Method
Black Beans	25	7	NATURAL
Black-Eyed Peas	8	6	NATURAL
Cannellini Beans	25	7	NATURAL
Chickpeas	35 to 40	15	NATURAL
Great Northern Beans	25	8 to 10	NATURAL
Kidney Beans	25	8 to 10	NATURAL
Lentils	7 to 8	unnecessary	QUICK
Navy Beans	20	8 to 10	NATURAL
Pinto Beans	25	8 to 10	NATURAL
Split Peas	8 to 10	unnecessary	NATURAL
White Beans	20	8 to 10	NATURAL

Vegetables

	Cooking Time HIGH pressure (minutes)	Liquid Needed	Release Method
Acorn Squash (halved)	8	1 cup	QUICK
Artichokes (medium, whole)	12	1 cup	QUICK
Asparagus	2	1 cup	QUICK
Beets (medium, whole)	15	1 cup	QUICK
Broccoli	3	1 cup	QUICK
Broccoli Rabe	3	1 cup	QUICK
Brussels Sprouts	4 to 6	1 cup	QUICK
Butternut Squash (1-inch cubes)	5	1 cup	QUICK
Cabbage (quartered)	4 to 6	1 cup	QUICK
Beets (medium, whole)	15	1 cup	QUICK
Cauliflower (whole)	12 to 15	1 cup	QUICK
Collard Greens	5 to 10	1 cup	QUICK
Corn on the Cob	2 to 3	1 cup	QUICK
Eggplant	3 to 4	1 cup	QUICK
Fennel (wedges)	4	1 cup	QUICK
Green Beans	3 to 4	1 cup	QUICK
Kale	4	1 cup	QUICK
Leeks (1-inch pieces)	4	1 cup	QUICK
Parsnips (1-inch chunks)	4 to 5	1 cup	QUICK
Potatoes (1-inch chunks or small whole)	6 to 8	1 cup	QUICK
Rutabaga (1-inch chunks)	4	1 cup	QUICK
Spaghetti Squash (halved)	12 to 15	1 cup	QUICK
Sweet Potatoes (1-inch chunks)	4 to 5	1 cup	QUICK
Swiss Chard	2	1 cup	QUICK
Turnips (1-inch chunks)	3 to 4	1 cup	QUICK

Slow Cooker Cooking Chart

Vegetables

	Slow Cook LOW	Slow Cook HIGH		Slow Cook LOW	Slow Cook HIGH
Artichokes (whole)	5 to 6 hours	3 to 4 hours	Green Beans	4 to 5 hours	2 to 3 hours
Beets (whole)	6 to 8 hours	3 to 4 hours	Caramelized Onions (sliced)	8 to 10 hours	4 to 5 hours
Broccoli (florets)	2 to 3 hours	1 to 1½ hours	Sweet Potatoes (whole)	6 to 8 hours	3 to 4 hours
Butternut Squash (large chunks)	6 to 8 hours	4 to 5 hours	Parsnips (sliced)	4 to 6 hours	2 to 3 hours
Cauliflower (florets)	5 to 6 hours	2½ to 3 hours	Potatoes (whole)	8 to 10 hours	4 to 5 hours
Corn on the Cob	5 to 6 hours	3 to 4 hours	Zucchini (sliced)	4 to 5 hours	2 to 3 hours

Beef

	Slow Cook LOW	Slow Cook HIGH		Slow Cook LOW	Slow Cook HIGH
Brisket (4 to 5 pounds)	8 to 10 hours	4 to 5 hours	Prime Rib Roast (4 to 6 pounds)	5 to 6 hours	3 to 4 hours
Chuck Roast (3 to 4 pounds)	8 to 10 hours	5 to 7 hours	Meatloaf (2 pounds)	3 to 4 hours	2 to 3 hours
Sirloin Roast (3 to 4 pounds)	3 to 4 hours	5 to 6 hours	Veal Shank (2 to 3 pounds)	7 to 8 hours	3 to 4 hours
Flank Steak (2 to 3 pounds)	8 to 10 hours	4 to 5 hours	Corned Beef (3 to 4 pounds)	9 to 10 hours	5 to 6 hours
Beef Short Ribs (3 to 4 pounds)	8 to 9 hours	5 to 6 hours			

Poultry

	Slow Cook LOW	Slow Cook HIGH		Slow Cook LOW	Slow Cook HIGH
Chicken Breast (boneless) (2 to 3 pounds)	2 to 3 hours	1 to 2 hours	Cornish Game Hens	8 to 10 hours	4 to 5 hours
Chicken Pieces (bone-in) (3 to 4 pounds)	4 to 5 hours	2 to 3 hours	Duck Breast (2 to 4 pounds)	6 to 8 hours	3 to 4 hours
			Whole Duck (4 to 5 pounds)	8 to 10 hours	4 to 5 hours
Chicken (whole) (4 to 6 pounds)	5 to 6 hours	2 to 3 hours	Turkey Breast (5 to 7 pounds)	5 to 6 hours	3 to 4 hours

Grains and Beans

	Slow Cook LOW	Slow Cook HIGH		Slow Cook LOW	Slow Cook HIGH
Grits	6 to 8 hours	3 to 4 hours	Wild Rice	6 to 7 hours	3 to 4 hours
Beans (dried)	10 to 12 hours	5 to 6 hours	Quinoa	2 to 3 hours	
			Farro		2 to 4 hours

	Slow Cook LOW	Slow Cook HIGH		Slow Cook LOW	Slow Cook HIGH
Lamb					
Lamb chops (3 to 4 pounds)	4 to 6 hours	2 to 3 hours	Leg of Lamb (bone-in) (4 pounds)	6 to 8 hours	4 to 5 hours
Lamb Shoulder (cubed) (2½ to 3 pounds)	6 to 8 hours	3 to 4 hours	Lamb Shank (3 to 4 pounds)	6 to 8 hours	4 to 5 hours
Pork					
Pork Chops (2 to 3 pounds; 2-inches thick)	5 to 6 hours	2 to 3 hours	Baby Back Ribs (5 to 8 pounds)	8 to 10 hours	5 to 6 hours
			Country Style Ribs (2 to 4 pounds)	6 to 7 hours	4 to 5 hours
Tenderloin (1 to 3 pounds)	3 to 4 hours	1 to 2 hours	Pork Sausages (1 to 2 pounds)	2 to 3 hours	1 Hour
Shoulder (6 to 8 pounds)	8 to 10 hours	5 to 6 hours			
Loin Roast (4 to 5 pounds)	4 to 6 hours	2 to 3 hours			
Ham (cured) (7 to 8 pounds)	4 to 5 hours	2 to 3 hours			
Fish and Seafood					
Codfish (1½ to 2 pounds)	1 Hour	30 minutes	Fish Chowder	4 to 5 hours	2½ to 3 hours
Flounder (1½ to 2 pounds)	30 min to 1 Hour	30 minutes	Seafood Stew	4 to 5 hours	2 to 3 hours
Halibut (1½ to 2 pounds)	1 Hour	30 minutes	Shrimp	30 to 60 minutes	
Salmon (1½ to 2 pounds)	1 Hour	30 minutes	Crab Legs (2 to 3 pounds)	3 to 4 hours	
Desserts *Use as a guide for converting traditional recipes*					
Fruit Compote	3 to 4 hours		Flourless Cake		2 to 3 hours
Bread Pudding	3 to 4 hours		Cake Mixes		3 to 4 hours
Cheesecake		1 to 2 hours	Pudding Cake (cooked in water bath)		2 to 3 hours

About the Author

Meredith Laurence grew up in Canada with a British mother and a Trinidadian father who both loved food and exploring cuisines from around the world. Meredith learned the same at a very young age and the rest has been history!

Now known as the Blue Jean Chef, Meredith has worked in the food world for over 20 years. After graduating from the New England Culinary Institute, she worked as a line cook at two Michelin-rated restaurants in France, as well as at the renowned Zuni Café in San Francisco and at Café Rouge in Berkeley, California. Meredith then went on to work as a culinary instructor, a food product consultant and as a test kitchen manager. She now works as the Blue Jean Chef on live television doing cooking demonstrations, giving viewers advice on cooking and equipping their kitchens.

Meredith is a best-selling author, with over one million books sold to date. In addition to her cookbook writing and appearances on television, Meredith also writes and appears in a cooking series called The Basics, which can be seen on YouTube (www.youtube.com/bluejeanchef). In over 100 episodes of The Basics, Meredith takes viewers through a series of easy cooking techniques and recipes, empowering even the most novice cook.

She splits her time between Canada and Pennsylvania, where she and her partner enjoy their dogs, playing golf, skiing, cooking together at home and exploring the restaurant scene wherever they find themselves.

Stay Connected with Meredith

Check out her **website** for more recipes and techniques: www.bluejeanchef.com
Like her on **Facebook**: www.facebook.com/bluejeanchef
Follow her on **Twitter**: www.twitter.com/bluejeanchef
Follow her on **Instagram**: www.instagram.com/bluejeanchef
Visit her on **Pinterest**: www.pinterest.com/bluejeanchef